# Essentials of
# grammatical theory

# Essentials of grammatical theory

A consensus view of syntax and morphology

D. J. Allerton

*Senior Lecturer in General Linguistics*
*University of Manchester*

Routledge & Kegan Paul
London, Boston and Henley

First published in 1979
by Routledge & Kegan Paul Ltd
39 Store Street, London WC1E 7DD,
Broadway House, Newtown Road,
Henley-on-Thames, Oxon RG9 1EN and
9 Park Street, Boston, Mass. 02108, USA
Phototypeset in V.I.P. Times by
Western Printing Services Ltd, Bristol
and printed in Great Britain by
Lowe & Brydone Ltd
Thetford, Norfolk
© D. J. Allerton 1979

British Library Cataloguing in Publication Data

Allerton, D. J.

Essentials of grammatical theory.
1. Grammar, Comparative and general
I. Title
415        P153          79–40659

ISBN 0 7100 0277 7
ISBN 0 7100 0278 5 Pbk

# Contents

v

Contents

mational relations, discontinuous constituents, deep
and surface grammar; problems of 'observational adequacy".

*Contents*

tence, clause, phrase, word and morpheme; scales of
realization and delicacy.

Contents

# Typographical conventions

New terminology is introduced with SMALL CAPITALS. New symbols are explained as they are introduced, except for the following conventions, which are used throughout.

## Linguistic data

Italics are used for quoted words, sentences, etc. in the text, e.g. *sing*.

Single quotation marks are used for quoted meanings, e.g. 'sing'.

Small capitals are used for "lexemes" (see chapter 10), e.g. SING (which embraces *sing, sings, sang*, etc.).

An asterisk before a quoted item indicates that it is non-occurrent, e.g. *\*an Italians*.

A question mark before a quoted item indicates that it is marginal, e.g. *?a Swiss*.

## Phonetic transcription

Languages written in an alphabetic script that affords a clear guide to pronunciation are given in their normal orthography. Other languages are transcribed using the symbols of the International Phonetic Association (I.P.A.), English being given in the version of Gimson (1962) based on an educated Southern English pronunciation, so-called Received Pronunciation (RP).

/ . . . / indicates a "broad" (phonemic) transcription.

[ . . . ] indicates a "narrow" (allophonic) transcription.

The symbols are exemplified below (from English unless specified).

# Typographical conventions

## Vowel sounds

a unrounded open front vowel; starting-point for English diph-thong /aɪ/

æ unrounded half-open to open front vowel of *pat, bad*

ɑ unrounded open back vowel; occurs long in *car, bard, part*

ɒ rounded open back vowel; occurs short in *pot, cod*

e unrounded half-close front vowel; occurs short and somewhat opener in *pet, bed*

ə (normally unstressed) half-close to half-open central vowel; occurs short in the first syllable of *above* and in the second syllable of *china*

ɛ unrounded half-open front vowel; starting-point for English diphthong /ɛə/

з (stressed) half-close to half-open central vowel; occurs long in *curse, curd, cur*

i unrounded close front vowel; occurs long in *key, peat, bead*

ɪ unrounded close to half-open centralized front vowel; occurs short in *pit, gist, bid*

o rounded half-close back vowel, as in French *faux*

ø rounded half-close front vowel, as in French *feu*

ɔ rounded half-open back vowel; occurs long and somewhat closer in *caught, paw, fall*

u rounded close vowel; occurs long in *coo, root, fool*

ʊ rounded close to half-open centralized back vowel; occurs short in *put, full, good*

ʌ unrounded half-open back vowel; occurs short and strongly centralized (even fronted) in *putt, cud, hull*

y rounded close front vowel, as in French *futur*

aɪ English diphthong, as in *buy, bite, lied*

aʊ English diphthong, as in *bough, bout, loud*

eɪ English diphthong, as in *bay, bait, laid*

əʊ English diphthong, as in *bow(-tie), boat, load*

ɛə English diphthong, as in *bare, laird*

ɪə English diphthong, as in *beer, weird*

ɔɪ English diphthong, as in *boy, quoit, Lloyd*

## Consonant sounds

b voiced lenis bilabial plosive of *bill, rib*

d voiced lenis alveolar plosive of *dill, rid*

dʒ voiced lenis palato-alveolar affricate of *Jill, ridge*

ð voiced lenis dental fricative of *this, writhe*

f  voiceless fortis labio-dental fricative of *fill, rift*
g  voiced lenis velar plosive of *(fish's) gill, rig*
h  voiceless glottal (cavity) fricative of *hill*
j  voiced palatal semi-vowel of *yellow*
k  voiceless fortis velar plosive of *kill, rick*
l  voiced (alveolar) lateral frictionless continuant of *lip, pillow, pill, salt*, further specified as:
ɫ  "dark" (back of tongue raised), as in *lip, pillow*
l  "clear" (front of tongue raised), as in *pill, salt*
m  voiced bilabial nasal of *mill, rim*
n  voiced alveolar nasal of *nil, run*
ɲ  voiced palatal nasal, as in French *agneau, montagne*
ŋ  voiced velar nasal of *sing, singer*
p  voiceless fortis bilabial plosive of *pill, rip*
r  voiced post-alveolar non-lateral liquid of *rill, rip, arrow*, further specified as:
ɹ  post-alveolar frictionless continuant (most speakers)
ɾ  post-alveolar flap (other speakers)
s  voiceless fortis alveolar (groove) fricative of *sill, kiss*
ʃ  voiceless fortis palato-alveolar (groove) fricative of *ship, fish*
t  voiceless fortis alveolar plosive of *till, kit*
tʃ  voiceless fortis palato-alveolar affricate of *chill, rich*
v  voiced lenis labio-dental fricative of *veil, sieve*
w  voiced labio-velar semi-vowel of *will, wail*
z  voiced lenis alveolar (groove) fricative of *zip, fizz*
ʒ  voiced lenis palato-alveolar (groove) fricative of *measure, rouge*
θ  voiceless fortis dental fricative of *thin, kith*
ʔ  glottal stop, as in German *die Uhr*, or in place of [t] in substandard English *bottle*

N.B. English voiced lenis plosives and fricatives are devoiced (i.e. voiceless lenis) in certain positions, e.g. word-final.


*Diacritics*

| ˜ (above a vowel symbol) | nasalized |
| : (after a vowel symbol) | long (relative to a "short" vowel) |
| ˌ (under a consonant symbol!) | syllabic |
| ' (preceding a syllable) | stressed |

# Preface

> Recent polemical writings have tended to obscure the fact
> that a vast amount of accepted knowledge is shared by
> nearly all scholars engaged in linguistic studies.
>
> Haas, 1973a: 74

It is in grammatical theory that the most important disagreements
have developed within linguistics. I have therefore felt it essential
that someone should try to bring out the common core of assumptions, methods of enquiry and knowledge shared by most general
linguists. Since, among linguists, what seems to matter most is their
differences, it is easy for them to forget that, for the newcomer to
the subject, what matters most is the broad areas of agreement.

This book is intended for the beginning student in linguistics,
whether undergraduate, postgraduate or non-curricular. It is specifically on grammar, in the sense of syntax and morphology; but the
introductory chapters place grammar in the setting of language as a
whole. An elementary knowledge of phonetics would be a helpful
preparation but is not essential.

The chapters are relatively independent of each other, and there
is necessarily a small degree of overlap in their contents. This means
that, although the chapters are recommended to be read in the
order in which they appear, it would be quite reasonable to change
the order somewhat, e.g. by taking chapter 10 earlier, or by moving
chapters 4, 8 and 11 closer together.

It is generally thought that an adequate scientific account should
be consistent, exhaustive and as simple as possible. In attempting
the difficult task of describing a "consensus view", I must have
fallen short on all three counts. But I have felt that the importance
of the task made it worth trying.

I have been constantly influenced by the broad and liberal but
systematic approach of W. Haas, who, besides encouraging me to
write this book in the first place, has kindly read and commented on

a number of chapters. I am particularly grateful, too, to D. A. Cruse, who has read practically the whole book and given me some very helpful suggestions. Different parts of the book have been read by Katharine Perera and by D. E. Hustler, to whom I would also like to express sincere thanks. Not least I would like to express gratitude to J. R. Hurford for some very useful criticisms. The responsibility for all shortcomings remains, of course, mine.

D. J. A.

*Chapter 1*

# The study of language

## Different views of language

Goethe once wrote:

> Everyone thinks because he can talk, that he can therefore talk about language.
> (Ein jeder, weil er spricht, glaubt auch über die Sprache sprechen zu können.)

and it is certainly true that most people hold decided opinions about language in general and about their native language in particular. This is understandable enough, in so far as we have all learnt to speak our own native language fluently, and this alone has provided us with words and expressions to talk about language, such as *speak, word, language, accent, put it another way, ambiguous*. Furthermore, most of us have learnt to read and write, linguistic skills which carry with them terminology like *letter, spell, prefix, sentence*. Many of us even learnt some form of traditional grammar at school and got quite used to looking at language and taking it apart, using a variety of technical labels, e.g. *verb, clause, infinitive, parse*, and we may have learnt to apply these labels to foreign languages as well as our own. So altogether we apparently have some grounds for regarding ourselves as entitled to talk about language.

However, about the same time that we learnt to talk, most of us also learnt to walk and have since become competent walkers. We have also acquired a terminology for talking about walking; we distinguish *walking, strolling* and *marching*, for instance, and we talk about someone's *gait*, and whether he walked *fast, straight, nervously*, etc. But how many of us can give a concise, step-by-step account of what the action of walking involves, of what bones, muscles, ligaments, etc. are involved and what they do, of how human decisions and energy are transformed into physical movement? In our defence, we would say that we feel this is the task not of the man-in-the-street but of the professional physiologist, anatomist, physicist or whatever the relevant speciality might be. So we are naturally led to ask why there should not be a specialist in language – in linguistics, in fact – to give us a technical account of his field and explain many aspects that the layman is incapable of explaining.

Language has, of course, already been studied for many centuries from a number of points of view, in particular by philosophers, by traditional grammarians and by literary critics. Ancient philosophers (the Stoics, the Alexandrians, Plato, Aristotle) all discussed the nature and origin of language. Although philosophy has at times taken language for granted, the twentieth century has seen philosophers concern themselves fundamentally with such problems as those of meaning, reference and truth (cf. the work of Russell, Ayer), and linguistic philosophy has used language as a key for clearing up misconceptions about theories of knowledge, existence, good and evil, and so on (cf. the work of Wittgenstein, Ryle and Austin).

Traditional grammar grew out of work by ancient writers on philosophy and language but more particularly out of works devoted to the study of Greek (e.g. Dionysius Thrax) and Latin (e.g. Varro, Priscian). As these became dead languages, so Latin and Greek grammars were able to become codified systems and gain extra respect because of the learned status of the works written in those languages. Thus traditional grammar was prescriptive, laying down rules for the "correct" use of the language (see below pp. 53–4); grammar had become part of the social etiquette, first of the learned world, and then later, when it was applied to "vernacular" languages like English, French and Russian, of the polite world.

The literary critic has always had to contend with language. Since the writer has language as his medium of expression, his work must be judged partly on the basis of his use of language. The ancient art of rhetoric similarly depended on an analysis of language texts and has provided some of the notions and techniques of the literary critic, e.g. metaphor, paradox.

In more recent times other specialists have devoted special attention to language. Psychologists, social anthropologists and sociologists, speech pathologists and computer scientists, to pick out just a few, have all studied linguistic problems associated with their own fields. But each specialist has been concerned with the particular aspects of language that touch on his or her own studies; the psychologist seeing language in part as a manifestation of mental activity or behaviour, the speech pathologist being interested in the normal process of language acquisition and retention and how various abnormal patterns deviate from this, and so on.

So most studies of language outside linguistics, whether ancient or modern, have a particular axe to grind and therefore, quite naturally, slant their account of language in a particular way. It is left to the (general) linguist to study language in a neutral unslanted way: to study language for its own sake. He is interested in its inherent nature, rather than in its importance for something else; he has no ulterior motive. While a philosopher may see language as an imperfect and misleading code for expressing logical relations, a psychologist may see language as a key to the understanding of the mind, or a literary critic may see language as a a medium for literature, the linguist just wants to know what language itself is like and how it works. It is, moreover, vital to have a neutral, unslanted account of language, because, although each outside specialist may see very deeply into his own problems, he will lack an overview and as a consequence may overlook many important points and issues. There is of course nothing to prevent a specialist taking the linguist's more general account and adapting it to his own particular needs.

## Different linguistic theories

So, accepting the need for a purely linguistic account of language, where precisely do we find it? The point of asking this question is that, although some writers would have it otherwise, there is no single, generally accepted body of linguistic theory, but rather a range of competing schools. Now it is the aim of this book to bring together the common aims, principles and methods of these various theories and to show that despite their differences there are more things they agree about than disagree about. It will nevertheless be necessary to begin with a very brief indication of the identity of these schools and of the principal points of disagreement between them. In this account reference will be made not only to schools as such but to a number of influential individual linguists who have had independent views of their own.

The most well-known, and probably the most influential, school during the 1960s and 1970s has been that of transformational-generative grammar. This theory was originally propounded by N. Chomsky in his *Syntactic Structures* (1957) and subsequently modified in *Aspects of the Theory of Syntax* (1965). The twin keynotes of Chomsky's approach have been the insistence on "generation", i.e. explicit specification of sentences and their structures through rewrite rules (see chapter 4), and the use of "transformations", rules for relating sentences with different structures or for relating the "surface structure" and "deep structure" of a single sentence (see also chapter 8). Transformational-generative grammar can, however, scarcely be regarded as a single school any more: a division of views opened up in the later 1960s between those, like J. D. McCawley, J. R. Ross, C. J. Fillmore and many others, who believe all syntax should be semantically based, thus merging semantics with "deep syntax", and those, like Chomsky himself and R. S. Jackendoff, who believe that a grammar should have independent "deep syntax" and semantic components, and that in the semantic interpretation of a sentence both "deep structure" and "surface structure" should play a part (see discussion in chapter 8).

The most direct influence on Chomsky in his work was Z. S. Harris, his teacher, with whom he developed the notion of transformation. Harris, one of the most original and systematic thinkers in linguistics, propounded a kind of transformation that partially agreed with Chomsky's earlier view, and one that we shall find fruitful; Harris also always stressed explicitness in a grammar.

We may trace Harris's and Chomsky's work back to the twin father-figures of American linguistics, L. Bloomfield and E. Sapir. They each produced an important book called *Language* in 1933 and 1921 respectively (although Bloomfield's is a revision of an earlier book). The two books illustrate the contrasting qualities of the two men: while Bloomfield's is attentive to language detail, careful to scrutinize any theoretical proposal he makes and sceptical about the utility of studying meaning, Sapir is more imaginative, more intuitive and more enterprising. While Chomsky's work can be seen as owing something to both, Harris is more directly a Bloomfieldian.

In fact the 1930s, 1940s and early 1950s were undoubtedly the era of Bloomfieldianism in the United States and the main alternative linguistic approaches available in North America today are provided either by individual post-Bloomfieldians like C. F. Hockett and the more transformationally inclined W. L. Chafe or by two schools arising out of Bloomfieldianism, tagmemics and stratificational grammar.

K. L. Pike first formulated the notion of a "tagmeme", a minimal grammatical pattern, in terms of which all grammatical structures have to be described. The idea was further developed by R. E. Longacre, who identified the "four fundamental insights of tagmemics" as the functional value of tagmemes (as subjects, objects, etc.), their grouping into sequences (syntagmemes), their occurrence at different "levels" (word, phrase, etc.) and the possibility for embedding and related phenomena ("level skips", "layering" and "loopbacks"; see chapter 9).

S. M. Lamb emphasizes levels of a different kind in his "strata", which are levels of abstraction or realization as well as of size unit, ranging from more abstract semantic and lexical units through morphemic units to phonemic units. The different units are linked through different kinds of realization, but also through rules of grouping called "tactics", which capture the structurings at grammatical and other levels.

So far we have spoken only of American linguistics, and it is to some extent true that American and European linguistics followed different lines in the pre-Chomsky era.

One unifying factor was their common heritage from Ferdinand de Saussure, the father of modern linguistics (if anyone was), whose planned *Cours de linguistique générale* was realized after his death by his pupils, in 1915. De Saussure was the first to distinguish clearly synchronic studies of a language – those that consider the state of a language at a particular point in time – from diachronic studies – which have the history of language change as their focus of attention. His other, perhaps more important, insights concerned the nature of the "language" that we study: that we should concentrate on the abstract linguistic system (*la langue*) rather than the actual speech (*la parole*) and the essence of a language is not in its external aspects – phonetic expression or semantic reference – but in its internal system.

De Saussure's most faithful followers form the Geneva school (C. Bally, A. Séchehaye, H. Frei, R. Godel), but the most logical development of his views is to be seen in the Copenhagen school, and particularly in the work of L. Hjelmslev. Linguistics becomes for Hjelmslev an autonomous discipline and is therefore given the new name of "glossematics", which describes language as an abstract system defined by its own internal relations. The theories of the Soviet linguist, S. K. Shaumyan, sometimes termed "applicational grammar", may too be regarded as embodying de Saussure's formal principles, but Shaumyan's grammar also claims to be generative in Chomsky's sense.

Equally close to de Saussure was the work of the pre-war Prague school. Inspired by the expatriate Russians, N. S. Trubetzkoy and R. Jakobson, but with important contributions from Czechoslovak linguists (V. Mathesius, B. Trnka, J. Vachek), the Prague school linguists made striking progress in the field of phonological theory. Since 1945 a new generation of Prague linguists (F. Daneš, J. Firbas) have made notable contributions to aspects of grammatical theory concerned with relations between sentences in a text (or "discourse") (see chapter 12).

In the United Kingdom it was J. R. Firth of the University of London who set the tone. Very few Europeans shared the extreme scepticism or pessimism about semantics felt by Bloomfield and his pupils in America, and Firth was even positive about meaning. He believed in studying language in the context of situation, and that meaning could be discerned at different linguistic levels. Firth also differentiated himself from Bloomfield in not giving undue weight to "chain" relations – or "bracketing" (see chapter 6) – compared with "choice" relations – or "labelling" (see chapter 7). Firth's most original pupil has been M. A. K. Halliday, whose work has been described as neo-Firthian but is mostly known now as "systemic grammar". Halliday further emphasizes the plane of "choice" relations, viewing language in general, and grammar in particular, as a whole system of choices or options with complex relations between them; he has also made a special study of textual relations along the same lines at the Prague school linguists.

To conclude our ultra-brief survey of approaches to linguistics we must mention two earlier European individual linguists, O. Jespersen and L. Tesnière. Jespersen, who was active throughout the first half of this century, besides his earlier phonetic work and his lengthy and erudite *Modern English Grammar*, wrote in a stimulating and insightful way in his general works, *The Philosophy of Grammar* (1924) and *Analytic Syntax* (1969). His notions of "rank" in the sense of a scale of modifiers, of "nexus" and the many transformational relations he exposed are still valid today and are implicit in much transformational-generative grammar.

Tesnière, like de Saussure, left his chief work, *Éléments de syntaxe structurale* (1959), to be published posthumously, but it is probably read more today than in the late 1950s when it appeared. Tesnière's insistence on a semantic basis for syntactic relations is much in sympathy with work by generative semanticists, and his notions of "actant" for grammatical roles like those played by subject, object, etc. and of the "valency" of verbs for such "actants" have found very wide acceptance.

Although it involves gross oversimplification, it might still be of some value to present a chart of the main streams of linguistic theory and their influences on each other (Figure 1). In any such guide all the names and schools are not of course equally important, and many omitted items will be just as significant as those included. But our only aim is to illustrate the diversity of approaches to the problems of linguistic (and, in particular, grammatical) theory.

However, having briefly sketched the extent and nature of these differences, we shall find no purpose in emphasizing them; what we do wish to emphasize is the common ground, the consensus, in so far as one exists. In recent years many linguistic works have been written in a polemical vein, criticizing and even ridiculing rival

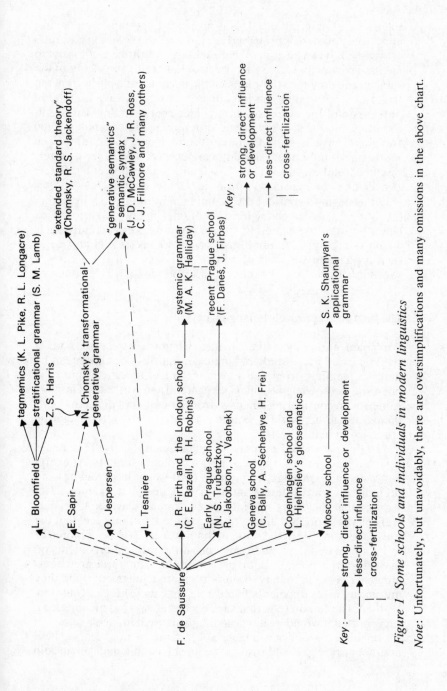

*Figure 1 Some schools and individuals in modern linguistics*

*Note:* Unfortunately, but unavoidably, there are oversimplifications and many omissions in the above chart.

theories and descriptions. This is no place to go into such details, and a study of these is probably best left until the common ground is established. It can be argued that such cut-and-thrust tactics (not to mention parries and feints) are a sign of the health and vigour of the subject, and doubtless they are. But the beginner or near-beginner in linguistics, not to mention the outsider, can be given a quite false impression of the extent of disagreement between linguists of different persuasions. Very often differences in terminology and treatment have obscured points of agreement. In addition, and more importantly, there are large areas which are never or rarely discussed, and yet which all or most linguists take for granted. These two kinds of consensus will form our object of study.

Let us begin to consider the common aims of linguists by asking the question: what characteristics of the linguistic approach to language study are shared by the different schools and individuals we have discussed? In establishing a consensus view in answer to such a question we shall of course be doing well if we carry a two-thirds majority of linguists with us on any particular point.

## The linguistic approach to language

We noted earlier how the linguist, whatever his persuasion, is single-minded in his study of language; but this does not mean he looks at language from one viewpoint only. On the contrary, the linguistic view of language may be regarded as a synthesis of insights gained from considering language from a number of different viewpoints. It will be useful to consider these aspects of the linguistic approach individually.

The linguist tries to examine language scientifically. This means first that he must be objective in his judgments about it. As everyday users of a language (or perhaps two) we all have feelings and prejudices about different items in it. I may, for example, feel strongly that so-called "split infinitives" should be avoided, or I may feel equally strongly that they should be used; or I may feel that the use of the word *gay* in the sense of 'homosexual' is to be deplored or to be applauded. Now there may be sound rational arguments on one side or the other (or both) in such disputes, but these arguments are generally used merely to support emotive judgments, and they are in any case arguments based on (appeals to) logic, tradition, aesthetics and so on (e.g. that such a word always has meant such a thing or that it would be illogical or ugly to use it in such a sense). If the linguist is to look at a language objectively he must ignore these non-linguistic rights and wrongs; he must look at language "in cold blood", as it were. This means that he must be empirical, taking as little as possible for granted and examining language anew, from first principles.

One thing the linguist can assume about language is that it is to some extent systematic; if no system at all lay behind it, it would hardly function. It is therefore essential for a linguistic account of a language to be systematic: this means being consistent, being thorough to the extent of exhaustiveness and at the same time keeping the account as simple as possible. These three criteria of consistency, exhaustiveness and simplicity (or economy) are universally accepted by linguists, though admittedly there are some differences of interpretation.

Part of the linguist's systematicness – and a somewhat misunderstood one – is his use of technical terminology. If language is regarded as a system, some technical terms are needed to describe the system. New concepts that are introduced by a science must be expressed with new words or with old words used in a new, technical way. Although it must be conceded that some schools of linguistics have built up an excess of terminology (e.g. *episememe, intensive, formative*), some terms are essential; but we shall try to keep to a generally agreed minimum (e.g. *morpheme, class, embedding*).

The danger of blurring linguistic judgment with emotion was one that the traditional grammarian fell prey to. His aim was, of course, different: he did not aim to describe language as it was, for its own sake, but rather to prescribe the form of language that should be used. This involves a presupposition that certain forms of a language or even certain languages are higher on a qualitative scale than others, Greek or Latin being "better" than a modern language, a standard language "better" than a dialect. A linguist totally rejects such judgments as without linguistic foundation; but he sees that they represent a social, anthropological or psychological datum, a view members of a community have about the language(s) they use and its varieties.

In saying that no one language is "better" in a linguistic sense than any other, the linguist is saying that all languages are of equal intrinsic value and interest. Whereas traditional grammar tended to regard all languages as corrupted versions of Latin or Greek, and logic to regard them as distorted versions of some ideal logical language, linguistics has traditionally stressed the differentness of natural languages. When translating, we typically find that items from the one language fail to match items from the other with any exactness: we may say the languages are NON-ISOMORPHIC.

Thus, in translating a simple English sentence like *They do like*

9

*brown carpets* into French, we find the following instances of a lack of one-to-one correspondence, i.e. non-isomorphisms:

(i) English *they* will not correspond to one French word, but to *on* if the persons involved are not identified, or, if they are, either to *elles* if they are all female or to *ils* if there is a male amongst them. (As linguists, we may note, without emotional involvement, that French, like many other languages, weights males more highly than females.)

(ii) French has no verb like *like* to contrast with the stronger *love*; *aimer* thus fails to provide a perfect translation.

(iii) French has no straightforward way of expressing the emphatic *do*, and thus contrasting *they do like* and *they like*.

(iv) The nearest colour word to *brown* is French *brun* which, however, designates a narrower band of colour excluding yellowish brown (*jaune*) and reddish brown (*marron*).

(v) It is impossible to translate the word *carpet* into French with a single word covering precisely the same area, since *tapis* would not distinguish carpet and lino, or carpet and wall-hanging.

(vi) Whereas the phrase *brown carpets* appears in English without an article, French must have either *les* or *des*.

(vii) The order of adjective and noun is different in French.

(viii) The form of the adjective is different after the noun *tapis* compared with some other nouns, e.g. *porte*, 'door'.

Thus neither the words nor the grammatical characteristics correspond exactly from one language to another, and linguists have generally highlighted this fact.

Indeed, perhaps as a reaction to the view of the traditional grammarian and logician, the linguist has tended to overemphasize the idiosyncratic nature of individual languages. In recent years, on the other hand, more attention has been given to the question of language universals, and the typical current view would be that a balance must be struck between what is language-specific and what is language-universal. Languages are very different and yet are somehow cut to a common pattern.

In looking at the differentness of languages, the linguist perhaps tends to align himself with the anthropologist. But in another matter – the distinguishing of descriptive and historical studies – he is more like the biologist. In the nineteenth century (when evolutionary biology was a dominating influence) the historical study of language held full sway. Great strides were made in tracing the history of the Indo-European language family (and others) by such figures as J. Grimm, F. Bopp, A. Schleicher and K. Verner. But the study of language change was so much taken for granted that H. Paul was able to say:

> Linguistic science is language history
> (Sprachwissenshaft ist Sprachgeschichte)

when it is clear in hindsight that for the linguist or for the biologist a historical study represents only one dimension; it is also necessary to study a language, or an organism, as a system at a given time. It was de Saussure who first saw this clearly: how irrelevant the history of a language can be to the study of the state of that language (*état de langue*) at a particular time. He pointed out how absurd it would be to design a panorama of the Alps, taking a number of different peaks as viewpoints; or (using his favourite analogy for language, the game of chess) how irrelevant it is to the current state of a game of chess what the previous moves have been (strictly speaking, at least one point of history is relevant: whether a player has already castled or not). It is now an accepted principle in linguistics that a clear distinction is made between SYNCHRONIC (or "descriptive") studies and DIACHRONIC (or "historical") studies of a language. No one would now maintain that diachronic facts are irrelevant for a synchronic study, or the converse (such "outside" evidence can be vital), but it is felt that any particular study should be clearly either synchronic or diachronic in its aim and manner of execution.

An equally important insight we owe to de Saussure is that each linguistic item needs to be considered not in isolation but in relation to the whole system of other items of which it forms a part. This was in reaction to the nineteenth-century tendency to trace the history of individual sounds, inflections and words. De Saussure always referred to a language as a SYSTEM, in fact a system of systems, but many other linguists, particularly Americans, have used the term STRUCTURE in an identical or largely overlapping sense, hence the term STRUCTURALISM. Some linguists, such as the Firthians (e.g. Allen, 1956), have reserved the term SYSTEM for "choice" relations and STRUCTURE for "chain" relations (see chapter 2). Using the term in the more general sense we may say that structuralism is a feature of the linguistic approach shared by most linguists, and we say this despite the fact it has sometimes been used as a (mildly pejorative) label for American linguistics of the pre-Chomsky era.

Unfortunately, the term STRUCTURE has become something of a vogue word in recent years, and, as a consequence, has not always had·as precise a meaning as it might. In linguistics we try to use it with a fairly specific meaning, in fact with a fairly literal meaning, akin to its original sense in the sphere of building. If we consider a building such as an ordinary house, it seems quite clear that there is more to it than the bricks, mortar, timbers, roof tiles, glass, etc. from which it has been built. Each of the component parts must be in the correct position relative to its neighbours: bricks are of limited value without mortar between them; an external door other than on the ground floor would be of limited use (except to intending suicides). But it is not purely a matter of relative position; structural relations are involved. The different parts of a window, for example, the uprights, cross-pieces, hinges, panes, and so on, must be of the correct number and of the right size and shape as well as being in the proper relative position, and together they must form a unified whole, a window: only then do they form a structure. These requirements – number of elements, type of elements, ordering of elements – are precisely those of a linguistic structure.

The analogy of building brings out some further points. The window, though on the one hand a whole structure of its own, is on the other hand a part of a larger structure: together with the other windows, doors and bricks it forms a wall, and of course the various walls themselves contract structural relations between themselves and with the roof. Thus we come to the idea of structures within structures, of a STRUCTURAL HIERARCHY, an essential aspect of the internal organization of a language. It is also clear that the same set of elements arranged in different ways may form different structures; this is taken for granted in building design. The same point is fundamental to grammatical structure, and it is one we learnt to appreciate at an early age when we were introduced to the riddle about Moses: that, if he was believed to be

(1) the son of Pharaoh's daughter,

then he must also have been believed to be

(2) the daughter of Pharaoh's son.

The two phrases needed to be understood with what we may call different BRACKETING (see chapter 6), something like

(1) the son of [Pharaoh's daughter]
          = X
(2) [the daughter of Pharaoh]'s son
          = X

where X is the name of Pharaoh's daughter.

The last aspect of the linguistic approach to language studying that we shall consider is given in the epithet FUNCTIONAL. When we say that the linguist takes a functional view of language, we mean that he tries to describe it in terms of the functions it performs. Language may be viewed as a tool, instrument or machine. No instrument or the like may be adequately described without taking its function(s) into account. (Imagine describing a bicycle pump to a human being who has never seen or heard of a bicycle.) The implication of this is that we cannot simply ask, "What is language like?" without also asking "What is language for?", "What does language do?" and "How does it manage to do it?".

It will probably be generally agreed that the main function of human language is communication, but it is less easy to say precisely what communication itself is. We might explain it best by considering some sample sentences:

Your dog's damaging my lawn.
I saw Gerald yesterday.

What purpose(s) would a speaker have in mind in saying such sentences? We might say he had some thought, idea or information in mind and used the sound pattern of the sentence, following the conventions of the language, to signal his meaning. He would normally perform such a speech-act when he assumed the information to be "new" and of interest to the addressee. For example, he would not normally utter the sentence

Your dog's got a short tail

with the same purpose in mind. He might use this sentence rather to induce his collocutor to provide some information about the subject introduced (the dog's tail). A more direct way to elicit information, of course, is with a question type of utterance, such as:

Is your dog healthy?
What's your dog's name?

These either ask whether a hypothesis is true, or ask for a particular piece of information. Both questions and statements may be addressed to oneself, and self-addressed language (whether the actual speech is suppressed or not) is probably the most important form of thinking. Most thought, in other words, may be regarded as self-communication. However, regardless of whether their purpose is to convey or to elicit information, to exchange information with another or with oneself, we may say that the utterances we have discussed so far have as their primary function that of communicating information: we may say that they have a COMMUNICATIVE function.

On the other hand what sort of information could be said to be conveyed (or elicited) by utterances such as those below?

(Good) morning!
Thank you (very much).
Welcome (to Manchester)!

It is true that the listener may deduce certain information, that the speaker is or is not being polite, from the first sentence that it is not yet lunchtime, from the last sentence that he is in Manchester, that the speaker is a speaker of English, etc. But all of this information emerges as a by-product; it is not the primary purpose of the sentences to convey it. Rather, these utterances are fully conventionalized social acts, like shaking hands or bowing one's head. Instead of being created by the speaker to convey specific information, they are what Lyons (1968: 177) calls "ready-made utterances" (de Saussure's "locutions toutes faites") and in fact constitute the prescribed or expected behaviour in particular social situations, such as meeting for the first time (or the first time on a particular day), receiving money or a gift, and so on. We may say that the speaker is adopting a particular role in a social activity such as meeting or giving, and that the utterance constitutes affirmation of his acceptance of this role. Such utterances may thus be regarded as having a (SOCIAL) ROLE-AFFIRMING function. Since they perform a function similar to that of the gestures we mentioned above, they might also be termed GESTURAL. (Malinowski used the term "phatic communion" in a slightly wider sense to include these utterances but also ones that have an element of information in them, so long as their primary purpose is social solidarity, e.g. *It's a nice day, isn't it?* )

Many utterances in fact combine a communicative aspect with a gestural (= role-affirming) one. Especially noteworthy in this respect are utterances that Austin (1962) called "performative" (see chapter 12). Examples are:

I name this ship H.M.S. *Independent.*
I beg you to reconsider.

Such sentences obviously involve role-playing, but there is also a clear communicative element. In the first example the actual name of the ship may be a closely guarded secret (as was the case for the *Queen Elizabeth II*); in the second, besides adopting the role of supplicant, I am clearly informing you of my wish that you reconsider.

Both communicative and gestural (social role-affirming) utterances have social functions in the sense that the utterances require an addressee (or listener) if they are to operate normally. There are some utterances, however, that in no way require an audience; in fact, they may occur more frequently when no audience is present. Consider utterances like the following, as said by the speaker to himself:

Those X scissors!
(where X is a variable with a number of values for different degrees of vigour)

Marvellous!
(either in delight or, ironically, in unpleasant surprise)

God, no!

Such utterances are said perfectly naturally in the absence of any addressee; indeed the only effect of the presence of an addressee is to restrain the speaker either in the values he gives to X, or from speaking altogether (the latter, presumably, because most societies place strict limits on the extent to which speakers are expected to talk to themselves – at least in company). Utterances like these, then, seem to provide the speaker with a linguistic way of giving vent to his emotions, particularly unpleasant ones like anger, disgust, and fear. If they can be used as an indirect substitute expression for aggressive behaviour or some other more "natural" outlet, they fulfil a useful function. This function is often referred to as the EXPRESSIVE function of utterances. It goes without saying that there are many utterances which combine an expressive function with a communicative and/or gestural (social role-affirming) one.

We may, therefore, say that the utterances of a language have three principal functions, but that these functions are not mutually exclusive. A command, for example, may combine all three. There are other minor functions, such as when language is used for aesthetic purposes in literature or for purposes of play in various linguistic games, but these seem to be secondary, derived uses. (Though we should note that Malinowski even regarded communication as a derived function, phatic communion or social solidarity being language's original purpose.)

When we maintain, therefore, that the linguist looks at language from a functional viewpoint, we partly mean that he examines it with a view to deciding how it operates to fulfil its principal function or functions. Since communication has always been assumed to be paramount, this has meant looking at language as a system of communication, and in the next chapter we shall see how it compares with other communication systems. It must also mean an examination of the way in which language enables members of a society to fulfil their social roles and to express their emotions, although these questions may be considered part of the more specialized fields of sociolinguistics and psycholinguistics respectively.

This is not all that has been meant by a functional view of language. It has been the practice not only to look at the functions of language or utterances in a language as a whole, but to consider also the functions of the units that go to make up the utterances. Thus each sound, syllable, word, phrase and so on may be said to have a particular function, a particular role to play in the language. The function of an English word like *the*, for instance, is obviously very different from that of a word like *dog*. Examining the function of such linguistic elements obviously means considering the part they play in the system of which they form part: we can observe, for instance, that *the* and *dog* make different kinds of contribution to noun phrases like *the dog, the dogs, a dog, dogs, the black dog, the same dog*, etc. But examining elements as parts of a system or structure is an insight we have already discussed under the heading of the "structuralist" approach. To a large extent, in fact, functionalism and structuralism may be regarded as pointing in the same direction: describing the function of an element means examining its use in a wider context, including the structure of which it forms part.

**Questions for study**

1 We referred above to some of the different linguistic schools. What are the advantages and the disadvantages of having competing hypotheses seeking to explain the same scientific data?

2 If linguistics is a science, should it be more like physics, like biology, or like a social science? Consider the different features of the linguistic approach and see how they apply in other sciences.

3 Is studying language like studying the law? Is language more like commom law or statute law, or both?

4 Think of three everyday words that are redefined in a technical sense in a science or technology you have studied.

5 Consider what points in the following sentence would present difficulties of translation into a language you know: *You have shown the box to your cousin, haven't you?*

6 Consider the structure of our daily eating routine. What part do such units as breakfast, main course, etc. play within it? What differences in structure are possible? (For a detailed analysis, see Halliday, 1961: 277–80.)

7 Do you find the view of language as a device for communication acceptable? Or would you follow Chomsky (1976: 69) in the view that "the 'instrumental' analysis of language as a device for achieving some end is seriously inadequate" and that "in contemplation, inquiry, normal social interchange, planning and guiding one's own actions, creative writing, honest self-expression and numerous other activities with language, expressions are used with their strict linguistic meaning irrespective of the intentions of the 'utterer' with regard to an audience"?

**Further reading**

On the history of linguistic studies: Robins (1967); Pedersen (1959); and Dineen (1967), chapters 4 to 12. On different approaches to linguistics: Bolinger (1975), chapter 15. On the linguistic approach to language: Lyons (1968), section 1.4.

*Chapter 2*

# Language as a semiotic system

## Some basic notions

In chapter 1 we took communication to be the principal function of language, but we gave only a rough indication of what we meant by "communication". To understand how language works as a system of communication – and particularly what part grammar plays within this – it will be useful to compare it with other such systems.

We said that communication involved transmitting ideas or information from person to person. This is most commonly achieved in human language by means of institutionalized patterns of speech sounds or of writing (usually on paper), each pattern conveying an agreed item of information. Each pattern thus forms a sign (or signal or symbol) representing the meaning; and the whole system of signs – often called a SEMIOTIC system – forms a code or language. We must begin by clarifying some of these notions within the field of semiotics, or sign theory. The terms SIGN and SYMBOL have been defined – prescriptively – in various ways, for example by Peirce and by de Saussure. It will be more helpful to us to take a descriptive approach, noting how the terms have been used, and, more important, precisely what distinctions need to be made.

In the field of folk meteorology, unusually clear visibility is often taken to be a SIGN of imminent rain (or of recent rain!); or a heavy clustering of berries on the holly tree, of a severe winter to come. In this sense, a sign is evidence providing an indication of something, based on a natural causal relationship; we say clearness MEANS rain, the berries MEAN a hard winter. Such cases are referred to by Peirce as INDICES.

The term SYMBOL, on the other hand, is often used, e.g. by de Saussure, to refer to a phenomenon that, though it may have a relationship of cause or of similarity to its meaning, is planned as an artificial representation of the meaning. For instance, in at least one type of central heating programme control box, the following symbols are used to indicate the temperature settings mentioned below:

'day setting'     'night setting'     '(early morning) boost setting'

Each item above symbolizes its meaning, and we note that the choice of form for the symbol is "motivated" in the following sense. Let us call the outward manifestation of a sign or symbol its EXPRESSION, and the meaning its CONTENT. We may say a symbol is "motivated" if it has a natural or cultural link between its expression and its content, so that an outsider could make an intelligent guess, if not as to what each symbol meant, then at least as to which symbol had which content, given the contents. For signs of this type Peirce uses the term ICON; we may say also they are ICONIC.

In natural human language, however, most words (e.g. *table*) or smaller meaningful units (e.g. *un-*) owe their meaning value not to any natural or cultural link but to pure convention. We say they are "arbitrary". Similarly it is purely by convention that, when an umpire at cricket raises his right hand, he is assumed to mean that the runs being scored are 'byes'. It is for such arbitrary signals that de Saussure reserves the term SIGN; Peirce, however, and, following him, Ogden and Richards (1949) use the term SYMBOL.

We summarize this rather confusing terminological situation in Table 1. Since we are taking a linguistic point of view, we shall, in the main, follow de Saussure in using the term SIGN for a linguistic element, but we also use it with Peirce's more general value.

A further distinction, first clearly made by Peirce, concerns the abstract and concrete aspects of a sign. If we were asked how many words were used in the previous sentence, we might answer, correctly, either seventeen or sixteen, depending on whether we count the word that occurs twice (viz. *a*) once or separately for each occurrence. The ambiguity of the question lies in the use of the word WORD, which may mean either 'word-type' or 'individual occurrence of a word = word-event'. This distinction is made more generally in relation to signs by referring to the "sign-type" as against "sign-event" or (more commonly) "sign-token".

The TYPE/TOKEN distinction is one of general linguistic importance and is paralleled by the distinction between CODE and MESSAGE. The

19

*Table 1 The use of terminology relating to sign and symbol'*

|  | Everyday term | Peirce | Ogden and Richards | de Saussure |
|---|---|---|---|---|
| *Over-all term*<br>Item standing for or indicating another item | ? sign | sign | sign | — |
| *Individual terms*<br>Item taken as evidence or indication of another (causally connected) item | sign, indication | index | — | — |
| Item used as arbitrary sign for individual item | symbol, sign (name, label) | index | symbol | signe |
| Item used as arbitrary sign for whole class | symbol, sign (word, name, label) | symbol | symbol | signe |
| Item used (for specific purpose) as motivated sign for class | symbol, sign | icon | — | symbole |

CODE is the overall inventory of signs in a system, together with the rules for their use; a MESSAGE, on the other hand, is an individual instance of use of the code. The difference between the two may seem so clear as to make confusion unlikely, but consider the use of the linguistic term SENTENCE in the following:

(1) A subject combined with a suitable predicate can be used as a complete sentence.
(2) He wrote down three sentences in Vietnamese.

In (1) we are referring to the code or language system; in (2) we are referring to an actual message or text.

We have tended to use the words CODE and LANGUAGE indiscriminately above, and of course they do refer to basically the same kind of entity. But in a stricter sense, which corresponds to everyday usage, as Cherry (1957: 7) points out, LANGUAGE refers to the fully developed natural human communication systems based on speech, whereas CODE refers to a set of rules for transforming messages from one sign-system to another or from one medium of a sign-system to another (see below pp. 28–9). Codes, moreover, are generally used for specific purposes on specific occasions.

We previously used the term SIGNAL in roughly the sense of 'sign' or 'symbol'; but it tends to be used in a slightly more specialized sense to refer to a complex sign, particularly in its physical manifestation as a sequence of sounds or pictures, or whatever it might be, frequently when it has been coded in some way. Thus a message in semaphore is a kind of signal. The precise medium in which the message is given is sometimes described as the CHANNEL of communication: semaphore, or even speech itself, could be a channel.

Any channel is subject to interference or, as it is termed by communications engineers, NOISE. Thus the wind blowing the semaphore signaller's flags, the sound of loud aircraft as a background to speech, or the sun shining brightly and making the traffic lights seem dim, would all be examples of noise. Fortunately, in most channels noise is allowed for by the presence of some degree of REDUNDANCY, that is, additional identifying characteristics of the information transmitted over and above the minimum required. In written language, for example, it is possible to obliterate letters or get them wrong while the message still gets through: there is enough redundancy for the receiver to identify the output as one involving one or more errors, and often to make the necessary corrections. In written English it is usually possible to reconstruct the true message, even when all vowel letters are lost, e.g.

Th*s *mp*rt*nt p**c* *f *nf*rm*t**n h*s b**n s*ppr*ss*d.

Redundancy is an important factor in grammar; most words which are mainly grammatical in function are redundant to a high degree, as the language of telegrams and newspaper headlines shows, e.g.

(The) MINISTER (is) EXPECTED (to) GIVE (his) DECISION BEFORE (the) DEBATE.

We should beware, however, of equating the redundant with the unnecessary. Not only is it essential to include some redundant items in a message in case of distortion by noise, but in spoken language, where the message is transitory and evanescent, the addressee is unable to span the whole sentence to ascertain its structure and therefore needs the redundant items as structural signals (see chapter 7). Moreover, the "redundant" items are omissible·only because English word order is grammatically distinctive and thus a structural signal in its own right. This means, of course, that it is self-defeating (and unnecessary) for radio news headlines to be given in the above form. It is interesting to note that, whereas the infinitival *to* in the above example would be omitted in a telegram, it would normally be included in a newspaper headline.

## Language-independent semiotic systems

We turn now to signalling systems independent of language, with which we shall compare it, the aim being to hit upon those characteristics which are essential to and characteristic of language itself. In referring to language-independent systems we obviously wish to exclude systems which are just alternative media for a natural language, such as written language, Morse, shorthand, Braille, etc. That these systems are language-dependent becomes clear when we realize that almost all messages in Morse, etc. have to be in English or French or some other individual language. We shall discuss them later in this chapter when we shall be considering language itself. For the present we must go right outside language, to look from the outside in, as it were.

Perhaps the most familiar — and probably most discussed — language-independent semiotic system is that of traffic lights. Let us consider first those temporary systems of lights that are used during road repairs, etc. In these systems only two lights are used, an upper red light and a lower green light, and only two messages can be sent, each light only being used by itself. The two messages with their meanings are: RED, 'stop', and GREEN, 'go'. Each message is thus unanalysable, both in its 'expression' aspect (the colour RED, the colour GREEN) and in its meaning or content ('stop' and 'go').

The situation is slightly different for the permanent kind of traffic lights that are most commonly found at crossroads. In these systems of lights (in the United Kingdom, at least) there are THREE individual lights, red, yellow (the so-called "amber") and green, but FOUR messages are transmitted with them: RED, 'stop'; RED + YELLOW, 'stop but prepare to go'; GREEN, 'go if safety permits'; and YELLOW, 'stop if safety permits'. While three of these messages again present simple (unanalysable) expression aspects, one breaks down into RED plus YELLOW. However, the content of this compound sign cannot be regarded simply as a sum of the meaning of RED and the meaning of YELLOW: in other words, it cannot be regarded as a sum of the meanings 'stop' and 'stop if safety permits' (or, as it is more generally interpreted, 'carry on going, unless you are forced to stop'!). It is clear that the sign RED + YELLOW has its own independent meaning of 'stop (but prepare to go)'. We must therefore say that this sign (but only this one) is analysable on the expression plane but unanalysable on the content plane, thus requiring two planes (or "levels") of analysis to capture this fact. In this it begins to approach the "double articulation" of natural human language, as we shall see below. We should perhaps note finally, in respect of traffic lights, that the relation between expression and content is probably arbitrary rather than motivated, although red in natural events is more likely a warning or danger signal than green.

The signs we see about our roads present a rather more complex picture. (We shall refer here to the standard signs used throughout Europe.) Whereas one or two signs seem to be unanalysable wholes, for example, the speed derestriction sign, the majority seem to break down naturally into component parts or features. Consider, for instance, the signs in Figure 2. We see at once that they

'No pedestrians'  'No cycling or moped riding'  'No right turn'

'Route for cyclists and
moped riders (compulsory)'  'Turn right'

'Pedestrian crossing'  'Side road (turning) on right'

*Key*

 = Blue  = Red

*Figure 2*

23

may each be analysed into an outer component meaning either 'no' = 'prohibition' or 'command' or 'take note' = 'warning' and an inner component designating either 'pedestrians' or 'cyclists/moped riders' or 'a turning on the right'. Each component may be regarded as a sign itself (the outer one being arbitrary, and the inner motivated), so that each whole sign is in fact composite. The situation here is rather different from the case of the red-and-yellow traffic light; that is complex in expression but simple (unanalysable) in content, whereas our road signs are analysable in both aspects. Thus, while the complex traffic light signal may be likened to a simple word made up of two sounds, the road signs are more like sentences or phrases made up of two words.

A further difference between traffic lights and road signs lies in their range; while traffic lights have very limited meanings and barely allow extension of the system, road signs are much wider in scope and form an extendible system. The set of signals used by the umpires in the game of cricket is intermediate in scope between these two extremes. There are considerably more messages than the four of the traffic lights, but there are not so many as there are road signs, and it is difficult to imagine the system being extended much. Some of the umpire's signals are clearly arbitrary, e.g. raising the right hand for 'bye', while others are clearly motivated, e.g. extending both arms as wide as possible for 'wide (delivery)'; but none of the signals seems to be analysable.

The cricket umpire's system does, however, offer one point of interest: whereas most of the signals are automatically addressed to the scorer in the pavilion, at least one – where he raises his right index finger to indicate that the facing batsman is 'out' – is addressed to the batsman. Now both traffic lights and road signs are invariably addressed without distinction to all drivers and riders (including those on Shanks's pony!) travelling along a public highway. This limited variation in the identity of the addressee places cricket umpires' signals one step nearer to natural language.

A symbol system on a much higher plane is that used in mathematical (or "symbolic") logic. The purpose of the system is to provide ways of expressing generalizations and abstractions in a more consistent and error-free way than by natural language. The capacity for general (even universal) application is achieved through the convention that symbols representing specific classes and types of elements have variable reference and are (re-)defined each time they are used. Symbols like *a* and *b* may thus represent anything from a chemical substance like *iron* to an abstract idea like *wisdom* or even some (generally assumed) non-existent entity like

*Pegasus*. Letters of the Roman alphabet (usually italic, e.g. $p$ and $q$) tend to represent sentences or propositions (e.g. the less-than-controversial *All men are mortal*). This variability of reference makes it possible for the system to be used to describe the general relations between a wide range of entities and propositions. Its chief interest to us at this point (for its further interest see chapter 11) is in its grammar or syntax; not only is it possible to combine different meaningful symbols to produce complex symbols (as in the case of road signs) but it is also possible to combine the same symbols in different ways, to produce different complex symbols. For example the following two expressions combine the same symbols but differ in value because of bracketing (which we may regard as a grammatical phenomenon):

(1) $(p \lor q) \land (r)$,  i.e. (either $p$ or $q$) and $(r)$.
(2) $(p) \lor (q \land r)$,  i.e. either $(p)$ or $(q$ and $r)$.

Mathematical symbols are similar in most ways to those of symbolic logic (the latter being, of course, in one sense just a branch of mathematics). An important shared feature is that of LINEARITY: complex messages must be transmitted in a pre-ordained order (through time, or from left to right, etc.) and must be read by the receiver in this order. The main differentiating characteristic of mathematical language is that, with the exception of set theory, the meanings of the symbols and their constructions are almost entirely quantitative.

A symbolic system in which the meanings of the symbols are much more specialized is that used in musical notation. The symbols are used not so much to describe, as in logic and mathematics, but rather to instruct which notes to play. The stave (*or* staff) notation indicates notes, with the duration shown by the type of note (crotchet, etc.) and the pitch shown by the position of the note on the stave; but there are separate symbols to denote loudness ($f, p$, etc.) and more subtle aspects of the sound quality, some of which are simply written words of Italian (*allegro, giocoso*). This Italian vocabulary might be thought to make the system partly language-derivative. But knowledge of this vocabulary is not limited to native speakers of Italian; while musicians who do know it are not thereby equipped, say, to bargain with a monoglot gondolier. The really unique characteristic of musical notation, however, is its range of meaning, which is entirely limited to (the playing of) types of sound and their combination. Thus, whereas for spoken language sound is the medium of expression, in musical notation sounds are the content. When people speak of "the language of music", on the other hand, they are generally referring to something rather different, to a

25

"meaning" in the sense of pictures, emotions and so on evoked by the music; but it is doubtful whether music can be used systematically in this way.

The question of systematicness is an important one. There is a whole range of potential interpersonal signals given by voice quality, gestures, posture, distancing from collocutor(s) and the like – phenomena that we may refer to as PARALANGUAGE and that are linked to, but to some extent independent of, spoken language. There can be no doubt that most gestures are meaningful in some sense. A nodding of the head can denote assent, an extreme opening of the eyes can denote surprise, a shrugging of the shoulders (sometimes accompanied by forward movement and upturning of the hands revealing the palms) can denote ignorance, and so on. But these signs tend to be an unorganized list rather than an integrated system. The meaningfulness of the other phenomena is less clearcut. What, for example, is the meaning of a nervous voice quality, and is it different from, say, an irritable one? Again, at what point does distancing from a collocutor become great enough to be interpreted as meaning coldness? These signals seem to be rather diffuse; they lack discreteness.

A further point relating to the status of the elements we have been discussing as meaningful signals is the degree to which they are intended and controlled. Considering for a moment spoken language, we would agree that we are at least half-aware of what we say; even if not all we say is pre-planned, at least we generally have a clear recollection of what we have or have not said (otherwise it would be unreasonable to ask someone to repeat what he had said). The same is *not* true of voice quality, gesture and the rest: people are generally quite unaware of having used them. Although they cannot be regarded as reflex actions like sneezes or laughter – after all they are not inherited behaviour but are learnt in a particular culture – nevertheless they are to a large extent unconscious acts.

We might ask finally about voice quality, gesture, posture and distancing: To what extent are they language-independent? Voice quality is language-dependent in the obvious sense that speech has to occur for voice quality to be audible; on the other hand, voice quality – or intonation for that matter – can be carried by such a semantically empty phonetic sequence as /m/. Gestures tend to be used to accompany speech-acts, e.g. handshaking co-occurring with the pseudo-question *How d'you do?*; but they may be used without speech. Posture, distancing and eye movement, on the other hand, tend to be more independent, although they are less clearly formed as systems.

### Distinctive characteristics of language

Having surveyed a range of language-independent semiotic systems and observed their similarities and differences, we now have sufficient perspective to assess the kind of communication system that natural human language is. We shall see that no one feature singles it out as unique, but that the combination of features it possesses – its "design features" (Hockett and Altmann, 1968) – puts it in a class of its own.

Consider first the question of DISCRETENESS. We have seen that natural human semiotic systems like voice quality or social distancing tend to involve the use of diffuse symbols representing points on a continuum (animal systems are similar; see the end of this section). Natural human languages, however, are symbol systems made up virtually entirely of discrete symbols. This applies to vocabulary and grammar, where each word or grammatical construction is completely distinct from every other: a thing may be big, medium or small, but not "bedium" or "medall" or any transition stage between them. It also applies to the sound system of a language, even though the speech sounds it works with form a continuum: an English speaker is interpreted as meaning *seat, sit, set* or *sat*, whenever he says /s/ and /t/ with an intervening vowel with tongue-front raising, even though there is an infinity of different front vowels he may utter.

Associated with the discreteness of a language is its LINEARITY. Given that language can use combinations of discrete signs, we see that the combinations involve sequencing along a particular dimension: time for speech, left-right or right-left, etc. for writing and so on. This has important consequences for grammatical arrangement.

As a third characteristic we may name what Martinet (1961: 17–19) terms "DOUBLE ARTICULATION". Whereas the permanent traffic lights have only one signal out of four (RED + YELLOW) that is complex in its expression aspect only, spoken human languages have vocabularies of thousands of lexical items, of which usually no more than perhaps twenty are minimum phonetic segments (e.g. English words like *a, awe, owe*), the remainder all being complex phonological sequences. This means that, in a complete description, a language needs separate (but related) accounts of its vocabulary and grammar on the one hand and its sound system (and/or writing system) on the other.

As regards ARBITRARINESS, we may say that the words in an ordinary human language that are clearly motivated are extremely limited in number. The vast majority have an arbitrary sound pattern: we see little similarity, for example, between the words for 'head' in French (*tête*), Spanish (*cabeza*), Turkish (*baş*) and Samoan (*ulu*). Non-arbitrary words are virtually limited to those denoting different kinds of sound like *rustle* or *crack*, or entities connected with those sounds like *cuckoo*. But even here, comparison of different languages shows that the sound system for a language imposes a kind of grid which impedes our ability to mimic sounds: as a result, while German dogs go *wawa*, /vaːvaː/, and French dogs (being chic) go *gnagna*, /ɲaɲa/, English-speaking dogs seem to fall into two types, those that go *bow-wow* and those that go *wuff-wuff*.

There are, however, elements of non-arbitrariness in odd places. Words containing close, front vowels ([i], [e], etc.) seem to be favoured for the concept of 'little, small', and words with open, back vowels for 'big, large'; but this trend is not without exceptions, as the words *small* and *big* themselves demonstrate.

The linguistic features we have been discussing are often compared to the difference between digital computers (the more common type) and analogue computers. In digital computers numbers are stored in a discrete fashion, being represented by partly arbitrary arrangements of electrical pulses; in analogue computers, on the other hand, numbers are represented by proportional voltages and are thus placed on a continuum. We may say that while the digital type is discrete and arbitrary, the analogue type is non-discrete and non-arbitrary; the former thus stands closer to natural language.

A further striking feature of language is its PLURALITY OF MEDIA, including the complex rules that hold for interchange between them. Whereas most other semiotic systems are limited to one medium (e.g. visual symbols for traffic lights and road signs, sound for the bus conductor's signals), human languages have a primary spoken form, but a whole range of derived ones – writing, shorthand, Braille, Morse, semaphore, etc. The complexity of the relations between these different media may be illustrated by the variety of ways in which a written language may relate to its spoken partner (cf. Haas, 1976: 181–97). The two may correspond at the level of meaningless distinctive sounds ("phonemes") or of meaningful units ("morphemes") or something near one of these (syllables, words), or of some combination of the foregoing; we might cite the English, Hindi and Chinese written languages as contrasting types. Although for some purposes writing has an equal status to spoken language, in many ways – in terms of child learning, of human history, etc., etc. – it is secondary and derived. Braille, Morse and semaphore are in a sense tertiary because they only relate directly to written language, e.g. *air* and *heir* have different values, not as in pronunciation. We might indicate some of the different media in which English may be represented as follows:

PRIMARY:       spoken language
SECONDARY:   written language    shorthand (e.g. Pitman's)
TERTIARY:      Braille   Morse (in sound or light)   semaphore
                    most secret codes

Language thus has a variety of different media to realize it, and yet the fundamental elements and their interrelations are virtually the same in all cases. The vocabulary and grammar of spoken English is substantially the same as for written English or for messages sent in Morse code: they belong to the language as a whole. The independence of a language from any one of its media may be seen as a consequence of the arbitrary relationship between its content and its expression.

We have left till last what is perhaps the most significant distinctive characteristic of language, its RANGE of meanings or use. All the other sign-systems we considered were fairly narrowly delimited: traffic lights and road signs had a fixed set of meanings which could be interpreted by someone travelling along a public highway; cricket umpires are the only people expected to use their particular signal system, and even they are unable to go beyond the first inventory of signs; even logicians usually define new signs in an *ad hoc* way. We may say that these other semiotic systems are limited in their use, limited in their semantic scope and limited in their number of possible messages.

Natural human languages, however, perhaps again as a result of the freedom they gain from arbitrariness, are quite unlimited in their use. I may speak to you in the street, in the garden, in bed or a thousand miles away at the other end of a telephone line; and I may leave a written message that you read ten minutes, ten days, ten months or even ten centuries later. Nor does language place any limit on the meaning of the message to be sent: I may talk to you not only about the here-and-now, but about the rice crop in South East Asia, or what Napoleon ate for breakfast; and (perhaps the most notable achievement!) I may lie to you. I achieve this limitless variety of messages by combining words into sentences in different kinds of combination with varying degrees of complexity. But perhaps the most important point is that, as a result, language is able to provide new messages on existing patterns, and thus to create infinite variety with finite means. Chomsky has always stressed this feature of "creativity" and has focused attention on the means that the grammar of a language provides for achieving this. Particular importance is attached to constructions involving embedding (e.g. *I believe that Mary hopes that Bill will decide that . . .*) and conjoining (e.g. *We bought potatoes and carrots and peas and . . .*). (See further, chapter 9.)

It is this breadth that is probably the most important factor differentiating human language from the various semiotic systems (or "languages") used by other species. A great range of species have been shown to have "language" of some kind (Sebeok, 1968: 165–522), but most of them are used for social-role asserting or expressive purposes, and their analysis faces many of the problems involved in describing the voice quality, gestures, etc. of human beings. Even the extensively studied language of bees (von Frisch, 1950; Wenner, 1968), which does seem to be primarily communicative in function, has a semantic potential that is limited to the location and richness of food sources. Animal languages are also generally characterized by lack of discreteness, lack of "double articulation" and lack of arbitrariness. Natural human language thus remains unique among systems of animal communication, and its uniqueness is hardly threatened by the relatively successful attempts of biologists to teach chimpanzees a simplified version of one of them (English). The achievement of human language lies in its having been invented and in its transmission to the whole of organized humanity.

**The organization of language**

Having seen how language compares with other semiotic systems, let us now consider how best to describe it as a system in its own right. Language comprises a system of symbols, each with a certain EXPRESSION and a certain CONTENT. The minimum units that are meaningful (content-ful) are signs but these can be subdivided in the expression plane into meaningless functional units called FIGURAE, e.g. phonemes, letters. These terms are Hjelmslev's but the following table indicates other terminology that has been used for the basic concepts:

| | | |
|---|---|---|
| Hjelmslev: | EXPRESSION – | CONTENT |
| de Saussure: | SIGNIFIANT – | SIGNIFIÉ |
| popular/informal: | FORM – | MEANING |

There is, here, a possible source of ambiguity; the word FORM, though commonly used to mean 'expression', was used by de Saussure, and, following him, by Hjelmslev, in a quite different sense to refer to the way in which linguistic items divide up their subject matter and are organized into a system. In this sense, FORM is contrasted with SUBSTANCE, the relationship these elements have to the matter or material of which they are composed, raw meaning or experience (Hjelmslev's "purport") in the case of signs, speech sounds (or written letters, etc.) in the case of figurae. As we saw in chapter 1 (when we discussed the translation of *They do like brown carpets* into French), each language maps an organized system of signs onto the unshaped world of our experience, dividing it into discrete semantic units. Similarly, for the system of figurae, the phoneme system which in part constitutes those signs divides up the total range of possible speech sounds, which form a variety of continua, into a discrete set of phonetic elements. For instance, in the area of voiceless front-tongue fricatives, French has /s/ v. /ʃ/, Castilian Spanish /θ/ v. /s/, and English /θ/ v. /s/ v. /ʃ/, shown schematically in Figure 3.

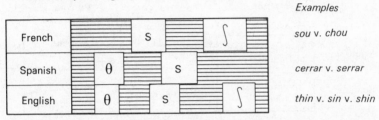

*Figure 3 Phonemic "form" imposed on a phonetic continuum (voiceless front-tongue fricatives)*

De Saussure thus saw linguistic form as the way language brought together sound (*signifiant*) and meaning (*signifié*) and organized them into a system of signs, giving each sign a value (*valeur*) which is defined partly negatively through its contrasts and rules for combination with other signs. We might represent his view as in Figure 4.

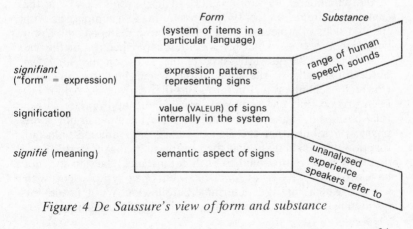

*Figure 4 De Saussure's view of form and substance*

The CONTENT of a sign is the sum of its "value" and its "significication".

Hjelmslev, however, took a more abstract, language-based view of substance, since for him unorganized experience, the raw material of meanings, was PURPORT, and substance represented the coming together of this purport with pure linguistic form, which incorporated de Saussure's VALEUR (value). On the expression plane, Hjelmslev set up a corresponding dualism EXPRESSION-PURPORT for the unorganized mass of speech sounds. He dropped de Saussure's notion of CONTENT, using the term in a quite different, general sense of 'signifié'. We might summarize his system as in Figure 5.

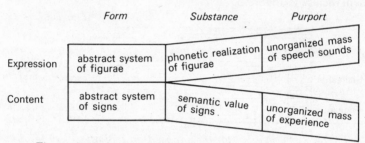

*Figure 5 Hjelmslev's view of form and substance*

In their views of the relation of expression and content, both de Saussure and Hjelmslev may be said to have taken a dualistic view, regarding the outward shape of a sign and its meaning or value as being somehow different entities, as though a sign had two parts to it, the phonetic expression ("outer" in Jespersen's view) and the semantic content ("inner"). De Saussure made a comparison with the two sides of a piece of paper. But he also made a comparison with monetary coins, which gives a different perspective: on the one hand, we see the outward shape of the coins; on the other, we observe the value of the coins in the system and their meaning (through exchange rates) in terms of other currencies. And it has been argued that this analogy is much more appropriate to the relationship of sound and meaning, since meaning is not some physical attribute that the sign possesses but rather a value or function or even activity that the sign participates in. In this non-dualist view (as represented by Firth, for instance) the sign does not have two sides to it – is not Janus-like – but one physical aspect with a value which may be determined, following Wittgenstein, by examining its use. Thus the dualism of the linguistic sign is rejected

32

for the same reasons that many modern philosophers (e.g. Ryle, 1949) have rejected the mind-matter dualism. There are, of course, other alternatives to the Cartesian dualism of mind and matter. In the idealist view (of e.g. Berkeley) only mind has real existence, matter being a theoretical construct of the mind; while in the materialist view mind is simply a rather special kind of matter and sensations represent the action of external objects on us (cf. Hobbes). The rejection of mind by materialists can be compared to the rejection of meaning by the Bloomfieldians (cf. chapter 1).

Despite these disagreements about the relationship between expression and content and the relationship between form and substance, it would generally be accepted that there is a good deal of truth in de Saussure's maxim (1962: 169):

Language is a form not a substance.
(La langue est une forme et non une substance.)

Let us return to de Saussure's chess. We know that, on the expression side, the precise details of size, material and even shape are not required for distinguishing a knight from, say, a bishop; as de Saussure himself points out, a wooden piece will do just as well as an ivory one and, if we lose the piece from the set, it could even be replaced by a piece having no resemblance to a knight, so long as we agree it has the value of a knight. This illustrates how value may be defined negatively – by differentness – the knight is anything that is different from a pawn, a bishop, a rook, etc.

On the content side, we know that, as compared with all the wide range of possible moves we might imagine chess pieces making, each piece has a clearly laid down potential; the knight, for example, may only move to a square that has a common side with one of the squares diagonally adjacent to its present square. A form is thus imposed upon it by the system of the rules of chess, and this includes not only its moves but its potential for taking other pieces, and, in the case of pawns, for transformation to another piece.

The form of a language similarly involves a system of values and of relations. It will now be our task to examine these different types of linguistic values and relations.

## Linguistic relations and values

If we consider the relations of a linguistic element – say an English word like *sky* or an English sound like [s] – we may do so from more than one point of view. A distinction is generally made between the following:

(i) SYNTAGMATIC relations, the relations the item has to its neighbours whenever it occurs; otherwise termed relations IN PRAESENTIA, or CHAIN relations.

(ii) PARADIGMATIC relations (de Saussure's term is "associative"), the relations the item has to competing items that might have occurred in its place; otherwise known as relations IN ABSENTIA, or CHOICE relations.

but room also needs to be found for a third type, what Haas (1966: 126–7) has called:

(iii) FUNCTIONAL relations, the relations an element has to the larger element within which it functions; these relations, unlike the other two which subsist between similar items (sounds to sounds, words to words, etc.), are PART-WHOLE relations.

Consider first the syntagmatic relations of our word *sky*. It would be abnormal to begin an utterance with this word in the singular, whereas the plural form *skies* would be quite possible, as in

*Skies* can be an indication of the weather.
*Skies* are difficult to paint.

However, *sky* would be perfectly normal at the beginning of an utterance if preceded by *a, the, that, every*, etc. Similarly, the English sound [s̰], unlike [ŋ], may occur initially in an English word, but if it does so it may not be followed by [b] or [θ], for instance. Such restrictions on sequencing are syntagmatic.

The paradigmatic relations of a word may be observed by considering the occurrence of *sky* in a typical sentence:

The *sky* looks very dark to me.

Here we might replace the word *sky* with *cloud, field, sheet, room*, etc., each time, of course, giving a sentence of different meaning. On the other hand, words of a different class like *big* or *explode* or *today* would be excluded, as would even the plural forms *skies, clouds, fields*, etc., so long as we maintained the verb form *looks* (as opposed to *look* or *looked*). Similarly, the sound [s] when used initially in English contrasts with [z], [ʃ], [l], etc. (cf. *sewn* with *zone, shown, loan*), but not with [ŋ].

The functional relations of an element involve the contribution it makes within the units of a higher level. When considering syntagmatic and paradigmatic relations, we looked at the occurrence of sounds and words within an utterance, a strictly non-linguistic unit. To examine the functional relations of *sky*, we need to look at its function within the sentence; or, for the sound [s], within the words and morphemes in which it occurs. Of course syntagmatic and paradigmatic relations are most frequently considered in this way, but the importance of this framework of a higher unit is often taken for granted and forgotten. Yet it is vital when we assess the distinctiveness of items, as we began to above under the heading of paradigmatic relations, or the size of our minimal units (e.g. *cranberry* = *cran-* + *-berry*?; [tʃ] = /tʃ/ or /t/ + /ʃ/?), as we might do under the heading of syntagmatic relations. In other words, examining functional relations means examining linguistic value.

Looking at linguistic function in a way akin to that in which we consider algebraic functions, we may think of functional values as deriving from the interaction of constants and variables. Thus, if we consider the initial element in a sequence of three forming a higher-level unit, this element may be taken as a variable with the others as a frame of constants, or it may be held constant while the other two are varied. Using the convention of algebra that $a$, $b$, etc. stand for constants and $x$, $y$, etc. for variables, we may represent this as follows:

1st element variable $x$ $b$ $c$
Number of element 1 2 3
1st element constant $a$ $x$ $y$

When we treat the first item as a variable $x$, we ask not only what may replace it but, more important, what is the effect of replacing it – what is its DISTINCTIVE VALUE? When on the other hand we treat the first element as a constant $a$, we ask to what extent it specifies or determines the nature of its neighbours – what is its DETERMINANT VALUE?

It is only by asking about distinctive value that we establish the difference between [l] and [ɹ] (e.g. *load v. road*) as being phonologically relevant in English (though not in Japanese) but the difference between [r] and [ɹ] (e.g. *road* as said by an (Eastern) Scots speaker compared with a speaker of British RP) as being irrelevant. We must further observe that some differences between sounds are non-distinctive, not because they are interchangeable, but because they can never occur in the same frame (cannot be replaced one for the other), e.g. British clear [l] and dark [ɫ], the former occurring only before vowels and /j/ and the latter everywhere else. This gives us three values which a difference may take in terms of distinctiveness (Figure 6).

In traditional phonemic theory the examples we have just discussed would be treated as follows: English [l] and [ɹ] would belong to different phonemes; [r] and [ɹ] would be free allophones of the

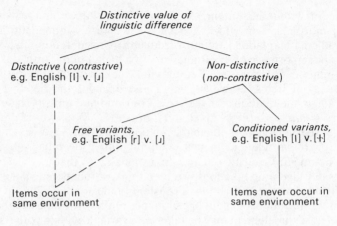

*Figure 6*

same phoneme; and [l] and [ɫ] would be conditioned allophones of the same phoneme.

Distinctive value applies equally to grammatical and lexical elements, i.e. to all elements that are meaningful. The word *more* in *more beautiful, more interesting*, etc. is distinctively different from (i.e. contrasts with) *less, most, very*, etc. On the other hand it might be regarded as a conditioned variant of *-er*, which occurs with the same meaning in *nicer, richer*, etc. But there is no possibility of *\*beautifuler*, etc. or of *more nice*, etc. There are, of course, borderline cases like *?tenser/more tense, ?quieter/more quiet*, but generally any given speaker uses either one form or the other for a particular word. Finally, if we compare the rival pronunciation of the *-est* of *nicest, richest*, etc. as /əst/ or /-ɪst/, we may take them to be (allomorphic) free variants (see further chapter 10); cf. also *patriot* with /eɪ/ or /æ/ as the first vowel, or *-d* as against *-n* in the past participle *mowed/mown*.

The determinant value of a sound may be illustrated with the glottal stop[ʔ] in some varieties of English. We are not concerned with the use of the glottal stop as a substitute for /t/ (or other voiceless plosives) but rather with its use by many speakers of Received Pronunciation (RP) at word and morpheme boundaries, e.g. [bə'nɑnə 'ʔaɪs] *banana ice*, [ju'gændə 'ʔeɪʃn̩] *Uganda Asian*. For the speakers in question the glottal stop only occurs at word boundaries between two vowels and is, of course, an alternative to the widespread intrusive/linking *r*. The glottal stop may be said to determine its environment: nothing may precede or follow it except a vowel, and a word or morpheme boundary must precede it. This example is actually a special case, because the marking of a boundary is not a necessary part of determinant value but a special subvariety, which we may call, following Trubetzkoy and Martinet, DEMARCATIVE. The example of English [s] considered above under syntagmatic relations showed that the occurrence of a sound may place limits on the occurrence of neighbouring sounds purely within a word or morpheme. The same applies to words and morphemes within the structures of phrases and sentences. If we examine the word *to* in a sentence like

I want to apply

we see that, although the distinctive value of *to* is negligible (what could replace it to give a similar sentence?), it has the clear effect of requiring a following member of the verb class and more explicitly a preceding member of the catenative verb class (including *need, hope*, etc. but not *examine, tire*, etc.).

It should be emphasized that distinctive value and determinant value are values not elements. It is therefore normal for an element to be categorized with respect to both values. Thus a word like *my* (or an English phoneme like /h/) is contrastive, cf. *the, a, his*, etc., but also determines the occurrence of a following noun (/h/ contrasts with /r/, /m/, etc. but requires a following vowel). So items which have determinant value but are almost lacking in distinctiveness are just an extreme case.

Distinctive value has been at the forefront of linguistic study. It was the idea behind the keeping apart of phonemic differences and (mere) phonetic (*or* allophonic) differences. More generally, Pike and others have spoken of the -EMIC and the -ETIC, applying the notion not only to minimal sound units (phonemes – allophones) and morphological units (morphemes – allomorphs) but also to syntactic units (tagmemes – allotagmas). Hjelmslev and others use the general terms INVARIANT for items that contrast (are subject to "commutation" – simultaneous change in expression and content) and VARIANT for items that are mutually substitutable without change of value. Determinant value has been less conspicuous, but it would seem to be involved in both Firth's notion of "syntagmatic prosodies" (1957: 137) and in the idea of grammatical or structural meaning (Fries, 1952: 106–9). It is exemplified most particularly by "grammatical markers" or "structural signals" (see chapters 5 and 7).

## Rules and tendencies

In a linguistic description we need an account of the linguistic elements, their values and relationships. But what *kind* of statement do we make about them? Having observed the data, do we simply present what we see as general regularities, or are we bold enough to frame RULES? A rule says that a certain relation holds in all cases, whereas a REGULARITY may assert something less than this. The difference may amount to nothing more than the degree of certainty or modesty felt by the linguist, but it may indicate his consciousness of the degree to which the rule/regularity needs to be restricted and qualified to cover apparent exceptions. On the other hand, if language is a well-defined system, then perhaps it should be capable of description in terms of rules.

Consider the following rules or regularities for English grammar:

(1) All noun phrases are either singular or plural (e.g. *the boy – the boys*).

(2) All proper nouns referring to single expanses of land occur in the singular without an article (e.g. *Lisbon, Portugal, Europe*).

(3) Noun phrases that occur as objects of the verb *injure* are animate, while those that occur as object of the verb *damage* are inanimate.

The first rule makes a strong claim – that there is a clear-cut distinction of number applying to all noun phrases (even presumably to ambiguous ones like *the sheep*) – but it is one that has a strong chance of applying, as it stands, to all possible cases. The second rule, on the other hand, will clearly have to be modified if it is to take account of certain exceptions, e.g. *The Hague, the Lebanon*; this modification might be achieved either by stating that non-contrastive uses of the article are excluded, or by listing the exceptions. However, can we be said to have a fully fledged rule, if exceptions have to be listed? Do we have anything more than a tendency?

During the nineteenth-century period of historical linguistics a controversy was initiated by the Neogrammarians' (*Junggrammatiker*) insistence that sound laws, i.e. patterns of phonological change, were "exceptionless" (cf. Pedersen, 1959: 277–310, especially 294f.). Apparent exceptions, they pointed out, could be attributed either to external interference of some kind (e.g. linguistic borrowings) or to the fact that the sound law had not been fully worked out in all its complexity (e.g. Grimm's Law needing to be modified by Verner's Law). The only other possibility was that the sound law was of a different, sporadic type which affected individual words as lapses, due to slips of the tongue, analogy and related phenomena (e.g. metathesis, popular etymology).

These points have some lesson for us in the question of grammatical rules, particularly in connection with our third example. Although we can agree that most examples follow the rules, e.g.

> John injured the passenger/guard/elephant, etc.
> John damaged the door/box/ring, etc.

What are we to say about cases like:

> ? John injured my poor car.
> ? That treatment damaged the child.

The fact that we encounter such borderline cases suggests that we are faced not with a clear-cut division but with what has been variously referred to as "shading" or a "cline" (Halliday, 1961: 287), or "gradience" (Bolinger, 1961): in other words, we do not categorize in terms of "yes" and "no" but in terms of "more" and "less". Such an approach to the data seems especially to be required for questions that are semantic rather than formal and grammatical. Indeed Haas (1973b: especially 147–8) suggests that we distinguish grammatical RULES from semantic TENDENCIES.

The issue of exactness – just how much is allowed by a language, and just how far linguistic data are grammatical and how far semantic – poses a particular problem for generative grammar, as we shall see (in chapter 4). If no distinction is made along Haas's lines, then in becomes necessary to distinguish different degrees of grammaticalness (Chomsky, 1961) including the so-called "semi-grammatical" (compare further Bazell, 1964). Returning (perhaps not totally unexpectedly) to the analogy of the game of chess, we may note that the rules of the game are fixed, while the tenets of good play can only be described as trends, probabilities and tendencies. It would be nice to think that grammatical patterns were as definite as the rules of chess, but we may find (see further chapters 3, 4, 11) that they are sometimes more like the tenets of good play.

## Questions for study

1 Is the word *word(s)* used in the meaning of 'type' or 'token' in the following:
  (a) There are some words that you should avoid using in a dissertation.
  (b) Your dissertation must not exceed 15,000 words.
  (c) You must correct the last word of your first sentence.
  (d) You should avoid overuse of that word.

2 Identify the redundancy in the following; decide whether it
  serves any purpose; and consider how, if at all, it might be
  remedied:
  (a) John defeated Bill more easily than George defeated Bill.
  (b) This is a new innovation, but I forecast it two years in
      advance.
  (c) John's been shot with a gun.

3 On the old-fashioned kind of bus with driver and conductor,
  the conductor could send the following messages on his bell:
  DING, 'stop at next stop'; DING-DING, '(re-)start';
  DING-DING-DING, 'don't stop at next stop'. Does this language
  have a separate "phonological" level? In other words, does it
  have a level of meaningless expression units?

4 "He didn't have to tell me – I could see it written all over his
  face." How much is this normally true, and how much an
  exaggeration? Is it a linguistic matter?

5 The word *language* is, of course, frequently used in a
  figurative or extended way, e.g. the language of music, the
  language of love, computer languages. How many of the
  distinctive characteristics of human language apply in these
  cases?

6 If, because of the calamitous emotional associations it had for
  me, I found myself unable to use the word *exam(ination)*, and
  regularly replaced it with my private word *clope*, how would
  my linguistic system be affected? (Consider its relations to
  other words.)

7 Consider the sentence *John will be at the party*.
  (a) Comment on the syntagmatic and paradigmatic relations
      of the word *will*.
  (b) Consider such forms as *won't, will not, couldn't, could not,
      may not, shouldn't, should not*, and assess the degree to
      which the items *not* and *n't* are free variants, conditioned
      variants or are in contrast in spoken English.

**Further reading**

On semiotic systems: Lyons (1977), sections 4.1 and 4.2 (also
Gaillie, 1952, and Cherry, 1957). On the distinctive characteristics

(or "design features") of language: Hockett and Altmann (1968). On the organization of language: de Saussure (1962), 97–140. On linguistic relations and values: de Saussure (1962), 150–75; Haas (1966). On rules and tendencies: Bazell (1964); Haas (1973b).

# Chapter 3

# The task of grammar

## The scope of grammar

Having attempted to understand something of the basic nature of human language, we are now in a better position to ask: what aspects of a language constitute its grammar? We have seen how language is a two-level semiotic system, being analysable separately for content and expression units: it has a set of meaningful content units (signs) and a set of meaningless expression units (figurae), each set with its own system of values and relations. Hockett (1958: 575f.) refers to the level of content units as "plerem111c", with its minimal units "pleremes" apparently embracing both items like *walk, the* and grammatical patterns like subject–verb–object. The level of expression units he describes as "cenematic", with its minimal units "cenemes" (cf. Hjelmslev's "figurae") presumably including phonemes, intonation patterns, etc., on the one hand, and the letters ("graphemes"), punctuation etc. of written language, on the other.

The division into plerematic and ceremetic is in many ways the easiest divison to make, although no ready terms to refer to it spring to mind apart from Hockett's. The plerematic level, the study of meaningful units, is generally subdivided into the areas of grammar (or syntax), lexis (or vocabulary) and semantics. But the precise relation of these subfields to each other and to plerematics as a whole is by no means clear: there is some overlap, and some areas are apparently left uncovered.

Let us consider first the relationship between grammar and semantics, which we touched on earlier (in chapter 2). A vital concept in both fields is the notion of a minimum plerematic unit, i.e. a minimum meaningful unit, or MORPHEME. The morpheme is not without its difficulties (as we shall see in the next section of this chapter), but it may be regarded as a fundamental unit in both grammar and semantics. Provisionally we may say that a morpheme may, on its own, form a simple word, e.g. *cat, pure*, or it may combine with other minimum meaningful units to form a word, as in *girls, girlish, girlfriend, impure*. Morphemes may be seen then, either directly or through composite words, as the ultimate constituents of sentences, at least in a superficial sense. But in what combinations and in what sequences may they occur together? The patterning of morphemes to make up sentences is generally described as the GRAMMAR of the language. Those who wish to use this term in a more general sense to refer to the system of the language as a whole (as in "a grammar of (say) Aztec") prefer to use the term SYNTAX in a broader sense too, to cover morpheme patterning within the sentence. The reason why we use morphemes, whether individually or in combination, is to convey meaning. SEMANTICS is the study of this meaning, embracing both the meanings of individual lexical items ("lexical semantics") and the meanings conveyed by grammatical morphemes (such as *than* and *-ing*) and grammatical patterns ("grammatical semantics").

The area of overlap between semantics and grammar (or syntax) is thus evidently in the question of grammatical patterns and their meanings. We might ask, for instance, whether the use of the English third-person pronouns *him, her, it, them* in sentences like the following is a grammatical or a semantic matter:

> The *man* was better than I gave *him* credit for.
> | | |
> |---|---|
> | *woman* | *her* |
> | *doctor* | *him/her* |
> | *book* | *it* |
> | *bull* | *him/it* |
> | *cow* (cf. also *ship*) | *her/it* |
> | *sheep* | *it/him/her* |

If it were a matter of grammatical rule, like, say, the use of *le* v. *la* with the French noun, we would need to set up noun classes for each type of agreement, something after the fashion of Strang (1962: 95), e.g. MASCULINE (*man, boy, bachelor*), FEMININE (*woman, girl, midwife*), COMMON (*doctor, person, adolescent*). But is there, even given this complex set of relations, a strict agreement at all? We need to appreciate that it only requires a minor semantic change, strictly one only in reference (i.e. perhaps only a change in the external world to which language refers), to make a difference in the agreement of a word: for instance, if men start becoming accepted into midwifery, the item *midwife* becomes COMMON. Moreover, a common noun like *neighbour*, as McCawley points out (1968: 133f.), only needs adjectival specification with, say, *buxom* or *virile* to make it unequivocally FEMININE or MASCULINE. In addition, the items which select either one pronoun or another do not do so randomly, but according to the view the speaker takes of the item referred to: does he personally know the particular bull referred to or, in the case of a vessel or vehicle, is he emotionally attached to it? We are dealing here with so-called "natural gender", where pronominal agreement is semantically and not syntactically based.

The general question of where semantics and syntax meet is one that has divided linguists constantly, and in recent years there has been disagreement on the issue amongst generative grammarians, Chomsky and others regarding certain matters as syntactic which generative semanticists regard as semantic. For example, McCawley, a generative semanticist (1968: 135), asks how it is that we can say

> I counted the boys.
> I counted the crowd.

but that we cannot say

> *I counted the boy.

This can best be explained, he claims, not by saying that the verb *count* is selectively restricted to objects that are syntactically plural (or collective), but by simply saying that its objects must denote "a set of things rather than an individual".

Bazell (1964) takes a different view from either Chomsky or McCawley. Like Chomsky, he wishes to distinguish the grammatical from the semantic – he speaks of "grammatical constraints" and "semantic restraints" – but he would put the border-line in a different place. He would agree with McCawley in regarding the noun-occurrence of *I counted the boy* as due to semantic features (it would be "non-grammatical"), but would regard some non-occurrences, e.g. *He seems sleeping*, as due to syntactic factors (they would be "ungrammatical"). Bazell would further distinguish grammatical "constraints", where there is no semantic "tie up", from grammatical "restraints", where there is.

Of course, in the view of all three linguists, sentences like

> The cross-eyed elephant slept in the hotel bed.
> That ice cube you just melted has shattered.

would be prevented by the nature of the real world, by a "referential obstruction". We might summarize the differences between them as in Table 2.

In distinguishing between grammatical and semantic deviance, Bazell pays attention to the question of corrigibility. If an impos-

*Table 2 Reason for deviance*

| Deviant sequence | Bazell (1964) | Chomsky (1965) | McCawley (1968) |
|---|---|---|---|
| *When he will come, . . . | *grammatical constraint* | *ungrammaticalness* | *grammatical violation* |
| *He seems sleeping. | *grammatical restraint* | *semi-grammaticalness*[a] | *? grammatical violation* |
| *He counted the dog. | *semantic restraint* | *semi-grammaticalness*[a] | *semantic selectional restriction* |
| *That ice cube you just melted has shattered. | *referential obstruction* | *referential obstruction* | *? referential obstruction* |

*Note:*
[a] Chomsky distinguishes different degrees of grammaticalness, ungrammaticalness being the end-point of the scale.

sible sequence has an obvious equivalent correct sequence (or set of them), then it is uniquely corrigible, e.g.:

*When he will come = When he comes.

This means of course that distinguishing the grammatical v. the ungrammatical is a clear-cut matter, whereas semantic deviance is a matter of degree. This ties up with Haas's notions of grammatical rules and semantic tendencies, which we discussed in chapter 2.

We cannot adequately disentangle the grammatical and the semantic without giving time to a further, related, distinction, that between LEXICAL and GRAMMATICAL. This is basically the difference between a dictionary and a grammar, and refers to two different functions meaningful items may have. On the one hand they may have a lexical function, in so far as they make direct reference to the world of the speaker (e.g. *knife, nice, night*); on the other they have a grammatical function in so far as they make a contribution to the structure of the speaker's utterance, having themselves mainly structural or relational meaning (e.g. *than, to, not*). Lexical and grammatical functions are in no way mutually exclusive, but most morphemes have predominantly the one function or the other. (These functions may be viewed as the plearematic level of operation of the distinctive and determinant values that we discussed in the last chapter.) Some morphemes have mainly lexical value, bearing a particular lexical meaning, and for these we use the term ROOT (see chapter 10); other morphemes, NON-ROOTS, have mainly grammatical value, marking particular grammatical structures and bearing grammatical meaning (Martinet (1961) has used the terms "lexeme" and "morpheme" for these two types). Root morphemes, having greater distinctive value, belong to large paradigms, to so-called OPEN SETS; grammatical morphemes (non-roots), having less distinctive value, belong to small paradigms, to so-called CLOSED SETS (or SYSTEMS). The former gives the speaker choices; the latter a framework for those choices.

Let us examine the substitution potential of the items in the following sentence:

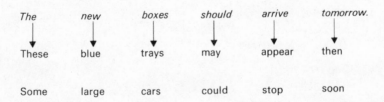

| *The* | *new* | *boxes* | *should* | *arrive* | *tomorrow.* |
|---|---|---|---|---|---|
| These | blue | trays | may | appear | then |
| Some | large | cars | could | stop | soon |

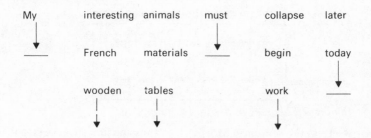

We see that the words *the* and *should* belong to closed sets, being replaceable by a couple of dozen items at most, whereas *new, boxes* and *arrive* belong to open sets, where the number of replacements is counted in hundreds, even thousands, and the number may be added to by new words entering the language as foreign loans or produced internally as neologisms; the adverb *tomorrow* seems to be intermediate. Words with larger paradigms normally carry more information, since they involve selection from a wide range of choices. Words with smaller paradigms, and therefore less lexical importance, tend to have a grammatical role.

Lexicology, or LEXIS, studies the lexical items that make up the vocabulary of the language, their phonological form, their morpheme structure (where they are other than single morphemes) and, most important, their lexical meaning. Grammar studies the structural function of morphemes, for which grammatical morphemes are highly significant, including the patterns that ultimately make up sentences and the meanings of grammatical structures. The boundary between lexis and grammar is, however, far from clear. Firstly, many grammatical categories have fairly concrete lexical meanings, e.g. 'plural', 'past' (see further chapter 11). Secondly, lexis is said to study particular facts of the kind that go into a dictionary, but some patterns above the word level are fairly idiosyncratic. Certainly idioms like *to and fro, a white elephant, to beat about the bush* (different as these are) must all be included in lexis. But what about semi-productive patterns like *have a* VERB (*have a look, have a try*, compared with *\*have a see, \*have an experiment*), and the irregularity of some prepositional usage, e.g. *tired of, interested in, bored with*, etc.?

A simplified indication of the relative position of grammar to adjacent areas is given in Figure 7.

Grammar is often subdivided into morphology and syntax. The word is taken as the dividing line. Morphology traditionally describes morphemes and their patterns of occurrence within the word; while syntax describes the structuring of morphemes and

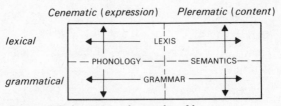

*Figure 7 Subareas in the study of language*

words within the sentence. Morphology thus accounts for the structures of complex words like *boys, loved, inexpensive, dentist, fire-engine, washing machine*. Syntax accounts for the structure of phrases like *very good, very good students, pass examinations*, and sentences like *Very good students pass examinations*. But the boundary between morphology and syntax is not so straightforward either. An element like *'s* in the English phrase *the man-next-door's daughter* seems to operate at phrase level in this example, but within the word in other cases (e.g. *John's daughter*). Inflections like *-s* in *The girl loves him* fall within the field of morphology as affixes within the word, but, on the other hand, they have an important role in the syntactic structure of the sentence, in helping to mark the subject through number concord, for example. As we shall see later (in chapter 10), inflection, though part of morphology, stands close to syntax; and traditional grammarians clearly distinguished inflection, or "accidence", from the lexical part of morphology, "word-formation". Figure 8 illustrates the basic divisions and overlaps within grammar and semantics.

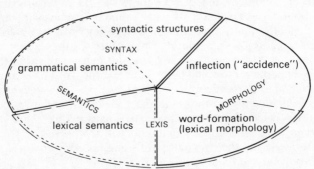

*Figure 8 Subareas of plerematics*

Whatever the precise areas of semantics, grammar, lexis, morphology and syntax, one thing they all share, as subareas of plerematics, is the morpheme as a basic unit. It is therefore necessary, as a next step in our approach, to consider the nature of this basic unit.

## The morpheme as a basic unit

It is clear that we need something like a morpheme as our basic unit in grammar. We have seen how in morphology words are broken down into smaller units. The words we listed above, for example, would need to be broken down as follows:

    boys = boy + -s
    loved = lov(e) + -ed
    inexpensive = in- + expens(e) + -ive
    dentist = dent- + -ist
    fire-engine = fire + engine
    washing machine = wash + -ing + machine

Some of the constituents are themselves capable of occurring as words in their own right, e.g. *boy, love*, and are usually termed FREE; the others, marked with a hyphen, only ever occur as part of a word, e.g. *-s, in-, dent-*, and are termed BOUND (see further chapter 10). But they are all "ultimate constituents", to use Bloomfield's term (1935: 161). The question arises, though, just how far we are to go in arriving at these ultimate constituents, or morphemes. This depends on what the essential requirements of our basic morpheme are: do they include meaningfulness, and, if so, of what kind?

Although Bazell (1949b), for instance, has argued that the morpheme is a "formal" or grammatical unit rather than a semantic one, a minimum meaningful unit would surely be the soundest base for plerematic studies. It is less easy to say what "minimum meaningfulness" is. We presumably need to identify each quantum of meaning with a particular phonological segment. What, for instance, if it were claimed that the word *pillow* consisted of two elements *pill-*, 'soft, padded', and *-ow*, 'small, portable rest/support'? We would enquire when, if ever, either of these elements occurred in other combinations with the same meaning. The answer in these cases would presumably be "never", but the matter is often much less clear-cut. This point can be well illustrated from the range of different verbs in English that may begin with *dis-* (phonologically /dɪs-/). We might set these out in four groups:

    (1) disarrange, disorganize, disagree, etc.
    (2) discern, discuss, distribute, etc.
    (3) dismay, distort, disturb, etc.
    (4) disappoint, disclose, discount, etc.

In group 1 we can recognize a recurrent element *dis-* with the meaning 'fail to carry out the required process/carry out the reverse

49

process'. There is also a clearly identifiable second constituent in each case (*arrange, organize, agree*).

In group 2, on the other hand, we find no clear semantic resemblance either between the members of the group themselves or between them and members of another group, and are consequently obliged to regard the phonological similarity as irrelevant (in present-day English); moreover the phonological "remainders" *-cern, -cuss* and *-tribute* have no semantic significance, either.

In group 3 we equally find incoherent remainders, *-may, -tort, -turb*, but this time it seems possible to detect a common strand of meaning running through the *dis-*'s, somewhat similar to that in group 1, involving 'failure or misdirection of a process'. So the remainders *-may, -tort* and *-turb* may have some semantic status attributed to them – that of UNIQUE morpheme (Hockett, 1958: 126–7), a morpheme that never occurs without a particular companion. Traditional examples are the *cran-* of *cranberry*, the *luke-* of *lukewarm*, the *-couth* of *uncouth*.

Finally, in group 4 we may also recognize a recurrence of the *dis-* of group 1, and at first sight the rest of each word is not a mere remainder but an occurrence of the already existent morphemes *appoint, close* and *count*. Our recognition of these items is, however, obviously illusory. The resemblance of our remainders to them is purely formal: there is no straightforward semantic connection between *disappoint* and *appoint*, *disclose* and *close*, or *discount* and *count*. At best, these occurrences of *appoint, close* and *count* can be regarded as pseudo-morphemes; more realistically, there is nothing to distinguish group 4 from group 3.

Summarizing, we have found:

(1) *disarrange*, etc.: MORPHEME +MORPHEME
(2) *discern*, etc.: single MORPHEME
(3) *dismay*, etc.: MORPHEME + UNIQUE MORPHEME
(4) *disappoint*, etc.: MORPHEME + PSEUDO-MORPHEME (the latter being a UNIQUE MORPHEME identical in form to another morpheme)

This seems quite a neat scheme; but, in practice, the lines between groups 2, 3 and 4 are difficult to draw. They involve considering the questions of whether a particular meaning can be identified as one that recurs in other contexts, and whether the sequence is exhaustively analysable. Unfortunately there often seems to be a cline (or gradience) involved. If we consider, for instance, English prepositional verbs with *look*, we find that the degree to which the use of the sense of sight is implied decreases as we progress through this list:

John looked at the professor.
John looked for the professor.
John looked to the professor (for an answer, etc.).
John looked after the professor.

At what point through these examples do we cease to identify the morpheme *look*?

A further problem in the identification of morphemes is that of contextual conditioning, homonymy and polysemy. It is clear that many morphemes have a meaning that varies somewhat from context to context: it is only by overlooking these minor differences and abstracting the common core that we can make generalization possible in language. For example, the word *bag* refers to quite a variety of different objects in *handbag, shopping bag, mailbag*, but there is an automatic variation in meaning according to context.

The different uses of the word *paper*, on the other hand, present a slightly different picture. We have three main meanings for *a paper*:

(1) 'a newspaper',
(2) 'a document',
(3) 'an academic lecture';

and the difference in meaning between them goes beyond any automatic change conditioned by the context of news media, official use or the academic world, respectively; there are special extra features of meaning in each case. Nevertheless, despite this specialization, we recognize a retained core meaning of 'important written or printed material for public use'. Such cases are referred to as POLYSEMY and the morpheme is described as "polysemous".

We meet a rather different phenomenon, however, when we examine an item like *race*, with its two meanings:

(1) 'ethnic group'
(2) 'speed competition'

Here it is difficult to see how anyone would wish to make a link between the meanings. The only course open is to say that two different morphemes are involved, both having the same phonological expression. This phenomenon is termed HOMONYMY. A distinction may be made, according to whether the sameness of expression is phonological, graphemic or both. Examples are:

(1) FULL HOMONYMY. Spoken the same – written the same: *race* –*race*; *plant* ('factory') –*plant* ('vegetable organism'); etc.

51

(2) HOMOPHONY. Spoken the same – written differently:
*night – knight*; *die – dye*; etc.
(3) HOMOGRAPHY. Spoken differently – written the same:
*lead* (/li:d/) – *lead* (/led/); *wind* (/wɪnd/) – *wind* (/waɪnd/); etc.

But usually these different phenomena are jointly categorized as "homonymy".

The distinction between homonymy and polysemy is not always easy to make. Is there, for instance, sufficient common meaning in the different uses of the word *suit* in *a suit of cards, a suit of clothes* and *a legal suit* to warrant a common morpheme?

In stressing the importance of the morpheme as a basic unit in grammar, we should not be unaware of the importance of the WORD. We leave a discussion of the precise nature of the word till later (chapter 10), but we should note at this stage that it is the lexical unit *par excellence*. It is the basic unit of lexis and has far greater independence than the morpheme. The contrast is particularly striking in inflecting languages like Latin, Russian and Sanskrit, in which root morphemes (e.g. Latin *mens-*, 'table', *am-*, 'love') lead a very sheltered life, going nowhere without the chaperonage of inflectional affixes. Even in English words are "prefabricated", as Bolinger (1975: 108–11) puts it, while morphemes are "semi-finished material"; in other words, morphemes can be so limited and lacking in definition that they only become fit for instant use when they are built into a word.

## Kinds of grammar

At the beginning of this chapter we tried to establish what part of a language constituted its grammar. We now turn to the question: how should this part of the language be described? This question is often made unnecessarily difficult for those coming from a background of traditional grammar, because of a misunderstanding about the nature or purpose of grammar and about its scope. "Grammar" as taught at school is likely to include anything from lexis through semantics, syntax and morphology to orthography and even pronunciation. This misunderstanding about the scope of grammar becomes natural enough, however, when it is considered how the word in its countable use ("*a* grammar") has been used to refer to a full account of a foreign language, as in "A grammar of French" (or Aztec, or whatever it might be), and how modern transformational-generative grammar, as we noted above, uses the term in a similar way.

The misunderstanding of the purpose of grammar is explicable in a different way: there are different kinds of grammar written for different purposes. We may distinguish three main kinds.

A PRESCRIPTIVE MONOLINGUAL (or normative) GRAMMAR aims to codify, in the form of rules, the usage of speakers of the standard variety of the language. The purpose is presumably to make possible the acquisition of the standard dialect by non-standard speakers. Such a grammar can have official force when, as in France, Spain and a number of other countries, there is a National Academy to commission it. In other countries it is the social prestige of the speakers of the standard dialect that ensures the standing of the grammar.

The chief difficulty with prescriptive grammars lies in the notion of "correctness". Starting simply as a codification of the dialect of socially (and, perhaps, also economically and educationally) superior speakers,[1] such a grammar invariably tends to drift towards the way the grammarian thinks people ought to use the language. This presumably arises from the grammarian's dissatisfaction with the arbitrariness of judging one linguistic usage as superior to another, and his urge to find a justification for his ruling. He looks for justification in different directions:

  (i)   to history, to some earlier stage of the language, e.g. the prescribed uses of *shall* and *will* as auxiliary verbs.
  (ii)  to some "culturally superior" language like Latin, e.g. only nominative forms to be used after the verb *to be* (*It's I* for *It's me*), or the prohibition of a "split infinitive" (this conflicting with the history of the language, since *to* was not part of the Latin infinitive).
  (iii) to logic, e.g. the rejection of "double negatives" as strong negatives because, logically, they are equivalent to a positive. (The real justification for the prescription is simply that educated speakers do not use the pattern.)
  (iv)  to a circular justification in terms of his own rules, e.g. the precept (in parody form) "Never use a preposition to end a sentence with !", based on the inadequate definition of prepositions as items that precede noun phrases (see below, p. 60).

This search for justification of prescriptions outside the language (in its present state) merely leads to the prescription of some artificial forms that no one uses naturally. It also leads to speakers misapplying prescriptions to cases they were never intended for, e.g. *He likes*

---

[1]   It constantly needs to be re-emphasized that it is the speakers or their status that is superior – not the dialect itself.

*you and I*. The only adequate kind of prescriptive grammar is one that bases its prescriptions on a genuine description of the recommended variety of the language, as it is actually used by its speakers.

A DESCRIPTIVE MONOLINGUAL GRAMMAR is a description of the system underlying the actual utterances produced by speakers of a language. It is the kind of description modern linguistics aims at. There is no attempt to legislate how speakers should behave, only to describe how they do behave linguistically. The purpose of such a grammar is to make explicit a thing that is implicit in a speaker-listener's use of his language but of which he is usually quite unaware, i.e. the set of rules underlying it. The average linguistically naive speaker of English is quite unaware, for example, that some verbs (e.g. *know, own*) are rarely or never used in progressive forms (e.g. *\*He's knowing the poem*), or that some verbs may be followed by an infinitive (e.g. *want, expect*) but others require a gerund (e.g. *enjoy, finish*). Yet that same speaker constantly makes use of the words in question in these ways, using them correctly without the least difficulty. He has a tacit or implicit knowledge of the grammar of English.

A BILINGUAL GRAMMAR is one which sets out to provide all the information about a language that is likely to be needed by a non-native learner. Ideally it should be slanted to take account of the nature of the learner's native language, highlighting, either implicitly or explicitly, or both, the points where the two languages contrast. In theory, a second language might be acquired in the same way as the first, simply through exposure to it, the so-called "direct method". But some degree of interference from the first language is inevitable, and conscious learning of patterns and rules does at least utilize the adolescent's or adult's superior intellectual powers relative to a child's. However, regardless of its value *vis-à-vis* pure language exposure, a bilingual grammar obviously needs to be based on an adequate description of the language (as it is currently used). At the same time it must be recognized that a bilingual grammar is bound by its very nature to be prescriptive: the foreign learner is not simply having an implicit knowledge made explicit; he is being given instruction in how to acquire knowledge of a language that is new to him.

Thus both prescriptive monolingual grammars and bilingual grammars depend ultimately on the provision of adequate descriptive grammars. We therefore need to turn our attention to the question of how to produce such a grammar. Halliday (1961: 241f.) distinguishes three kinds of descriptive grammar:

    (i) TEXTUAL: a grammar that sets out to describe a finite text or "corpus".

(ii) EXEMPLIFICATORY: a non-textually-based grammar that describes the potential structures of the language, giving examples.
(iii) (TRANSFORMATIONAL) GENERATIVE: a non-textually-based grammar that provides a mechanism or set of rules for specifying the sentences of a language and their structure. Such grammars may, but need not, include transformations (rules for relating different structural patterns to each other; see chapter 8).

The second and third types agree in focusing on the grammatical potential of the language, whereas the textual type is based on a corpus – perhaps a short conversation, perhaps a poem, etc. – while at the same time relating the parts of the text to the relevant aspects of the language's grammatical potential. The corpus-based grammar was the norm for pre-Chomskyan American linguistics, which gave importance to the methods of collecting the data, collating them and "discovering" a grammar and phonology for those data (Hockett, 1958: chapters 12, 14 and 15). Hence the concern with "grammar discovery procedures" (Longacre, 1964). We may refer back to a pair of notions we introduced in chapter 2, and say that, whereas a textual grammar is more concerned with particular messages, the other two types are more concerned with the overall code. De Saussure and later Chomsky use different terminology to refer to broadly the same distinction – code v. message, theory v. practice or potential v. actual – but there are differences in the way their distinctions are made:

|  | *Potential* | *Actual* |
|---|---|---|
| Communication theory | code | message |
| de Saussure | la langue | la parole |
| Chomsky | competence | performance |

De Saussure (1962: 23–39) distinguishes *la langue* ('language') from *la parole* ('speech') on two bases. Firstly, *la langue* is the essential underlying system, while *la parole* is the totality of actual speech-acts made using the system; secondly, *la langue* embraces the common features shared by the social community, while *la parole* is the totality of linguistic contributions made by individual speakers. It is worth separating out these two factors: potential system v. actual use of the system, for which we might use Chomsky's terms COMPETENCE and PERFORMANCE; and LANGUAGE of the community v. IDIOLECT of the individual. The individual speaker's linguistic habits can be as systematic as the system of a whole language.

Chomsky (1965:4) feels the need to distinguish his notion of competence from *la langue*. He criticizes de Saussure's notion as apparently envisaging "merely a systematic inventory of items". This criticism seems a little harsh, in view of the fact that, for de Saussure, in *la langue* it is not the individual signs that are important, but their differences, values and relations: "Ainsi, dans un état de langue, tout repose sur des rapports" (1962:170). ("Thus, in a language, viewed statically, everything is a matter of relationships.") But for Chomsky it is vital for language in its ideal form, competence, to be seen as a system of (generative) rules which account for the speaker-listener's ability to handle an infinite number of possible sentences – most of which he has never heard before – and to assign to each of them a grammatical structure, a phonological form and a meaning. And this handling capacity applies to both input (understanding, reading, etc.) and output (speaking, writing, etc.). It is this ability to handle infinite variety with a finite system of rules that gives language its creativity and makes it essential to regard it as "rule-governed behaviour". We can disagree with Chomsky about just how much is produced by rule and how much is rote-learnt, or about how much is a matter of absolute rule and how much is a matter of tendency, analogizing, blending, etc., but we must all, I believe, accept the fact that the grammatical system of a language involves rules in some sense, and that these rules must allow for infinite recursion (to account for structures such as *the cat that killed that cat that . . .*).

The precise relationship between competence and performance is, however, rather difficult to characterize. Performance is simply use of competence to produce a message: it is the behaviour governed by the rules. But not only is it a matter of chance which particular messages are sent (they may be atypical and unrepresentative, as is well known by the corpus-based linguist, frantically waiting for the desired items and structures to be uttered); also the utterances that do occur may be in a pretty poor shape, affected by (to cite Chomsky's (1965:3) list) "memory limitations, distractions, shifts of attention and interest, and errors . . .". As a rather extreme example of the kind of text that can be "performed" by quite "competent" speakers of a language, we might cite the following (for a further example, see Quirk, 1968:180):

> Well, I was . . . er . . . wondering if you – or at least, if not
> yourself, then – you know sort of . . . one of your . . . mmm
> . . . colleagues, so to speak . . . that you might . . . kind of,
> well, consider, anyway, the . . . er . . . possibility of . . . well
> of . . . signing my . . . er – but of course you wouldn't know
> . . . mm what was involved in the . . . er . . . well, anyway,
> would you sign it for me?

Even when they are unaffected by these factors, individual utterances are still a matter of performance; and if they are in perfect accord with competence, they might be termed IDEAL PERFORMANCE. How linguistic change is to be accounted for within such a framework is problematic. For de Saussure all change first takes place in *la parole*. When, for example, speakers of earlier English began using the prepositions *to* and *for* in a largely redundant way with dative noun phrases (*give the book to the man*, etc.), they were presumably at first committing an error of performance. But at precisely what stage did these errors become incorporated into a new competence, where use of the prepositions became the norm? The boundary between competence and common performance error is impossible to draw with precision. Moreover, bearing in mind the difference between idiolect and language, we must take care not to set such an ideal standard for competence that no speaker's performance ever matches it.

The task of a grammar, then, is to account for a speaker's competence, and probably also for some aspects of his performance. To achieve this, a purely exemplificatory type of grammar will not be enough; the grammar will have to be generative, at least implicitly. This may not be too much of a problem, because, although only Chomsky and his followers set out to be generativists, it is now claimed that tagmemics (Cook, 1969: 144, 158f.) and systemic grammar (Hudson, 1974) are generative in principle. Generation ceases to be so much of an issue, if complete explicitness is recognized by all as the aim. (We shall take this point further in the next chapter.)

The really basic problem for the grammarian, however, is how to get at his native speaker's competence. The difficulty is that we cannot ask the native speaker to introspect directly and intuit the grammar for us. After all, his knowledge is purely tacit. He does have intuitions about grammar, but very often these result from a particular training he has received or his own, sometimes misdirected, speculations. As Chomsky puts it (1965: 8), "it is quite apparent that a speaker's reports and viewpoints about his behavior and his competence may be in error" (cf., however, Allerton, 1970).

This difficulty of access to competence and the consequent difficulties of investigating grammar make it all the harder for us to be sure when we have found the best grammar. Indeed, is there a best grammar at all? The answer given to this question depends on the philosophy of the linguist. As in most sciences, the view may be taken that there is an ultimate truth (*the* grammar) just waiting to be discovered; alternatively, taking a more pessimistic view of epis-

The task of grammar

temology, it may be felt that truth is an illusory goal and that probabilistic statements are the most that can be expected. While the former view accepts competing theories and models as only a temporary state of affairs, the latter view sees them as in the very nature of things. These two views have been known in linguistic circles as the "God's truth" and "hocus-pocus" positions respectively, the labels being attributed by Joos (1957: 80) to F. W. Householder. As is obvious, the present book inclines to the latter view, that an element of truth may be found in a number of different grammars and that inadequacy is a more serious fault than inconsistency.

## Questions for study

1 Would you say, on the basis of the following examples, that number in English nouns was a semantic or a grammatical category?
   (a) *these (five) peas; these (?five) cornflakes; these (\*five) oats; this porridge*
   (b) *The police like/\*likes it; the government like/likes it; the chairman likes/\*like it*
   (c) *The shirt is narrow; the trousers are narrow*

2 Consider how you would analyse the following words in terms of morphemes and unique morphemes: *horrid, morbid, solid, stupid; portable, readable, probable.*

3 Consider the following prescriptions:
   (a) Don't say *It's me* – say *It's I.*
   (b) The possessive form of *Bess, Ross,* (etc.) is *Bess', Ross',* (etc.) not *Bess's, Ross's,* (etc).
   (c) *To substitute A for B* means the same as *to replace B with A*; and so saying *to substitute B with A* is wrong.
   (d) *He don't* is wrong and should be replaced with *he doesn't.*
   What is the reason usually offered for each prescription? Is it justified? To what extent is the prescription explicit? To what extent would it assist communication?

4 How do you imagine speakers come to use the forms listed below?
   (a) Between you and I, he's a fool.
   (b) Linguistics are very interesting.
   (c) I read Alan's and your article.

58

5  What are the limitations of:
   (a) a textual grammar?
   (b) an exemplificatory grammar?

6  In an ideal performance, what would the speaker cited on p. 56 have said?

**Further reading**

On the scope of grammar: Lyons (1977), sections 10.1 to 10.4; Halliday (1966a). On the morpheme as a basic unit: Bloomfield (1935), chapter 10; Hockett (1958), chapter 14; Bolinger (1975), chapter 5; Lyons (1977), section 13.4 (homonymy and polysemy). On kinds of grammar: Halliday (1961), 241f.; Chomsky (1965), sections 1.1 to 1.2; de Saussure (1962), 23–39.

*Chapter 4*

# Generative grammar – rules and descriptions

---

**Judging the adequacy of a grammar**

We have accepted that it is the main aim of a grammar to provide an account of the native speaker's competence in producing and understanding sentences in accordance with the patterns of his language, and that the account the grammar gives must be explicit. But *how* explicit must it be, and how is the explicitness to be assured? Generative grammar lays claim to offer the only systematic method of providing full explicitness. We must examine this claim in detail.

For full explicitness there seem to be two requirements. Firstly, everything should be fully spelt out, with nothing left to the imagination; the descriptions used should have an unequivocal meaning and the relationships between the different descriptions should be clear. Traditional grammar would obviously be inadequate on this score; for example, the definition of NOUN as 'the name of a person, place or thing' is not one that can be applied precisely (it seems wrongly to include *you, here*, etc. but equally wrongly to exclude *activity, blueness*, etc.); and the rule that prepositions precede nouns is only a half-truth (the reference should be to noun *phrases*, and prepositions do not always precede them anyway, e.g. in interrogatives or relative clauses, leaving aside the postposition *ago*).

Secondly, for full explicitness, there must be fullness and depth of coverage. Otherwise, how can we know precisely which cases our rules apply to? Again, traditional grammar falls short, because there were several issues which it failed to cover adequately or failed to tackle at all, e.g. negation, non-finite clauses, count v. mass nouns.

In the view of the generative grammarian the two requirements can only be satisfied if two conditions are met:

(a) if the grammar GENERATES the sentences of a language,
   i.e. specifies exactly what sequences are sentences in the

60

language (are "grammatical") and thus, by elimination, those that are not. A grammar satisfying this requirement is said to be OBSERVATIONALLY ADEQUATE, and a theory providing such grammars is said to have WEAK GENERATIVE CAPACITY.

(b) if, for each sentence it accepts as "grammatical", the grammar GENERATES (i.e. assigns) a description explicating its grammatical pattern, thereby indicating its component parts, the relations between these parts and to other possible parts, etc. (i.e. its grammatical relations). A grammar satisfying this requirement is said to be DESCRIPTIVELY ADEQUATE, and a theory providing such grammars to have STRONG GENERATIVE CAPACITY.

These seem reasonable demands to make, but the interpretation of them may give rise to difficulty.

Although traditional grammar came nowhere near satisfying the requirements of generativity, some pre-generative linguists did. Precise specification presumably demands a mathematical type of formulation, and we find this for instance in Jespersen's *Analytic Syntax* (1937) and in the work of Harris ("From morpheme to utterance" (1946) and *(Methods in) Structural Linguistics* (1951)).

Jespersen offered formulae to describe the various syntactic patterns of English in concise form. However, although they are often extremely insightful, his analyses are based on structural labels that are mainly defined by exemplification. He has different sets of symbols to indicate functional roles (subject, verb, object, etc.), "rank" (primary = head word, secondary = modifier, tertiary = modifier of modifier, etc.), syntactic features (negative, connective, etc.) and structural relations (apposition, speaker's aside, etc.). The precise relationship between these different labels is, however, not always clear, and it is certainly not possible to use the formulae to specify the full range of English sentences.

Harris comes nearer to full explicitness. His formulae are given in equations which represent constructions, e.g.:

$$N^1\text{-}s = N^2$$
$$TN^2 = N^3$$

(The formulae are cited from the 1946 work of Harris. There are some differences, particularly of superscript numbering, in his 1951 version.) In each case the right-hand side is the label for the construction, which may be a single element (thus justifying its status as a construction; see below pp. 112f) or may be represented by the sequence of classes given on the left-hand side. Thus the first example means that the noun complex $N^2$, while it may be realized by single elements that are $N^2$ in their own right (*milk, steel, pride*, etc.), can also consist of a sequence of $N^1$ (*bottle, book, advantage*, etc.) followed by the noun plural inflection *-(e)s*. In other words, *milk* and *bottles* are equivalent in some respects, both being capable of occurring after certain determiners, for example:

I need some/more milk.
I need some/more bottles.
*I need some/more bottle.

Similarly, for the second equation, a proper noun like *John* or *Manchester* is equivalent to *the men, the cities, the people* (or *the man, the city*, since $N^2$ in this position embraces $N^1$). Harris's equations thus relate to each other and allow themselves to be interpreted as specifying constructions that build up inside larger constructions until a sentence-level construction ($N^4V^4$) is reached. However, there are a number of serious weaknesses in Harris's procedure. Firstly, his subclassification of the major syntactic classes is inadequate: although verbs are subclassified, some types are left unaccounted for (e.g. ditransitive), while nouns are not subdivided into countable and uncountable, despite the recognition of the need for this shown by the formulae quoted above. Secondly, the non-productive and semi-productive constructions found within morphology (e.g. *en-large* but not *en-small*; see chapter 10) are not adequately handled. Thirdly, concord and similar relations (see chapter 7) are specifically excluded. Finally, some sentence patterns, such as passive, are not properly treated; and for these Harris later went on to develop his theory of transformations.

## Finite-state grammars

Thus the work of Jespersen and Harris (and even later work such as that of the tagmemicists, of the stratificationalists and of the postwar Prague school) may be regarded as semi-explicit. Chomsky's objective of a GENERATIVE grammar represents the first thoroughgoing attempt to come to grips with the problem of grammatical explicitness. In *Syntactic Structures* (1957: 24) Chomsky suggests that "the simplest type of grammar which, with a finite amount of apparatus, can generate an infinite number of sentences" is a FINITE-STATE or MARKOV-PROCESS grammar (the latter after the Russian statistician Markov). While finite-state grammar is not a serious candidate for an adequate grammar and has rarely been proposed as a model for describing a syntactic system (Hockett's *Manual of Phonology* (1955) is the only use of it ever cited, though the diagrams of Hockett (1958: 290–2) and Harris (1951: 353) have it implicitly), it does merit some consideration.

A finite-state grammar is a grammar that is an abstract device but one that may be viewed as a kind of machine. The machine has a finite number of states and the capacity to change from one state to another as it registers different symbols. Among these states, one is the inital state ($S_0$) and there is at least one final state ($S_F$). Different diagrammatic conventions are possible for representing a finite-state grammar, but we shall represent each state as a point and each symbol as a line between points. Figure 9 is an example.

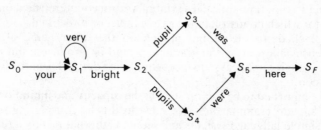

*Figure 9*

Instructions for this language will be of the form ($S_1$, $S_2$, $a$), to be read as "proceed from state $S_1$ to state $S_2$, registering the symbol $a$". Such a finite-state grammar would represent a language that permitted the sequences

> Your bright pupil was here.
> Your very bright pupil was here.
> Your very very bright pupil was here.
> etc.

> Your bright pupils were here.
> Your very bright pupils were here.
> Your very very bright pupils were here.
> etc.

We described the finite-state grammar as "registering" these sequences; we might equally have used the verb SPECIFY. It is important to note that these terms are said to be neutral with reference to the question of whether the symbol sequences are regarded as an input or output. (Chomsky (1957: 48) suggests that the term GEN-ERATE is equally neutral, but some writers (e.g. Wall, 1972) seem to equate it with "produce" and contrast it with "recognize" or "accept".)

In other words, it does not matter whether we regard the machine as being programmed to emit symbols as it passes from state to state (the output model) or we regard it as being prepared to read symbols on a tape fed to it and pass from state to state accordingly (the input model). In the output model tapes would be fed out, thus simulating the speaker (writer); in the input model tapes would be fed in, thus simulating the listener (reader). The simulation of the speaker/listener only applies at an abstract level, i.e. to his capacity for operating with that sentence as a potential sentence in his grammar, not for using it on a particular occasion in a particular context. In the input model a sequence on the tape would be rejected as ungrammatical if a symbol were encountered next on the tape for which no instruction was available, or if the final state was not reached; in the output model, on the other hand, all the sequences allowed by the grammar would be produced, but only these – ungrammatical sequences thus being defined negatively, by omission.

It is important to be clear just what the capacity and limitations of a finite-state grammar are. We may do this by considering some very simple language systems and seeing with what facility a finite-state grammar may generate them. We shall use algebraic letters to represent morphemes. (For simplicity's sake, we refrain from labelling the states.)

1 (i) *"infinite a" type language.* Each string is a sequence of *a*'s varying in number between one and infinity. Such a sequence may be generated by using a loop of the type:

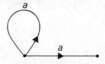

Note that, although this allows us to choose as many *a*'s as we wish, a separate line is necessary for the final *a*, to bring us to the final state. (To produce just one *a*, the loop is bypassed.)

1 (ii) *"finite a" type language.* Each string is a sequence of *a*'s, with a minimum of one and a specified maximum (in our example, four). A finite-state grammar may generate this language as shown in Figure 10.

Note that the loop is unusable here, because it would place

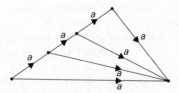

*Figure 10*

no limit on the number of *a*'s selected. We are therefore
obliged to utilize a method of allowing for a variable number
of *a*'s that involves deciding from the outset how many
*a*'s are to be generated in the particular string being pro-
cessed and choosing a path accordingly. An even less attractive alternative would be that shown in Figure 11.

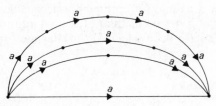

*Figure 11*

2  (i)  *"infinite a/b" type language.* This language, allowing any
sequence of *a*'s and/or *b*'s, may be generated with a
slight modificaton of Figure 11, as Figure 12 shows.

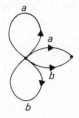

*Figure 12*

2  (ii)  *"finite a/b" type language.* This language, in which each
string is a sequence of *a*'s and/or *b*'s with a maximum
(say of four, once again), may be generated with a
variation of 1 (ii). (The reader should attempt to produce
the required revisions.) But it only achieves this in a
complex way.

3 (i) *"infinite $a^n + b^n$" type language*. In this language (discussed in Chomsky, 1957) every string consists of a given number of $a$'s up to infinity in a number followed by the same number of $b$'s. A loop would be necessary to allow the number of $a$'s to range up to infinity, and a similar loop would be necessary to allow the number of $b$'s to be infinite; but there would be no way of ensuring that there should be the same number of $b$'s as $a$'s in any one string. A circuit such as that proposed in Figure 12 allows an infinite range for the quantity of $a$'s and/or $b$'s without making them equal. On the other hand, a circuit such as Figure 13 ensures the right quantity of $a$'s and $b$'s but must put them in alternating order. We are thus forced to the conclusion that *a finite-state grammar is incapable of generating the infinite $a^n + b^n$* type language. The basic reason why a finite-state grammar is incapable of achieving this is that it has no method of storing information (how many $a$'s have been selected) for later use.

*Figure 13*

3 (ii) *"finite $a^n + b^n$" type language*. This finite version of type 3 (i) *can* be generated by a finite-state grammar, but only with great complexity. If the specified maximum number of $a$'s and $b$'s is four, for instance, something like Figure 14 must be envisaged.

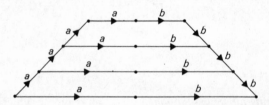

*Figure 14*

4 (i) *"infinite abba"* ('mirror-image') *type language* (also discussed in Chomsky, 1957). In this language, each utterance consists of a freely chosen sequence of $a$'s

and/or *b*'s followed by a similar sequence in the reverse order. The language allows sequences of the type *aa*, *bb*, *abba*, *baab*, *aabbaa*, etc., with no limitation on length. A finite-state grammar is incapable of generating this language too, again because of the inability of finite-state grammars to store information for later use.

4 (ii) *"finite abba" ('mirror-image') type language.* The finite version of the mirror-image type language can again be generated, though again only through complex means. We could display a grammar specifying a maximum sequence of six (3 + 3) symbols (Figure 15).

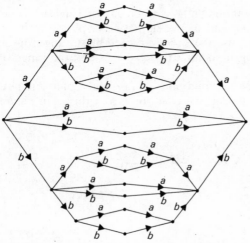

*Figure 15*

The "*a*" languages are of little linguistic interest, since they only contain one item of vocabulary, *a*. Languages involve a choice by the speaker-listener between different meanings. (Even the bus conductor's language described in the "Questions for study" of chapter 2 involves a system not so much like Figure 16 as like Figure 17, where each sequence of rings (or buzzes) represents a different choice.) However, all of the other artificial languages we have considered contained two items of vocabulary and restrictions on sequences that have analogues in natural human languages. Any difficulty a finite-state grammar has in dealing with them must therefore be considered a significant failing.

In this connection it will be useful to consider the applicability of

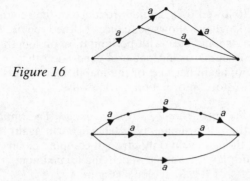

*Figure 16*

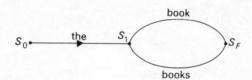

*Figure 17*

finite-state grammar to a fragment of English syntax, a highly
schematic account of the simple noun phrase in its specific (i.e.
non-generic) uses. We shall proceed by starting from simple cases
and building up complexity as we extend the range of examples
covered.

The simple definite noun phrase with countable nouns may be
singular or plural. We could represent this as in Figure 18.

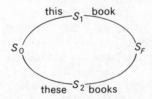

*Figure 18*

(We here ignore the analysis of *books* into *book* + *-s*, and simply
take *book* to represent COUNT NOUN SINGULAR and *books* to represent COUNT NOUN PLURAL; the choice of the lexical item *book* as
opposed to *pen, pupil*, etc. is not at issue.) Demonstrative determiners, however, are sensitive to number, and so for them, taking
*this/these* as examples, we need something like Figure 19.

*Figure 19*

Combining *the* with *this/these*, we get:

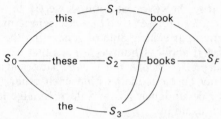

*Figure 20*

A mass (non-count) noun like *ink* may occur with a mass determiner like *enough*, with *the* and with *this*; *enough* also occurs with *books*. We may accommodate these possibilities as in Figure 21. Finally we

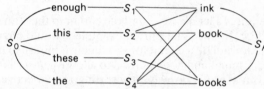

*Figure 21*

may incorporate the singular count determiner, represented by the indefinite article *a*, and the mass-only determiner *much*, to give the scheme of Figure 22.

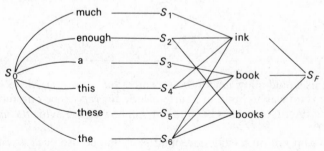

*Figure 22*

In this scheme we have provided enough intermediate states ($S_1$ – $S_6$) to cater for the different ranges of choice that each determiner imposes: for example, *much* allows only *ink*, while *enough* allows *ink* or *books*, *a* only *book*, etc. A finite-state grammar is thus able to allow for complex relations of co-occurrence between adjacent elements.

Difficulties arise, however, as soon as we try to accommodate restrictions of choice imposed by a non-adjacent item. We saw that a finite-state grammar is incapable of generating the languages of types 3(i) and 4(i) above. Chomsky argues that certain constructions in English, e.g. *if–then, neither–nor*, pattern in a similar way, in that they may be embedded within each other to produce a nested series of dependencies as in a mirror-image language. We might cite as an example:

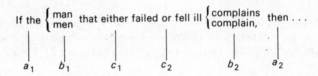

where $a_1$ requires a later $a_2$, etc. and the earlier in the string $a_1$ is the later $a_2$ will be. In our noun-phrase example it would obviously be necessary to formulate a circuit for an adjective phrase to intervene between determiner and noun phrase, to allow for *the ((fairly) new) pens*, etc. But there is no way of inserting the adjective without losing the required information about determiner selection of noun type, unless we use a separate adjective circuit for every path.

A further problem is that of optionality: this can be generated using loops, e.g.

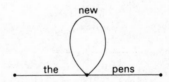

but this would allow *new* to be repeated (*ad nauseam*). Moreover, there is no way to build in a further loop for *very* to be entered on only if the first loop has been taken, i.e. how do we avoid *the fairly pens*?

To sum up: finite-state grammar is of limited use because of its inability to deal adequately with discontinuous dependencies and with optional elements. What is needed to achieve adequate generative capacity is a more powerful device, which is not tied to generating symbols in purely consecutive order. Recalling the difficulty a finite-state grammar had with the $a^n + b^n$ languages, we might now imagine a more abstract device, less tied to a serial order, which might simultaneously specify items at different points in the string. Although such an abstract device cannot easily be represented visually, it might schematically look like Figure 23, with each loop on the *a* circuit somehow simultaneously specifying a paired (later) loop on the *b* circuit. One such device which is capable of this, because it is more powerful and more abstract than a finite-state grammar, is a REWRITE (RULE) GRAMMAR.

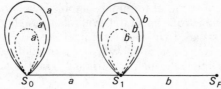

*Figure 23*

## Rewrite grammars

A rewrite grammar can be best appreciated in the form in which it is usually presented, i.e. rewrite rules. Each rule takes a symbol or symbols (on the left of an arrow) as input and converts them to a different sequence (on the right of an arrow), giving the format:

$W(+X) \rightarrow Y (+Z)$ [where + means simply 'followed by' and the parenthesis denotes optionality.]

Now each step in a finite-state grammar can be presented in this form, with the current state given on the left and the symbol emitted or read together with the new state on the right, e.g.:

$S_1 \rightarrow a + S_2$

In fact, every step in a finite-state grammar is of this form, referring to one symbol of the text and two symbols representing states (in the final rule, the final state $S_F$). We may refer to the "text symbol" *a* as a TERMINAL SYMBOL and the "state symbols" $S_1$ and $S_2$ as NONTERMINAL (or "AUXILIARY") SYMBOLS. A rewrite-rule grammar, however, has a capacity for a much broader variety of rules. Particularly important are its capacities:

   (i)  to have a rule generating more than one terminal symbol, in effect, $S_1 \rightarrow a+b+S_2$, or $S_1 \rightarrow a+S_2+b$;

  (ii)  to have a rule generating purely non-terminal symbols, i.e. rules equivalent to $S_1 \rightarrow S_2+S_3$. This obviously makes the grammar more abstract, giving it greater capacity for storage and computation;

(iii) to have a rule rewriting two (or more) symbols at a time. Basically, then, a rewriting grammar consists of: an initial symbol (equivalent to an initial state), often designated as $S$ or $Z$; a set of non-terminal (=intermediate or auxiliary) symbols; a set of terminal symbols (=the "vocabulary" of the language data); and a set of rules relating all the symbols. Each rule rewrites one or more non-terminal symbols either as further non-terminal symbols or as terminal symbols, until eventually, when all relevant rules have been applied, a string of terminal symbols is generated. Thus we develop a string from an initial symbol, through a sequence of intermediate stages, to its final state, the TERMINAL STRING, when it consists exclusively of terminal symbols. The whole series of strings from initial symbol through to terminal string is termed a DERIVATION.

For example, for the grammar

1. $Z \rightarrow A + B$
2. $A \rightarrow M$
3. $A \rightarrow N$
4. $B \rightarrow P + Q$
5. $B \rightarrow R$

the initial symbol would be $Z$, the non-terminal symbols $A$ and $B$, and the terminal symbols $M, N, P, Q, R$. Possible derivations (giving the rule number in parentheses) would include:

| | | | | |
|---|---|---|---|---|
| $Z$ | | | $Z$ | |
| $A + B$ | (1) | | $A + B$ | (1) |
| $M + B$ | (2) | | $A + R$ | (5) |
| $M + P + Q$ | (4) | | $N + R$ | (3) |

(It should be noted that the order of application of the rules is irrelevant so long as the conventions of rewriting are observed.) The complete range of possible terminal strings is

$$M + P + Q, \quad M + R, \quad N + P + Q, \quad N + R.$$

We can now see how this applies by generating the languages we considered above.

1 (i) *"infinite a" type language* (allowing any sequence of $a$'s). A rewrite grammar may generate this language with the following rule(s) (where the brace { represents a free choice):

$$Z \rightarrow \left\{ \begin{array}{l} a \\ Za \end{array} \right.$$

A rule like this which allows repeated application through having one symbol appearing on both the left-hand and right-hand sides is termed RECURSIVE. This covers all the possibilities of the finite-state loop, but allows many other possibilities in addition.

Through the abbreviatory device of the parenthesis ( ) (indicating two possible rewritings with or without the bracketed symbol), the above rules may be conflated to

$$Z \rightarrow (Z)a.$$

1 (ii) *"finite a" type language* (with a maximum of four *a*'s). This language may be generated in an equivalent way to that proposed for a finite-state grammar, i.e.:

$$Z \rightarrow \left\{ \begin{array}{l} a \\ a \left\{ \begin{array}{l} a \\ a \left\{ \begin{array}{l} a \\ aa \end{array} \right\} \end{array} \right\} \end{array} \right\}$$

which again may be conflated using parentheses to

$$Z \rightarrow a(a(a(a))).$$

2 (i) *"infinite a/b" type language* (allowing any sequence of *a*'s and/or *b*'s). This language is generated by

$$Z \rightarrow (Z) \left\{ \begin{array}{l} a \\ b \end{array} \right\}$$

2 (ii) *"finite a/b" type language* (with a maximum of four *a*'s/*b*'s). This language is generated in a manner similar to 1 (ii) above by

$$Z \rightarrow \left\{ \begin{array}{l} a \\ b \end{array} \right\} \left( \left\{ \begin{array}{l} a \\ b \end{array} \right\} \left( \left\{ \begin{array}{l} a \\ b \end{array} \right\} \left( \left\{ \begin{array}{l} a \\ b \end{array} \right\} \right) \right) \right)$$

3 (i) *"infinite $a^n + b^n$" type language* (requiring the same number of *b*'s as *a*'s). Unlike the finite-state grammar, the rewrite grammar is perfectly capable of generating this language. It may do so very simply with the rule

$$Z \rightarrow a(Z)b.$$

A sample derivation using this rule is:

$$Z$$
$$a\,Z\,b$$
$$a\,a\,Z\,b\,b$$
$$a\,a\,a\,b\,b\,b$$

This accomplishes precisely what the finite-state grammar could not because it uses the possibilities of generating more than one terminal symbol at once and of developing two different points in the string simultaneously.

3 (ii) *"finite $a^n + b^n$" type language* (with a maximum of four *a*'s/*b*'s). This language is generated in a similar manner to that used for a finite-state grammar:

$$Z \rightarrow a(a(a(a(ab)b)b)b).$$

4 (i) *"infinite mirror-image" type language*. Once again a language beyond the capacity of a finite-state grammar is generated by a rewrite rule grammar, thus:

$$Z \rightarrow \begin{Bmatrix} a(Z)a \\ b(Z)b \end{Bmatrix}$$

4 (ii) *"finite mirror-image" type language* (with a maximum of six symbols). This language may again be generated relatively simply, thus:

$$Z \rightarrow \begin{Bmatrix} a\left(\begin{bmatrix} a\left(\begin{Bmatrix} aa \\ bb \end{Bmatrix}\right) a \\ b\left(\begin{Bmatrix} aa \\ bb \end{Bmatrix}\right) b \end{bmatrix}\right) a \\ b\left(\begin{bmatrix} a\left(\begin{Bmatrix} aa \\ bb \end{Bmatrix}\right) a \\ b\left(\begin{Bmatrix} aa \\ bb \end{Bmatrix}\right) b \end{bmatrix}\right) b \end{Bmatrix}$$

Once again we may note that the finite version of a language may appear to give greater complexity than the infinite; but this is largely because we have gone without non-terminal symbols and conflated everything to one rule. We should not be too concerned in any case, since human languages have not been observed to place arbitrary limits on the number of items in a grammatical sequence. Any such limits can be described as a matter of performance (see chapter 3).

The schematic English noun phrase discussed above may also be generated by a rewrite grammar. We may simply convert the finite-state pattern to a set of rewrite rules:

$$S_0 \begin{cases} \textit{much} & + S_1 \\ \textit{enough} & + S_2 \\ \textit{a} & + S_3 \\ \textit{this} & + S_4 \\ \textit{these} & + S_5 \\ \textit{the} & + S_6 \end{cases}$$

$$S_1 \rightarrow \textit{ink}$$

$$S_2 \rightarrow \begin{cases} \textit{ink} \\ \textit{books} \end{cases}$$

$$S_3 \rightarrow \textit{books}$$

$$S_4 \rightarrow \begin{cases} \textit{ink} \\ \textit{book} \end{cases}$$

$$S_5 \rightarrow \textit{books}$$

$$S_6 \rightarrow \begin{cases} \textit{ink} \\ \textit{book} \\ \textit{books} \end{cases}$$

Alternatively, we may simplify, by dispensing with the non-terminal symbols:

$$S_F \rightarrow \begin{cases} \textit{much} & \textit{ink} \\ \textit{enough} & \begin{cases} \textit{ink} \\ \textit{books} \end{cases} \\ \textit{a} & \textit{book} \\ \textit{this} & \begin{cases} \textit{ink} \\ \textit{book} \end{cases} \\ \textit{these} & \textit{books} \\ \textit{the} & \begin{cases} \textit{ink} \\ \textit{book} \\ \textit{books} \end{cases} \end{cases}$$

Although these rules patently succeed in generating the correct sequences, it may be felt that they are somewhat duplicative. But this is only one out of a number of possible rewrite grammars for these data. The truth is that not only can a rewrite-rule grammar accomplish all that a finite-state grammar can and more; it has even

75

been shown to be equivalent to a Turing machine (Wall, 1972: 280–2; Bach, 1974: 196–7). A Turing machine is an abstract mathematical system so powerful that it can provide for any clearly defined system, e.g. the set of the squares of all integers, opening moves at chess, the possible constituency of Parliament in terms of party strength, and so on. In other words, an UNRESTRICTED rewrite grammar gives us an *embarras de richesse*. There is no doubt of its observational adequacy, but we must be concerned about it from two points of view:

(i) It is so powerful a system that it is quite general and not especially attuned to the needs of linguistic systems, paying no heed to the general constraints that all languages seem to observe, e.g. related elements tending to appear adjacent to each other.

(ii) We have so far seen no evidence for its descriptive adequacy – its ability to assign correct grammatical descriptions.

It is to this second point that we must now turn.


## Phrase-structure grammars

How can a generative grammar be made not only to specify the strings that form sentences in a language but also to assign the required grammatical descriptions? This is what is required, if the grammar is to be totally explicit (as outlined above, pp. 60–1). The obvious way is to make the non-terminal symbols, that are in any case required in a rewrite grammar, act as the grammatical labels and to make the relationships between these non-terminal symbols mirror the grammatical relationships to be described.

Thus, a simple noun phrase (=NP) pattern without the complications of those discussed above, instead of being generated directly as

$$\text{NP} \rightarrow \left\{\begin{matrix} the \\ my \\ any \end{matrix}\right\} \left\{\begin{matrix} book \\ books \\ ink \end{matrix}\right\}$$

could rather be generated by using intermediate non-terminal symbols to indicate the grammatical classes (Determiner = Det), thus:

(1) NP→   Det + Noun

$$(2)\ \text{Det} \rightarrow \left\{\begin{matrix} the \\ my \\ any \end{matrix}\right\}$$

$$(3)\ \text{Noun} \rightarrow \left\{ \begin{array}{l} \textit{book} \\ \textit{books} \\ \textit{ink} \end{array} \right\}$$

A commonly accepted (though by no means fully adequate[1]) form of representation for grammatical description is the LABELLED TREE DIAGRAM. In this each symbol represents a grammatical item or category, with sequential relations represented from left to right, and constituency relations from top to bottom. It will now become clear that a set of rewrite rules can be used to generate a set of non-terminal symbols in such a way that they may automatically be built up as a tree-diagram representation of the sentence being generated. This can be done, providing the following procedure is strictly observed.

1 For each sentence being generated, starting with the initial symbol, write down every stage of the string as it is developed by the application of successive rules, e.g. (for our simple noun phrase):

| NP | | | | (alternatively) NP | | | |
|----|---|------|-----|----|---|------|-----|
| Det | + | Noun | (1) | Det | + | Noun | (1) |
| *my* | + | Noun | (2) | Det | + | *ink* | (3) |
| *my* | + | *ink* | (3) | *my* | + | *ink* | (2) |

(The number of the rule that has been applied to produce a particular string is given in parenthesis.) This series of strings constitutes the DERIVATION (or DERIVATIONAL HISTORY).

2 To form the tree diagram, place the initial line of the derivation at the top of the tree; then, checking line by line which symbol or symbols have replaced a symbol that has disappeared from the preceding line, write the replacing symbol(s) under the disappearing one and join them to it with a line or lines, as necessary; continue this procedure until the last line of the derivation is reached. This would give, in our example:

---

[1] One of the self-imposed restrictions on conventional tree diagrams is their limitation to two dimensions (a limitation of most graphic media). This is a potential source of problems, e.g. with "discontinuous constituents" (see chapter 6).

Each label on the tree diagram which has lines joining it to lower symbols is termed a NODE. This notion is important, because the use of an identical node is, as a general principle, the only way of indicating a shared syntactic characteristic. Thus if, for example, our rule 1 had been extended to:

(1')
$$NP \rightarrow \begin{cases} Det + Noun \\ Name \end{cases}$$

and we had added a fourth rule

(4) Name → *John, Mary*

we might have developed a tree:

This would mean that only the node NP represents the syntactic similarity between the elements *my ink* and *John*. The similarity between Noun and Name (and even between Common Noun and Proper Noun) is something that the intelligent reader may intuit, but which the grammar has not explicitly stated.

It will be noted that the same tree diagram is arrived at regardless of which derivation is chosen. Thus the rules do not need to be ordered (except intrinsically, i.e. by what appears on the left- or right-hand side in each rule), since the same tree diagram is arrived at anyway; the tree diagram captures the essentials of the rules as they are used.

However, certain conventions will need to be followed, if this procedure is to be applied successfully. In particular, two restrictions must be placed on the form of rewrite rules if structural descriptions – in the shape of tree diagrams – are to be automatically specified:

(1) *Only one symbol should be replaced in any given rule*. Otherwise it is unclear which higher symbol is the node to which the new symbols are to be attached. For example, putative rules like:

$AB \rightarrow CDE$

or

Det + Noun → Art + Adj + Count Noun

78

would be unacceptable, since it would be impossible to decide which new symbol to attach to which old symbol (Figure 24). We could certainly *guess* what joins to make, but this is not good enough; we are looking for full explicitness.

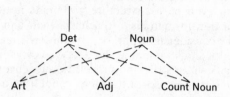

*Figure 24*

(2) *No symbol should disappear without being replaced.* This amounts to a ban on deletions (or at least on deletions without a zero symbol – the zero symbol (ø) can be reckoned as a replacing symbol). Such a ban is necessary to ensure that every tree is fully developed to the stage of being supplied with terminal symbols. Rules such as:

$$ABC \rightarrow AB$$

or

$$\text{Det} + \text{Noun} \rightarrow \text{Det}$$

(to derive *any*, for instance, from *any ink/books*) would result in unacceptable outputs like the following:

Rules that produce unacceptable trees must be prescribed. If we observe the above restrictions, then our rewrite-rule grammar will assign grammatical descriptions automatically. Such a grammar is, however, no longer an unrestricted rewrite grammar, but a special subvariety of rewrite grammar termed a PHRASE-STRUCTURE GRAMMAR.

Phrase-structure (or PS) grammars have been given much attention because of their property of automatically achieving descriptive adequacy through their automatic linking of rules and tree

79

diagrams (via derivations). They are clearly more restrictive than unrestricted rewrite grammars, and hence more suited to the specific description of a natural human language; on the other hand, they are more powerful than finite-state grammars, which we have seen are incapable of generating all aspects of a language. We shall later see that even phrase-structure grammars need supplementation – with transformations – to achieve their aim.

Let us now consider how phrase-structure grammars cope with one of the difficulties we met in the data we considered for finite-state grammars, viz. restrictions on the co-occurrence of subclasses. Returning to our examples of the English noun phrases, we might look at this very restricted set of data:

This book     that book     this page     that page
these books   those books   these pages   those pages

NB: *this books, *those page, etc.

Clearly, subclasses of determiner and noun need to be developed to accommodate the restrictions on combination we find in these data. We might consider the following rules:

(1) $\left.\begin{array}{l} \end{array}\right.$ NP $\rightarrow \begin{cases} \text{Det}_{sg} + \text{N}_{sg} \\ \text{Det}_{pl} + \text{N}_{pl} \end{cases}$
(2)
(3) $\text{Det}_{sg} \rightarrow$ *this, that*
(4) $\text{Det}_{pl} \rightarrow$ *these, those*
(5) $\text{N}_{sg} \rightarrow$ *page, book*
(6) $\text{N}_{pl} \rightarrow$ *pages, books*

However, this partial grammar would generate the following structural descriptions (amongst others):

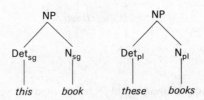

In this analysis the only grammatical feature that the two sample noun phrases share is that they are both noun phrases. As we saw above, the grammar does not tell us that $\text{Det}_{sg}$ and $\text{Det}_{pl}$, or $\text{Det}_{sg}$ and $\text{N}_{sg}$, have anything in common (though as intelligent readers we might have assumed this). As far as the grammar is concerned, we have merely developed two kinds of noun phrase, each with two constituents, and these could equally well have been written $W + X$

*and Y + Z*. In a fully explicit grammar nothing must be left to the intuition of the user, and he cannot be expected to know in advance the meaning of symbols like $Det_{sg}$. Although in practice such informative labels are utilized, in theory every label is defined within the grammar by the set of rules that develop it, e.g. $Det_{sg}$ here means no more than the class of elements *this, that*.

How, then, can we make explicit in the grammar the fact that each kind of noun phrase has both a determiner and a noun, i.e. is a sequence of the same two classes, but of different subclasses? To solve this problem, we need a special kind of rule, a CONTEXT-SENSITIVE RULE. All the rules we have used so far have been CONTEXT-FREE, in the sense that a symbol could be rewritten wherever it occurred. If, however, we wish to limit the application of a rule to certain contexts, we can write it in the form:

$X \rightarrow Y + Z$ / in the context $P - Q$
or, in short, $X \rightarrow Y + Z / P - Q$

These formulations are both equivalent to:

$$P + X + Q \rightarrow P + Y + Z + Q$$

where, although only one symbol is rewritten, other symbols $(P, Q)$ occur with it, but remain unchanged in the context. The context that determines the application of the rule may be "to the left" (preceding) or "to the right" (following), or both. In other words, $P$ or $Q$ may have the value "zero" or "null". If both $P$ and $Q$ are null, then the rule is no longer context-sensitive but context-free. Therefore a context-free rule may be regarded as a special case of a context-sensitive rule.

Grammars which contain at least one context-sensitive rule are termed CONTEXT-SENSITIVE GRAMMARS. Otherwise they are CONTEXT-FREE GRAMMARS. As with their component rule types, context-free grammars may be regarded as a more restrictive subclass of context-sensitive grammars; whereas context-free grammars only permit context-free rules, context-sensitive grammars allow both context-sensitive and context-free rules. We may thus establish a hierarchy of grammars in respect of the restrictiveness of their rules:

MORE RESTRICTIVE finite-state grammars
⬆ context-free phrase-structure grammars
⬇ context-sensitive phrase-structure grammars
LESS RESTRICTIVE unrestricted rewrite-rule grammars

Let us now apply the notion of context sensitive rule to our particular case. Let us assume, for the sake of argument, that the grammatical feature of number belongs in the first place to the noun. We might write a set of rules as follows:

(1) NP $\rightarrow$ Det $+$N
(2) N $\rightarrow$ $\begin{cases} N_{sg} \\ N_{pl} \end{cases}$
(3) Det $\rightarrow$ $\begin{cases} Det_{sg}/ -N_{sg} \\ Det_{pl}/ - N_{pl} \end{cases}$
(4) $Det_{sg} \rightarrow$ *this, that*
etc. (as in our previous rules)

The greater descriptive adequacy of such a set of rules (in particular of the context-sensitive rule 3) becomes evident as soon as we consider the tree diagrams generated for the noun phrases we considered above:

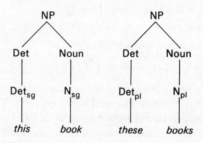

Comparing these two tree diagrams, we see that the similarity between the two noun phrases is indicated not only in the shared noun-phrase node, but also in that the identity of the constituents is recognized with the common nodes "determiner" and "noun".

We must assume that any phrase-structure grammar of a natural language will need to make extensive use of context-sensitive rules. Languages contain a multiplicity of phenomena that involve co-occurrence restrictions. Such phenomena (which are discussed in more detail in chapter 7) include government, such as the selection of grammatical case in a noun by a preposition or verb, and concord, such as that of number between a finite verb and its subject.

One further detail concerning our context-sensitive rule 3 requires mention. In the above version of the rule we specified separate contexts for the occurrence of $Det_{sg}$ and $Det_{pl}$. In practice there is a convention whereby the context specified for one or more variants or subclasses, and the last is assumed to occur "elsewhere", i.e. in all the remaining contexts. Our rule 3 might therefore be reformulated as:

(3') Det→ $\begin{cases} \text{Det}_{pl} - N_{pl} \\ \text{Det}_{sg} \end{cases}$

The "elsewhere" element is generally chosen as such on the basis of its higher frequency and/or its occurrence in a wider range of contexts and/or its being viewed as the "unmarked" member of the set (see chapter 8). In this instance, singular can be regarded as unmarked in the sense that (i) it is marked mainly by the absence of the plural suffix rather than by a suffix of its own, and (ii) it is the form of the noun that occurs when grammatical number does not apply, e.g. in compounds (cf. *fly – flies – flycatcher*).

The difference between context-sensitive and context-free rules is a generally recognized one. We should, however, be aware that there is another important point of difference to be found amongst the various rules proposed for phrase-structure grammars. If, for example, we compare rules 1 and 2 in the grammar we have just considered, we find that they are quite different in their effect:

*Rule 1* describes the construction called "noun phrase", telling us that it consists of a determiner and a noun in that order. This is a SYNTAGMATIC or CONSTITUENCY rule.

*Rule 2*, on the other hand, describes the class "noun" and tells us that we must distinguish two subclasses, singular and plural. This is a PARADIGMATIC or SUBCLASSIFICATION rule.

Constituency rules map out the grammatical structure of a particular (part of a) sentence; subclassification rules, on the other hand, force on us a choice of alternatives, of which we only select one in any particular case. The latter rules thus give rise to "unitary branchings" like

$$\begin{array}{c} | \\ \text{Noun} \\ | \\ \text{Noun}_{sg} \end{array}$$

where the lower element is not really a constituent of the higher.

Rules catering for optional elements present us with a kind of rule that seems to be a blend between a constituency and a subclassification rule. They are normally expressed using a parenthesis, e.g.:

Verb Complex → Verb (Verbal Adverbial)

(The types of adverbials referred to here would be those of manner or degree, e.g. *sleep (soundly), suffer (slightly)*.) The parenthesis used in such cases is often regarded as a kind of abbreviating device (cf. Koutsoudas, 1966: 9). Such a rule is said to be equivalent to

$$\text{Verb complex} \rightarrow \begin{cases} \text{Verb } + \text{ Verbal Adverbial} \\ \text{Verb} \end{cases}$$

The latter formulation is, however, misleading in suggesting that we have a choice involving the verb, since the latter is compulsory. We should rather say that we have an obligatory constituent and an optional one.

It is also worth distinguishing a further type of rule that is neither a constituency nor a subclassification one. Examples are

$\text{Det}_{sg} \rightarrow$ *this, that*
$\text{Noun}_{sg} \rightarrow$ *book, ink*

These rules, which we might call LEXICAL REALIZATION rules, have been called "terminal rules", because they introduce "terminal symbols" (see above, p. 71f). Their special status is recognized in that they do not occur in Chomsky (1965) and works following this model: lexical elements are introduced in a quite different way.

A further difference within the rule types of a phrase-structure grammar should be mentioned. Some rules involve subclassification in terms not of subclasses but of syntactic features, e.g.

$\text{Noun} \rightarrow [+\text{Noun}, \pm\text{Common}]$
$[+\text{Common}] \rightarrow [\pm\text{Count}]$

The reasons for the introduction of such syntactic features are discussed in chapter 7.

## The adequacy of phrase-structure grammars

By considering the array of rule types permitted within phrase-structure grammars, we have in effect been considering their potential for grammatical description. Clearly phrase-structure grammars are far superior to finite-state grammars, both in their ability to generate all the required kinds of sentence and only these (i.e. observational adequacy) and in their ability to assign the right kind of grammatical description (i.e. descriptive adequacy). However, almost all generative grammarians have claimed that simple phrase-structure grammars are – without some modification – inadequate to the task of describing human languages. This view is based on the difficulties encountered by phrase-structure grammar in describing certain kinds of sentential relations. These difficulties of descriptive adequacy, it is generally proposed, can only be overcome by supplementing the phrase-structure rules with transformational rules.

Basically, two kinds of linguistic phenomena present the greatest difficulties to a purely phrase-structure grammar:

    (a) transformationally related structures ("transformations" in the narrow sense),

    (b) discontinuous constituents.

Difficulties are also caused by embedded structures, which are discussed in chapter 9.

Transformationally related structures may be exemplified by such related patterns as:

(1) $\begin{cases} \text{Cromwell took the castle.} \\ \text{The castle was taken by} \\ \text{Cromwell.} \end{cases}$ (ACTIVE V. PASSIVE)

(2) $\begin{cases} \text{Cromwell took the castle.} \\ \text{Cromwell's taking (of)} \\ \text{the castle.} \end{cases}$ (SENTENCE V. NOMINALIZATION)

(3) $\begin{cases} \text{Cromwell took the castle.} \\ \text{It was Cromwell who took} \\ \text{the castle.} \end{cases}$ (UNMARKED V. CLEFT-SUBJECT)

Each of the above sentences bears a transparently simple meaning relationship to the fellow member of its pair. Yet the members of each pair differ in their outward shape by more than just one morpheme. In the first pair, for example, both noun phrases change their position, the preposition *by* is inserted and the verb *take* is expanded to *be taken*. Such a relationship, where a complex difference in form corresponds to a simple difference in function, we term transformational. (See further chapter 8.) Clearly such members of a related pair (or triple, etc.) need to have a large common element in their structural description. But this is almost impossible to achieve by phrase-structure means. By the same token, the active-passive ambiguity of such phrases as

    the shooting of the hunters (Chomsky, 1957)

    the love of God (Lyons, 1968)

is also difficult to account for, so long as we rely on tree diagrams derived from phrase-structure rules.

Discontinuous constructions present difficulties for a phrase-structure grammar, because tree diagrams can only represent relationships between adjacent elements. Thus, in a sequence $XYZ$ it is only possible to indicate a relationship between $X$ and $Y$ or between $Y$ and $Z$, as in Figure 25a and b.

A pattern such as Figure 25c is not permitted by the conventions of tree diagrams, limited as these are to two dimensions. If, therefore,

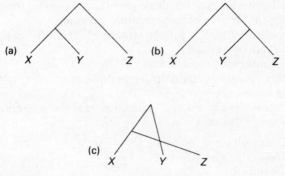

*Figure 25*

we wish to represent such a relationship, as in Figure 26, we can only do this by using two tree diagrams, one to indicate the underlying syntactic relationship (or "deep structure"; see further chapter 8) and one the overt uttered sequence (or "surface structure"). These

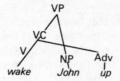

*Figure 26*

two will have to be related by a rewrite rule that is not of the phrase-structure type, since it does not further develop the tree but rather relates two different trees thus:

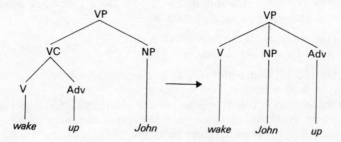

Such a rule is termed "transformational". We should observe that, although the underlying structure here gives rise to an actually occurrent phrase, this is not always the case, cf. *\*wake up him*

(assuming *him* is unstressed). In the latter case, the transformational rule would be OBLIGATORY rather than OPTIONAL.

Most generative grammars that have been written have contained a transformational component. Transformations have had a wide variety of functions in these grammars, as we shall see later, but we may generalize and say that their main purpose has been to relate one or more SURFACE STRUCTURES with DEEP STRUCTURES that have differed from the surface structures in the following respects:

(i) the occurrence in deep structure of semantic elements with no simple overt realization, e.g. (= 'Question');

(ii) the non-occurrence in deep structure of semantically empty surface-structure elements, e.g. *do* in *I do not like it*;

(iii) the sequencing of elements (as in our example above).

However, in order to perform their function of relating different tree diagrams (for the same sentence), transformational rules must necessarily be freed of the restrictions we imposed on phrase-structure rules (see above, pp. 78–9). This liberation has, however, one unfortunate effect: the grammar ceases to be a phrase-structure grammar and in effect becomes an unrestricted rewrite-rule grammar, or at best a hybrid between the two. We decided above that the unrestricted rewrite-rule type of grammar was too generally applicable and too powerful a system to give an enlightening account of human language. We are therefore faced with an unenviable choice between an enlightening grammatical model that lacks generative capacity (finite-state grammar or unmodified phrase-structure grammar) and an unenlightening grammatical model that does have the required generative capacity.

There seems to be an inbuilt conflict between on the one hand the generative capacity of a grammatical theory – its need to provide grammars that are both observationally and descriptively adequate (i.e. that both generate all the required sentences and assign them structural descriptions) – and on the other what Chomsky has termed "explanatory adequacy" – the need for the over-all linguistic theory (in terms of types of rule and their organization) to reflect something of the universal limitations on language *vis-à-vis* other systems. Observational and descriptive adequacy require us to go beyond finite-state grammar to phrase-structure grammar, including context-sensitive rules, and to supplement this with transformational rules – and possibly also with further sophistications such as "global rules" and "surface constraints" (see chapter 8). Explanatory adequacy, on the other hand, requires that we have a more restricted theory than a mere unrestricted rewrite-rule system; and yet Peters and Ritchie have, according to Bach (1974: 202), shown that a transformationally supplemented phrase-structure grammar is equivalent to this.

Such a dilemma is enough cause for us to wonder about the need for generativeness itself. The desire for generativeness, we may recall, arose from a desire for full explicitness. But there are doubts we might entertain about the feasibility of explicitness at each level of generative adequacy.

Is observational adequacy a practical proposition? What it takes for granted is that there should be an agreed number of sequences that are clearly grammatical. Leaving aside the problems of disentangling "grammatical" and "semantic" that we discussed at the beginning of chapter 3, and concentrating on purely grammatical deviance, could we get native English speakers ιo agree on the grammatical acceptability of (a), (b) and (c) below?

(a) This house will have been being built for two years.
(b) It's starting raining.
   (cf. It's started to rain; It's started raining; It's starting to rain.)
(c) I cooked John some meals. (cf. I cooked some meals for John.)
   I ironed John some shirts. (cf. I ironed some shirts for John.)
   I transplanted John some wallflowers. (cf. I transplanted some wallflowers for John.)
   I marked John some books. (cf. I marked some books for John.)

Such data as these would suggest that it might be impossible – even for the idiolect of one speaker – to lay down precise limits for what is permitted or excluded in a language. If this is the case, is a generative grammar, which rigidly distinguishes what can or cannot occur, a suitable linguistic model?

Is descriptive adequacy a practical proposition, at least in so far as we think in terms of tree diagrams as our descriptions? If we consider only a very simple sentence like

John kissed Mary yesterday.

we will find that a whole series of suggested analyses can be applied to it. Figures 27 to 29 are just a tentative sample.

No one of these tree diagrams is totally adequate as a representation of the underlying grammatical structure of the sentence; but neither is any one of them totally uninformative. For example, while Figure 27 brings out the strong sequential link between (main) verb and auxiliary, Figure 28 accounts for the co-occurrence restriction be-

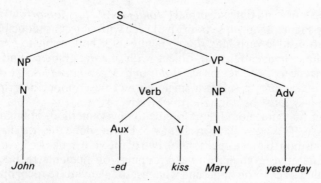

*Figure 27 A la Chomsky (1957)*

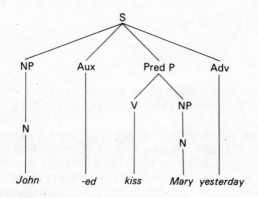

*Figure 28 A la Chomsky (1965)*

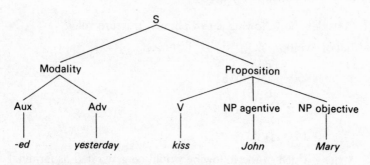

*Figure 29 A la Fillmore (1968)*

tween tense and time adverbial (*\*John kissed Mary tomorrow*); and while Figure 28 groups (transitive) verb with object as reducible to an intransitive verb (e.g. *sleep*), Figure 29 is better able to explain the interchangeability of object with passive subject and the occurrence of the reciprocal *John and Mary kissed*. So perhaps it is premature to select a single correct description; descriptive adequacy must be a long-term objective.

Our first aim should therefore be to devise methods of linguistic analysis. This we shall do in chapter 5. Having done this, we shall be in a position to make decisions on two of the vital issues we have met in generative grammar: what groupings of elements to bracket together as constructions, and what lists of elements to recognize as classes. These matters will occupy us in chapters 6 and 7. We shall then be able to turn our attention to transformations in chapter 8. A consideration of the question of size units in grammar ("rank") in chapter 9 will then complete our survey of the more fundamental grammatical problems.

## Questions for study

1  Produce a finite-state diagram for the "finite *a/b*" type language described in paragraph 2 (ii) on p. 65.

2  One of the problems confronting finite-state grammars is how to specify optional elements without allowing them to become recursively repeatable. A finite-state grammar of a different kind (from the one discussed in this chapter) might register symbols not between states (in the conventional way) but at each state. Could the optionalities contained in, for instance, *the ((fairly) new) pens* then be specified more easily? (Try with pencil and paper!)

3  Consider the following set of phrase-structure rules:

Initial Symbol: Z

$$(1) \quad Z \to \begin{cases} P \\ (M)\ C\ (S) \\ B\ (S) \end{cases}$$

(2)    $C \to H\ T$
(3)    $S \to N\ V$
(4)    $M \to (I)\ A$

Specify which of the following would be generated as terminal strings by the rules (i.e. would be "grammatical" in terms of them) and give the structural description (in the form of a tree diagram) assigned by the rules to each string generated:

| | | | | | | | | | | |
|---|---|---|---|---|---|---|---|---|---|---|
| (a) | A | H | T | N | V | (e) | B | | | |
| (b) | P | | | | | (f) | B | N | V | |
| (c) | I | H | T | N | V | (g) | I | A | B | |
| (d) | B | S | | | | (h) | I | A | H | T | N | V |

4 Write a single set of rules to generate all and only the sentences and associated labelled tree diagrams specified below:

(a) The two sentences:

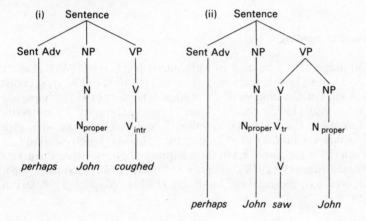

(b) As for (a), but with any NP having the following structure instead of being simply a proper noun:

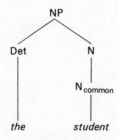

(c) Make the grammar permit *Jane* to occur in place of *John, a* in place of *the, fainted* in place of *coughed, welcomed* in place

of *saw,* and *lecturer* in place of *student*; and permit sentences
without a sentence adverb.
(N.B. It will be necessary to use context-sensitive rules.)

5 Identify any discontinuous constituents in the following: *in
three weeks' time, the most able student in the class, afraid of
having disturbed not only the children but also the neighbours.*
(If you find this difficult now, return to it after chapter 6.)

6 Draw a tree diagram to represent the simple "traditional
grammar" analysis of the sentence *John kissed Mary
yesterday*, and compare it with the analyses discussed at the
end of chapter 4.

**Further reading**

On judging the adequacy of a grammar: Jespersen (1969), chapter
28; Harris (1946), sections 1.0 to 3.9; Chomsky (1965), sections
1.4 and 1.6. On finite-state grammars: Chomsky (1957), chapters 4
and 5; Wall (1972), chapter 9 (on "Type 3 grammars"). On rewrite
grammars: Bach (1974), chapters 2 and 8. On phrase-structure
grammars: Chomsky (1957), chapter 4; Lyons (1968), section 6.2;
Bach (1974), chapter 3. On the adequacy of phrase-structure grammars: Chomsky (1957), chapter 5; Postal (1964); Lyons (1968),
section 6.6; Postal (1972); Bach (1974), chapter 5; Allerton
(1978a).

*Chapter 5*

# Grammatical analysis

---

## Description and analysis

We have seen in chapter 4 that a generative grammar presupposes not only an inventory of the sentences of a language, but also a grammatical description to go with each sentence. But how can the validity of these descriptions be ensured? How can we even know what the most appropriate mode of representation is for grammatical descriptions, tree diagrams, lists of features or whatever else? The only sure method is to scrutinize the sentences and carefully examine the relations between them and the relations between their parts. Grammatical descriptions need to be justified, and the only way of justifying them is by a kind of grammatical analysis. There is, of course, no automatic way of hitting upon correct grammatical descriptions, but the least we should aim for is that, when we arrive at a description, we have some ways of showing why it is a reasonable description.

It is the aim of grammatical description to reflect the native speaker's grammatical competence, to account for his ability to use his language on the grammatical level. We referred in chapter 3 to the native speaker's "implicit" or "tacit" knowledge of the grammar of his language. The difficulty is that the native speaker is by definition unaware of this knowledge and, if directly asked grammatical questions about his language, is likely to respond either with puzzlement or with imperfectly remembered fragments of prescriptive traditional grammar (which is the bad grammar we are trying to improve on!).

In the face of this situation, some transformational generative grammarians have reacted by avoiding naive informants and concentrating on their own grammatical judgments and those of fellow-linguists. The danger is, of course, that they simply confirm each other's prejudices, and that statements like "I find X intuitively correct" are presented as arguments.

Post-Bloomfieldian structuralists responded to the problem in a different way: by simply avoiding all grammatical and semantic intuitions and describing only what can be directly observed. This anti-mentalism (deriving from a behaviourist psychology) is found in Bloomfield, e.g.:

> A morpheme can be described phonetically, since it
> consists of one or more phonemes, but its meaning cannot
> be analyzed within the scope of our science. (1935:
> 161)

but it is principally his disciples (Bloch, Trager, Hill, Harris) who take it to its logical conclusion. This is a totally corpus-based approach, where all the linguist does is identify the minimum grammatical units (morphemes) and describe their distribution relative to each other. Distributional studies, however, although they do have an important part to play, cannot alone provide an adequate grammatical analysis, since, ignoring meaning as they do, they are bound to remain largely superficial. A very large number of distributional patterns can be found in any corpus, but there is no way of knowing which of these are significant, without taking meaning into account; and different patterns which (sometimes) have the same form will never be distinguished without meaning. Thus Harris was only able to distinguish the grammatical patterns of his sentences

> She made him a good husband.
> She made him a good wife.

by going beyond distributionalism to transformational relations.

It is possible, fortunately, to take a view on the role of intuitions that is intermediate between that of the transformationalists mentioned above and the post-Bloomfieldians: that *some* linguistic questions can legitimately be put to the naive native speaker ("naive" in the sense that he or she is free of prior grammatical training or prejudices). Naive native speakers are not normally aware of grammatical patterns. They may well have feelings, e.g. that the sentences

> One boy pretended to write his essay.
> That dog tried to chew its bone.

are somehow similar, but they are unlikely to be able to specify further, and their feelings remain vague presentiments.

We can expect the naive native speaker to speak with greater awareness on questions that relate directly to meaning. He knows what things mean (more or less) the same and what things are clearly different in meaning. Thus he should be able to tell us that

Manchester is where I prefer to stay.
It's Manchester where I prefer to stay.
The place where I prefer to stay is Manchester.

all mean more or less the same (there are, of course, differences in emphasis and style). Also he should be able to detect the two possible meanings of

I used the book in the library.

although we cannot necessarily expect him to say that the ambiguity attaches to the grammatical patterning rather than to a single lexical item. We can think of our naive native speaker as working on the principle that, as a rule, each different sentence has a different meaning, and as having the ability to pick out cases where the rule does not hold, viz.: sets of synonymous sentences; and sentences that are ambiguous.

We can, however, also legitimately put one kind of question to our informant that is at least partly grammatical in its nature. We may ask: Is X (a particular sequence of words) a possible (grammatical) sentence in the language? This question is only partly a grammatical one, because, as we saw in chapter 3, there are a number of different reasons why the sequence may be rejected. We might summarize them as follows:

1 *linguistic reasons*: because the envisaged meaning must be expressed differently (the correct expression is given in parenthesis in the example). The tested sequence has a fault that is:

   (a) *grammatical*
       *The waiter a request made.
       (cf. The waiter made a request.)
       *The waiter made much requests.
       (cf. The waiter made many requests.)
   These would be ungrammatical sequences for Bazell (1964).
   (b) *lexical or locutional* (giving an effect of non-idiomaticalness), e.g.:
       *The waiter made a question.
       (cf. The waiter put/asked a question.)
       *The waiter gave a request.
       (cf. The waiter made a request.)
   These would be non-grammatical sequences for Bazell.
2 *referential reasons*: because the speaker cannot envisage any

meaning for the sequence (and thus there is no correct version) except for a meaning that is:

(a) *non-occurrent*, i.e. beyond any experience he can foresee, e.g.:

*The water made a request.

*The waiter flooded out of the tap.

(b) *nonsensical*, either analytic or contradictory, e.g.:

*The water was wet.

*The water was dry.

So, whenever a speaker rejects a sequence, we as linguists must decide whether it contains a linguistic fault and, if so, whether that fault is grammatical. A useful guide is whether the non-permitted sequence has an obvious correct version, and how it differs from the original.

We must obviously concentrate, however, on those sequences that are accepted as grammatical. To explain their grammatical character, we need to understand how they are related to each other. Which sentences are grammatically the same and which are grammatically different? Clearly, some pairs of sentences differ only in the identity of one of their lexical items, e.g.:

The waiter opened the door.

The waiter opened the window.

If this lexical one is the only difference between them, then they are grammatically identical. Even if we make further lexical changes, e.g.:

The manager opened the window.

grammatical sameness is preserved.

How can we tell, though, whether we have inadvertently made a change in grammatical structure alongside our lexical change? For example, the two sentences

The waiter injured the guest with a kick.

The waiter injured the guest with a limp.

differ in more than just the identity of their last word; the grammatical status of the whole phrase *with a kick* differs from that of *with a limp*. This grammatical difference will probably be felt by the naive native speaker, but he is unable to be clear or definite about it. The question is: how can we show, in a clear way, that there is a difference? How can we justify the native speaker's and our own intuitions?

In these examples we can observe that the two sentences differ in the positions in which they allow an adverb like *seriously* to occur.

Both sentences allow *seriously* to precede the verb *injured*, but otherwise the adverb must be used as follows:

> The waiter injured the guest seriously with a kick.
> The waiter injured the guest with a limp seriously.

Moreover, our two original sentences have differing passive versions, i.e.

> The guest was injured by the waiter with a kick.
> The guest with a limp was injured by the waiter.

Now these new sentences we have considered are in a sense minimally different from our original sentences, the first pair involving simply insertion of an extra adverb, the second pair conversion (or, as we shall later say, TRANSFORMATION) to the passive. This all suggests that grammatically different sentences will have different sets of minimally different related sentences. In other words, the grammatical pattern of a sentence determines what related sentences it will have, and testing for the possible occurrence of these related sentences is one way of testing the grammatical character of our original sentence(s).

We are considering here the possibility of grammatical tests for ascertaining the grammatical character of a sentence, at this stage simply to categorize it as the same or different compared with another sentence. Such a test is not the same as what the post-Bloomfieldian structuralists referred to as a "discovery procedure". By this term, linguists meant a procedure, envisaged as almost automatic, by which a description could be built up step by step on a systematic basis (cf. Longacre, 1964). Such an ambition has now largely been given up, and is often (somewhat unjustly) derided. But, in any case, our aim is much more modest, simply to provide some useful tests for same v. different.

If a botanist is asked whether two specimen leaves are botanically the same, he can examine and test for various attributes (the overall shape, the kind of edge), he can dissect the leaf to examine its internal structure, he can check for the presence of various acids, enzymes, etc. The chemist will proceed in a similar way, if asked which two of three sample substances are the same, by weighing, heating, checking for solubility, etc. Neither scientist will claim to have an automatic procedure, but they both need to have a battery of tests to apply. The grammarian also needs such a battery of operational tests.

**Grammatical tests**

Perhaps the most important tool in all linguistic studies is SUBSTI-
TUTION for a given element; it is at the heart of the study of paradigmatic relations (discussed in chapter 2). We assume that an examination of the range of different substitutes for an element gives an
insight into the function of the element in the context where substitution is being tried out. The reason for this is that by looking for
substitutes we find a total list of alternatives that forms the class to
which the element belongs, and we see what other elements our
element under consideration has to be kept distinct from. An analogy would be the different materials we could substitute for carpeting on a house floor; these might include linoleum, vinyl flooring,
wood parquet, etc., each of which contrasts with carpeting in its
characteristics, but shares with carpeting membership of the class of
floor coverings.

Consider now a linguistic example, the word *pencils* in the following sentence:

John brought in some brown *pencils* for us yesterday.
↓
*pens*
*chairs*
*dogs*
*eggs*
etc.

Each of the substitutes gives a sentence that any native speaker will
recognize as minimally different from the original. The substitution
list, which disregards lexico-semantic factors, gives us a provisional
grammatical class, and thus marks a step in building up a picture of
the grammatical character of the sentence.

We might also have tested substitutions for *some*:

John brought in *some* green pencils for us.
↓
*the*
*my*
*many*

But what if we had proposed *useful* or *strange* as substitutes for *some*
in this case? We would probably feel that we had replaced *some* with
something rather different, or, in other words, that we had not
carried out a straight substitution of an element so much as omitted
one element and inserted another. How can we demonstrate this?

As a general rule, different constituents occur side by side in a
structure, but elements of the same class do not do so except with

some marker of co-ordination such as *and, but, or.* Thus we have the following sequences:

| | | |
|---|---|---|
| some green pencils | BUT NOT | *some the pencils |
| the green pencils | | *some my pencils |
| some red pencils | | *green red pencils |
| etc. | BUT | green and red pencils |
| | | green or red pencils |

Turning to *useful* and *strange* we find:

some useful green pencils
some strange green pencils

AS WELL AS: useful green pencils
strange green pencils
N.B. useful but strange green pencils.

In other words, since *useful* and *strange* occur not only apparently in place of *some, the, my* but also side by side with them, they are best regarded as cases of insertion with simultaneous omission, rather than straight substitution.

The other main kind of improper substitution is when the apparent straight substitution has the effect of changing the sentence structure in some way. We saw an example of that earlier when we simply replaced the word *kick* with *limp*. For a substitution to be valid, then, the sentence must be essentially the same grammatically before and after the operation. To check on this sameness we can either go direct to our informant or carry out operational tests on our test sentences. (There is here, in theory, a danger of infinite regress, but in practice this gives rise to little difficulty.)

The dangers of inadmissible examples that we have just considered apply not only to substitution but also to the other tests we are now going on to consider.

EXPANSION is a test which can be regarded as a special kind of substitution. Instead of replacing one element with a similar single element, we replace it with a complex sequence. An example is:

John brought in some *green* pencils for us.

*pale blue*
*mushroom-coloured*
*post-office red*
etc.

In such cases the expanded sequence represents the same kind of element as the word it replaces, but a larger version of it, so to speak. As a larger version, it is not therefore exactly the same as the element it replaces, but the difference lies in the internal structure of the replacing sequence; in their external relations to the rest of the sentence the original item and its expansion must be equivalent.

REDUCTION is the converse of expansion. In this test we examine a sequence of words (or morphemes) in our test sentence and seek a single element to replace it, if this is feasible. It should be feasible when the sequence under consideration has coherence and can act to some extent as a unit; in such cases it is usually regarded as a "construction" (as we shall see in our next chapter). Consider:

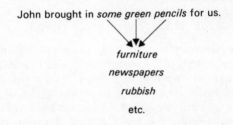

Each reduction brings about a simplification of the grammatical structure of the sentence, in that while the external relations of the affected constituent are left undisturbed, its internal structure is reduced to the status of a single element.

In expansion and reduction, as in substitution, it is essential to preserve the grammatical character of the sentence as a whole; it is equally essential to ensure that any proposed expansions or reductions are not really uses of omission with simultaneous insertion. Improper reductions could be exemplified by:

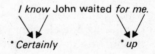

A pseudo-reduced structure with *certainly* would not allow optional insertion of *that* after it, whereas *I know* would; and the pseudo-reduction *up* could actually occur side by side with the original construction *for me*.

The operations of INSERTION and OMISSION (or DELETION) are also related to substitution, but in a less obvious way. Insertion may be regarded as substitution of an overt element for a zero, i.e. introducing a new element; and omission (deletion) as the reverse, substitution of a zero for an overt element, i.e. removing an old element. Insertion may be illustrated with:

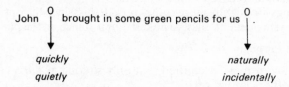

Different kinds of adverb are introduced at different points in this example. The precise points where such insertions are possible is one of the grammatical characteristics of the sentence under consideration. Neither kind of adverb could, for instance, be inserted between *brought* and *in*; although it would have been possible to make a comparable insertion of *quickly* or *quietly* in, for instance:

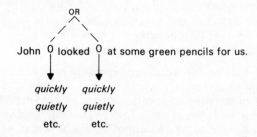

This suggests that *brought in* and *looked at* differ in their grammatical character (and there is plenty of other evidence to support this point).

Insertion is a useful indication of the coherence of two words in a sentence. Broadly speaking, the greater the potential for insertion between them, i.e. for interrupting them, the less connected or coherent they are; but the less they allow insertion, the more closely connected they are.

Omission involves testing whether the sentence can occur without the element under scrutiny. (We shall prefer this term to "deletion", reserving the latter for the description of the language, rather than for the description of analytic procedures.) In the sample sentence:

John brought (in) some (green) pencils (for us).

we can observe that any (or all) of the parenthesized elements may

101

be omitted and still leave behind a sentence of comparable structure (except as regards the omitted element itself). One value of the omission test is obvious: it indicates which elements in a sentence are optional, and therefore less essential.

But things are slightly more complex than this, since the optionality of different elements may be linked. For instance, in the phrase:

some fairly sharp pencils

the word *sharp* may be omitted, but only so long as *fairly* is also omitted; otherwise we get

*some fairly pencils.

On the other hand, *fairly* may be omitted on its own, leaving *sharp* where it is.

A different case is provided by the words *for us* in our original example. These two words may be omitted jointly, but neither one may be omitted on its own, cf.

John brought in some green pencils for us.
John brought in some green pencils.
*John brought in some green pencils for.
*John brought in some green pencils us.

We may say that the two words are capable of joint omission but not of individual omission.

The tests of insertion and omission have an obvious relationship to expansion and reduction, respectively. For example, above we expanded *green* to *pale blue*, but we might just as well expand it to *pale green*. This is a perfectly legitimate expansion, though of a special kind (we shall later call it "endocentric"), in that the expanded form contains the original item within it. At the same time we can, from a different point of view, regard it as a case of insertion. To be specific, we have expanded the adjective phrase by inserting an adjective modifier. In the reverse case, we would reduce a structure by omitting one of its component parts. There is no contradiction here, nor even a duplication; we are simply describing two different aspects of the same phenomenon.

PERMUTATION (or TRANSPOSITION) differs from the substitution-related tests we have considered so far, in that it does not involve any change in the identity of the words in the test sentence, but only in their ordering (or sequence). Thus, in our sentence, the word *in*, or independently the phrase *for us*, may be moved to different positions in the sentence, keeping the essential grammatical character of the sentence intact:

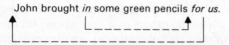

John brought *in* some green pencils *for us*.

The freedom of an element to move around a sentence free from its neighbouring elements suggests that the element has no specially close association with them. On the other hand, if a word can only make such movements along with a fellow-word (e.g. *for* with *us*), this is evidence for the closeness of these two items. The phrase *some green pencils* may also be moved as an integral unit to the initial position in the sentence, although this gives a special, contrastive, effect.

Just as insertion and omission were linked to expansion and reduction, so also is permutation linked to both insertion and expansion. The permutation of elements resulting from the transposition of an item can also be explained as a combination of omission in one position and insertion in another. Thus all of these tests are interrelated. It is of little consequence, however, precisely how any one of these tests is described; the important thing is to fix on a set of tests, however described, and apply them consistently to the sentences or structures that are being compared.

In actual fact any of the above operational tests could be (and has been) described as a TRANSFORMATION. This term, as we explained earlier, is a technical term in generative grammar and elsewhere, and we shall discuss it more fully later (in chapter 8). Provisionally, though, let us say that it will be useful to limit applicability of the term to operations which are complex in a sense that those we have so far considered are not. Each of our previous operations has involved one simple change, either in the identity of a single element or in its sequencing; that is what we meant by describing the sentences before and after the change as "minimally different". Underlying our discussion was an assumption that a minimum change in the form (i.e. expression aspect) of a sentence implied a minimum change in meaning – a very natural assumption. The converse, however, does not always hold: we can have a complex change in the form of a sentence corresponding to a simple (in a sense "minimal") change in meaning or grammatical structure.

We may consider the following examples as typical of this complex kind of formal change that we shall refer to as "transformational":

John brought in some green pencils for us.
Who did John bring in some green pencils for?
It was some green pencils that John brought in for us.
Some green pencils were brought in for us by John.

If we take the first of the above sentences as our "theme" sentence, and regard each of the others as a "variation" on the theme (or a "transform" of the original sentence), we observe that in each case there has been a complex change in form, involving a combination of substitution, expansion, etc., and yet there is a minimal change in content. In the second sentence, for instance, the verb *brought* is resolved into its components *bring* and *-ed*, the *-ed* is permuted to pre-subject position to join an inserted verb *do, who* is substituted for *us* and transposed to initial position; but the only change in meaning is to convert an asserted pronoun *us* to a queried pronoun *who*.

Transformationally related structures abound in languages. It is therefore essential to provide for these more complex sentence relationships in our battery of tests.

## Grammatical patterns

Since we assume that the infinity (or at least immeasurably large number) of sentences in a language can be reduced to a finite number of structures, our first step must be to use our grammatical tests to ascertain which sentences have which patterns. At the most elementary level, we might imagine that, given, say, twelve sentences (numbered 1 to 12) and three different patterns (A,B,C), all we have to do is simply assign each sentence to a pattern, e.g.:

| Structure A | Structure B | Structure C |
| --- | --- | --- |
| Sentence 1 | Sentence 3 | Sentence 4 |
| 2 | 7 | 11 |
| 5 | 8 | 12 |
| 6 | 10 | |
| 9 | | |

At a more sophisticated level, however, we shall need to recognize that there are not simply a number of entirely separate structures, but rather sets of interrelated patterns. One sentence must be characterized as simultaneously exhibiting a number of different grammatical patterns or features. For example, a sentence (or clause) might be categorized as: (i) command, statement or question (the latter subcategorized as *yes–no* or *wh-* question); (ii) affirmative or negative; (iii) copular ("equational"), intransitive or transitive (the latter subcategorized as monotransitive, ditransitive, etc.).

Other pattern differences may characterize not the sentence as a whole but one subpart, such as the verb or a particular noun phrase. Take, as an example, the four English words:

*policemen, criminals, watched, have*

Any grammar we give must show, of course, that they may be used to form the sentences:

| | |
|---|---|
| Policemen have watched criminals. | (1) |
| Criminals have watched policemen. | (2) |
| Have policemen watched criminals? | (3) |
| Have criminals watched policemen? | (4) |
| Policemen have criminals watched. | (5) |
| Criminals have policemen watched. | (6) |

and that, for instance:

*Policemen criminals watched have.

is not a possible sentence. Secondly, a grammar would recognize that only three grammatically different sentence-types, (1)–(2), (3)–(4) and (5)–(6), can be distinguished. But further investigation will show that, while (3)–(4) differ from (1)–(2) simply in the feature of statement–question, (5)–(6) differ from them in at least two points, verb pattern (causative) and aspect. Moreover, the question forms of (5)–(6) will not be:

*Have policemen criminals watched?
*Have criminals policemen watched?

They need the introduction of the grammatical element *do*:

Do policemen have criminals watched?
Do criminals have policemen watched?

We can further see the same difference of aspect between:

Policemen have watched criminals.
AND: Policemen watch criminals.

as we see between

Policemen have had criminals watched.
AND: Policemen have criminals watched.

A comparision reveals that the difference is shown by the use of the grammatical word *have* in combination with a difference in the morphological form of the word *watch/watched*.

Grammatical patterns, then, are ways of combining words (or morphemes) into larger units with more complex structure and more complex meaning. The meaning of the whole is a composite of the meanings of the individual words plus the meaning of the pattern. The pattern or structure itself is marked by a combination of:

(a) choosing the right classes of words,
(b) putting the words in the required sequence,
(c) using the appropriate grammatical items like *do* and *have*,
(d) choosing the appropriate form of the words, with the right inflectional morphemes, such as *-ed*, *-s* (see further chapter 10),
(e) where appropriate, choosing the right accentual pattern.

These different features that mark a grammatical pattern or structure may be referred to simply as GRAMMATICAL MARKERS or, to use Fries's (1952: 69–71 *et passim*) term, STRUCTURAL SIGNALS. Fries illustrates them from Lewis Carroll's well-known Jabberwocky verse in Alice's adventures *Through the Looking-Glass*. The first stanza runs:

'Twas brillig, and the slithy toves
   Did gyre and gimble in the wabe:
All mimsy were the borogoves,
   And the mome raths outgrabe.

This whole sequence is grammatically clear (assuming that in line 4 *outgrabe* is interpreted as a past-tense verb, to agree with the previous past tenses), and this is entirely due to devices of the kinds mentioned above under (a) to (e). What the passage lacks is not grammatical structure but lexical content – as Alice herself says:

"It seems very pretty . . . but it's *rather* hard to understand!
. . . Somehow it seems to fill my head with ideas – only I don't exactly know what they are!"

The grammatical structure of a sentence may thus be a very real thing to the native speaker-hearer, and it will be our task in the following chapters to decide how this should be described.

**Questions for study**

1 Find out what psychological issues divide "mentalists" from "mechanists" or "behaviourists". In what ways might different stands on these issues influence the linguist's approach? Is language a mental phenomenon, a physical phenomenon, or both? (Or is this whole question unhelpful?)

2 For what kind of reason – grammatical, lexical or referential – are the following non-occurrent or marginal?
   (a) *John is a geographical student (cf. medical student).
   (b) *This Antarctic giraffe is a geography student.
   (c) *John are a geography student.

3 On the basis of the tests of substitution, etc., show, in each of the following sets of sentences, which sentence is grammatically the odd man out compared with the other two:
   (a)  (i) They are afraid to eat.
       (ii) They are interesting to eat.
      (iii) They are unpleasant to eat.
   (b)  (i) I enquired where the artist worked.
       (ii) I stayed where the artist worked.
      (iii) I knew where the artist worked.
   (c)  (i) The soldiers blocked up the passageway.
       (ii) The soldiers opened up the passageway.
      (iii) The soldiers ran up the passageway.
   (d)  (i) Margaret was driven to the motorway.
       (ii) Margaret was escorted to the motorway.
      (iii) Margaret was opposed to the motorway.
   (e)  (i) James hated speeding motorists.
       (ii) James hated assisting motorists.
      (iii) James hated towing motorists.

4 We saw in chapter 4 that the sentence *John kissed Mary yesterday* had at least three competing analyses. Consider which of these three analyses would be favoured by the following evidence in terms of operational tests:
   (a) The verb *kissed* can only be replaced by other words that are similarly inflected for past tense (normally in *-ed*) or, if *yesterday* is eliminated, by words inflected for present tense (normally in *-(e)s*).
   (b) The sentence has a passive transformation, *Mary was kissed by John yesterday.*
   (c) The sequence *kissed Mary* may be reduced to, for instance, *panicked, misbehaved, fainted*; but if a similar reduction is attempted for *John kissed* (to, for instance, *Kiss, Hit*), the type of sentence is changed (to a command), not to mention the problem of *yesterday*!
   (d) The word *yesterday* may be permuted to initial position; and in some styles of English it may appear between *John* and *kissed*. But it cannot occur between *kissed* and *Mary*.

5 Using traditional grammatical labels, identify the class of each of the nonsense words in the Jabberwocky verse quoted at the end of the chapter, indicating the structural signals which mark the item as belonging to that particular grammatical class. Attempt a description of some of the grammatical structures you meet, referring to the five features listed on page 106.

**Further reading**

On description and analysis: Harris (1951), chapters 15 and 16; Haas (1973b), section 7.1. On grammatical tests: Haas (1954). On grammatical patterns: Fries (1952), chapters 4–8.

*Chapter 6*

# Constructions – the problem of "bracketing"

## Constructions and constituents

We have set ourselves the aim of describing the grammatical patterns that characterize sentences. There is good reason to believe that we cannot achieve this at one fell swoop. It is not just that sentences are structurally very complex, but that they have built into them a whole hierarchy of substructures (and sub-substructures, etc.). We may recall (from chapter 1) that linguistic structures are like building structures in this respect: that a sentence is like a house in not simply being an assemblage of its ultimate constituents, morphemes in the case of language, or bricks, timbers and glass (etc.) in the case of a house. Each word or morpheme, as an ultimate constituent of its sentence, exhibits what Bolinger (1975: 136–7) terms "togetherness" towards one or more of its neighbours, forming jointly with it/them an intermediate structural unit such as a phrase. In describing sentence structure we must take account of intermediate structural elements, the linguistic analogues of walls, windows and the like. This is the syntagmatic axis of syntax.

Bloomfield (1935: 160–1) suggested a distinction between IMMEDIATE CONSTITUENTS and ULTIMATE CONSTITUENTS. He proposed breaking down a sentence stage by stage: first a sentence into its immediate constituents, then those constituents into their immediate constituents, and so on until the ultimate constituents, morphemes, are reached. An ultimate constituent is thus simply a special kind of immediate constituent, viz. one that cannot be analysed any further. At each stage where analysis does take place there is a set of constituents[1] and the larger element of which they

---

[1] The non-ultimate constituents might be termed "intermediate constituents". These are the ones which require "auxiliary" or "non-terminal" symbols (see chapter 4).

are constituents; Wells (1947: section 7) and Hockett (1958: 164) refer to this larger element as the "constitute", but it is more generally referred to as the CONSTRUCTION.[2] This view of constituents and constructions may be represented diagrammatically as in Figure 30.

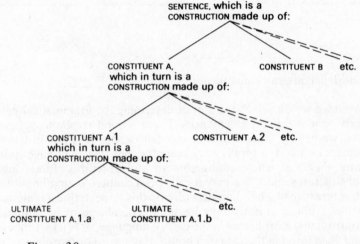

*Figure 30*

In this view every constituent is thus also a construction, except for ultimate constituents (morphemes) at the bottom of the tree diagram; and every construction is also a constituent, except for the sentence at the top. We thus have a hierarchy of constructions and constituents.

A linguistic example may make the point clearer. Figure 31 shows how we might think of the composition of the sentence *My sheep eat three times a day.* In this tree-diagram representation, each junction of lines, or NODE, represents a construction (and thus a point where a non-terminal symbol is needed). We have not labelled the nodes; they could of course be assigned a label reflecting their position in the tree (as the nodes in the previous diagram were), but this information can be derived from the tree as it stands. Such a tree diagram is notationally equivalent to a representation with hier-

---

[2]  Wells and Hockett reserve the term "construction" for the construction-TYPE, applying the term "constitute" to individual occurrences or TOKENS (cf. chapter 2).

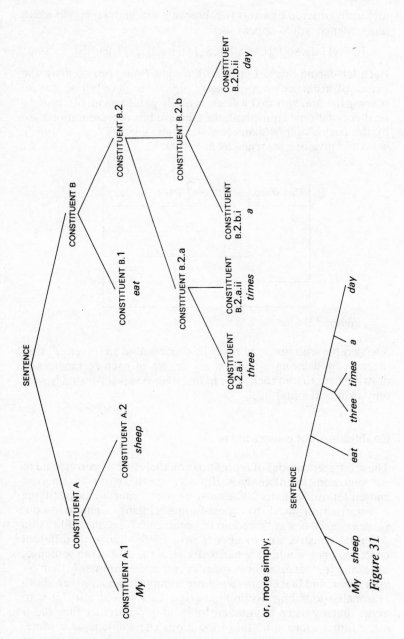

or, more simply:

*Figure 31*

archically ordered brackets (i.e. brackets within brackets) in which our sentence would appear as:

[[[My] [sheep]] [[eat] [[[three] [times]] [[a] [day]]]]].

Each left-facing bracket pairs with a right-facing one to mark the extent of a particular constituent; and there is only one way of reading the brackets that will successfully pair them all off. Using a further notational equivalent, the Chinese box representation used by the post-Bloomfieldians (e.g. Hockett, 1958; Gleason, 1961), we could give our sentence as in Figure 32.

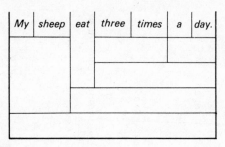

*Figure 32*

Such a representation may easily be converted to an (inverted) tree diagram by drawing a node in the centre of each rectangle and drawing lines to join each node to the other nodes separated from it only by a horizontal line.

**Establishment of constructions**

These different modes of representation therefore all correspond to the same constituent analysis. But why was this particular analysis chosen for our sentence? The most frequent criterion for justifying a construction used by (post-Bloomfieldian) immediate–constituent analysts was "freedom of occurrence", i.e. the ability of a potential construction to appear in a (wide) range of different contexts. They would have had to argue, in the case of our sentence, for example, that *three times a day* occurs more commonly than *eat three times*, and that *my sheep* is more common than *sheep eat* – both reasonable-sounding assumptions; but they would also have to argue that *my sheep* has greater freedom of occurrence than *sheep eat*, a rather more doubtful proposition. The whole issue is somewhat obscured by the lack of precision involved in the notion of "freedom of occurrence": in theory, we are supposed to gauge the variety of different contexts in which a sequence may occur, but it is never made clear what counts as a difference of context – a difference in lexical item, a difference in word-class, a difference in structure, or whatever else.

We are on more secure ground if we can use some of our operational tests for establishing constructions. The obvious one to use is reduction. For instance, *my* + *sheep* can be reduced to *they* with no change in the value of the rest of the sentence; and, in fact, in most contexts where it occurs, the phrase *my sheep* may be reduced to either *they* or *them*. Similarly, *eat* + *three times a day* may be reduced to *overeat* or *gorge*, or *starve*.

Reduction does not work, however, for our other constructions, and here we must turn to a second test, joint omission. It is true that *a day* may be reduced in our sentence to *daily*, but *daily* can obviously be analysed as two morphemes *dai-*(=*day*) and -*ly*; even *twice* as a "reduction" of *three times* seems to contain a *twi-* element (=*two*) and a -*ce* morpheme (cf. *once, thrice*). What we can say, however, about both of these constructions is that they can only be omitted, if at all, as constructions; their individual parts may not be separately omitted. Consider:

> My sheep eat three times a day.
> My sheep eat three times.         [omitting *a day*]

but the following are impossible:

> *My sheep eat three times a.     [omitting *day* alone]
> *My sheep eat three times day.     [omitting *a* alone]

Consider further reduction as follows:

> My sheep eat three times.
> My sheep eat.            [omitting *three times*]

but the following are impossible:

> *My sheep eat three.     [omitting *times* – only possible
>                     with a new meaning for *three*]
> *My sheep eat times.         [omitting *three*]

As a final example of an irreducible construction we may consider the drastically cut-down version of our sentence:

> They eat.

There is no single-word statement sentence in English, and therefore the reduction test cannot apply; but, if we imagine our sentence occurring in mid-text, surrounded by other sentences, then probably

we could jointly omit the whole sentence construction *they + eat*
and leave our text intact.

Figure 33 summarizes the results of our reduction and joint-
omission tests.

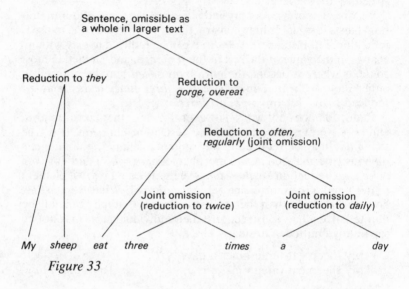

*Figure 33*

Each of the nodes we have proposed thus has some justification
in terms of our operations. Let us emphasize again, though, that
the operations were not a means of discovering a constituent
analysis, but merely a way of checking that the analysis had some
validity.

What we have been doing, then, is identifying certain operational
tests as diagnostic of constructions, viz.:

(1) reduction
(2) joint (but not single) omission, to which we may add:
(3) joint (but not single) transposition (i.e. permutation).

This last test is closely associated with the second. In the sentence
discussed above, for example, the construction *three times a day* can
not only be jointly omitted but can also be transposed, as a unit, to
initial position. This is commonly the case for English adverbial
phrases, cf. *in general, during Christmas.*

In a language like German, where word order is less fixed, other
constituents, such as noun phrases, may be moved around the
sentence. A German sentence like:

114

| 1 | 2 | 3 |
|---|---|---|
| [Der Lehrer] | [gibt] | [jeden Montag] |
| 'The teacher' | 'gives' | 'every Monday' |

| 4 | 5 |
|---|---|
| [dem Schüler] | [ein Heft]. |
| '(to) the pupil' | 'an exercise book' |

may be reordered by putting any of the constructions 3, 4 or 5 in place of construction 1 and moving the latter to a position immediately following item 2 (the verb). The elements that may be permuted in this way (Glinz (1952: 86–9) speaks of the "Verschiebeprobe") are always constructions with the status noun/adverbial phrase, and not isolated words like *jeden* or *Montag*.

All we have done so far, however painstakingly, is to establish which bits of a sentence go together as constructions and thus jointly form higher-level constituents. It should be obvious from the outset, however, that this is only one aspect of the grammatical patterning of a sentence. (Even traditional grammar did much more than this.) It is clear, for example, that the two phrases in Figure 34, despite their identical immediate constituent structure, have a very different internal make-up and a different potential for occurrence in sentences:

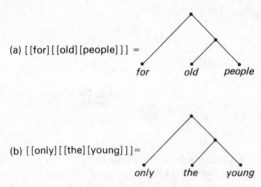

(a) [[for][[old][people]]] =    for    old    people

(b) [[only][[the][young]]] =    only    the    young

*Figure 34*

These structures seem to differ from each other in at least two ways: the classes of element that are involved; and the relationship between them. Together with tree or constituent structure itself, i.e. the domain of the constructions, this gives us three kinds of differences between grammatical patterns.

115

A useful touchstone for recognizing syntactic differences is syntactic ambiguity; and this can be caused by any of our three factors:

(i) *the domain of constructions, or* BRACKETING, e.g.:

    (the) Peruvian silver tray

which has at least two interpretations that differ only in the "togetherness" of the constituents (Figures 35 and 36). We might also distinguish a third interpretation (Figure 37),

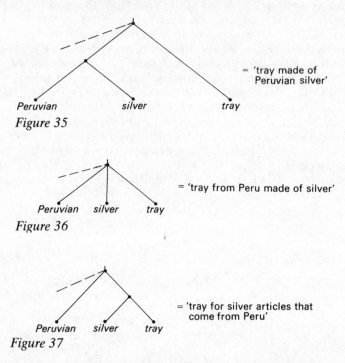

= 'tray made of Peruvian silver'

*Peruvian*    *silver*    *tray*

*Figure 35*

= 'tray from Peru made of silver'

*Peruvian silver tray*

*Figure 36*

= 'tray for silver articles that come from Peru'

*Peruvian silver tray*

*Figure 37*

but this phrase would have a markedly different stress pattern (with *silver* accented as opposed to *tray*), and *silver tray* in this case could be interpreted as a single lexical item. (Another example would be *the son of Pharaoh's daughter*, discussed in chapter 1.)

(ii) *the class(es) of constituent in the constructions, or* LABELLING, e.g.:

    (Holmes saw) the door open.

where the phrase in question is in any case the complement of the

116

verb *see*, and where the domain of the constructions cannot be varied, but where there is an obvious ambiguity according to the value of the word *open* (Figure 38). This ambiguity can only be accounted for if we assume that the word *open* belongs to two different classes – "verb" and "adjective" – and that the labelling forms part of the grammatical description of the phrase. Alternatively, there are two different words *open* (for discussion see next chapter). (A further example would be *Make this car fast*, where *fast* is ambivalent.)

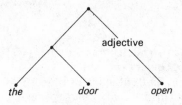

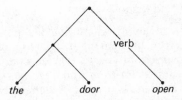

*Figure 38*

(iii) *the relationship between the constituents*, or FUNCTION, e.g.:

(John should) find Jane a good secretary.

In this case the ambiguity stems from the fact that the verb *find* may occur in either of two different constructions, in each of which it contracts different relationships to its following noun phrases (and to some extent has a different lexical meaning itself). The function of *Jane* in the interpretation given in (a) below is similar to that of *a good secretary* in interpretation (b):

(a) 'find Jane to be a good secretary'
(b) 'find (= obtain) a good secretary for Jane'

Both over-all patterns can be represented with the same labelled tree diagram (Figure 39), but what the diagram fails to show is the

117

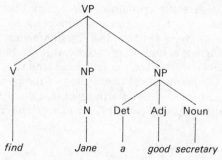

*Figure 39*

relationship of the two noun phrases to the verb: whether they have the function DIRECT OBJECT (meaning 'mental focus') + OBJECT COMPLEMENT (meaning 'current state of object'); or INDIRECT OBJECT (meaning 'beneficiary') + DIRECT OBJECT (meaning 'affected'). Tied up with these interconstituent relationships is the fact that for the (a) meaning the first noun phrase is obligatory, while for the (b) meaning it may optionally be deleted: in other words, the sentence

John should find a good secretary

must have the (b) meaning, where *find* is equivalent to 'obtain'. Thus the function of an element is a factor independent of its position in a construction. (For a further example, consider the three possible meanings for *John's photograph*, depending on different relations between *John* and *photograph*.)

Of these three different aspects to grammatical structure, we shall consider the domain of constructions and the relationships between their constituents (=their function) in this chapter, but postpone the question of class until chapter 7.

**The analysis of constituent patterns**

We saw in chapter 4 that generative grammarians have differed considerably in their proposals for the constituent-structure (phrase-structure) descriptions of the same sentence. Even the analysis of a single set of constituents within a construction can give rise to difficulty. The noun-phrase example that follows would be treated by transformational-generative grammarians as having the adjective introduced transformationally (deriving from the same source as *car that is new*); but they still face the problem of what the surface-structure representation of the noun phrase should be. Let

Constructions – the problem of "bracketing"

us consider the single case of a noun phrase with three elements, a determiner (e.g. *a*), an adjective (e.g. *new*) and a noun (e.g. *car*).

In theory four different constituent analyses are possible for such a noun phrase, and every one has something to be said for it. We can represent the four different analyses as in Figure 40.

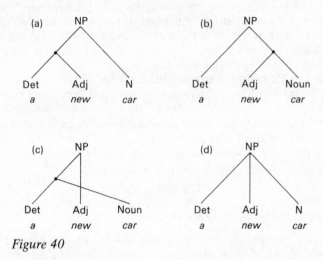

*Figure 40*

Solutions (a) and (b) can both be said to be based on the reducibility of *a new car* to *a car*, but to differ on the question of which subpart reduces to a single element:

a new → a
*or*: new car → car

All we can be sure of is that *new* is omissible, and our decision on which analysis to accept must therefore be based on other evidence.

Arguments for (a) seem to be based on semantic considerations, i.e. the contributions to the meaning of the noun phrase that the different elements make. It can be argued that *car* is the semantic centre (or "head") of the noun phrase, and that *a* and *new* should be grouped together as modifiers. The fact that two elements have a similar relationship to a third is not, however, a strong argument; and, in any case, they do not have the same relationship to *car*, since in this combination *new* is omissible while *a* is not. Analysis (a) therefore seems the weakest.

The arguments in favour of analysis (b) also seem to have a semantic foundation, but this time a more secure one. It is suggested that *new* and *car* unite to form a single concept: so that quite often

119

there is a single-word noun corresponding in meaning to the adjective-plus-noun sequence, e.g. *youth = young man, hamlet = small village*. (We are not here thinking of such "tight" combinations as *sweet pepper, black pudding*, which are best regarded as compound nouns (see chapter 10).) The fact that the adjective is semantically linked to the noun, and not to the determiner, has the consequence that there are individual co-occurrence restrictions of adjective with noun, stemming from the actualities of the real world, e.g. *dry shirt, ?dry idea, \*dry water*, but no such restrictions for determiner-adjective combinations.

The two elements in our noun phrase with the closest grammatical links are *a* and *car*. Firstly, they are mutually dependent on each other for their occurrence, whereas they can occur without *new*. Secondly, if we consider possible substitutions for each of them, we find (as we saw in chapter 4) that it is necessary to set up grammatical subclasses to account for co-occurrence restrictions such as:

| | | |
|---|---|---|
| a car | BUT | *a traffic |
| this car | | *this cars |
| some cars | | *some car [where some = /səm/] |
| some traffic | | *these traffic |

The combination of determiner-plus-noun could therefore be thought of as the core of the noun phrase with the intervening adjective one of a number of possible optional expansions. This view would be represented by solution (c).

The difficulty with analysis (c) is that it is not a normal tree diagram. The format of tree diagrams is governed by a precise set of conventions – it is studied in a branch of mathematics – and the crossing of tree lines is prohibited. The kind of constituent we have proposed in analysis (c) is a "discontinuous constituent", and we shall discuss this notion below. Provisionally let us simply note that, to accept the notion, we would need to modify or reject the accepted format of tree diagrams.

Having seen the various advantages and disadvantages of our first three solutions, it is easy to appreciate the attractiveness of solution (d). In this analysis the three elements are considered as equally closely related, and, therefore, although they all belong to the noun-phrase construction, no two of them form a "lower-level" construction – there is no lower node. This account of the constituent pattern thus gives no expression to the differing roles of the three words within the construction; but perhaps this should be taken care of within our third dimension of grammatical patterning, relationships between elements in a construction (see below).

Early Immediate Constituent analysts felt the need to choose a

solution from amongst (a), (b) and (c) (and (c) was only a last
resort), because they had a preference for constructions of two
constituents. This is implicit in Wells (1947), explicitly stated by
Bloch and Trager (1942: 67) and found natural by Gleason (1961:
142). But the preference for binary constructions is far from universal: Pike and the tagmemicists (as well as Halliday in systemic
grammar) have always spurned "binarism", and Longacre (1960)
explicitly contrasts Immediate Constituent Analysis with String
Constituent Analysis; Chomsky, though proposing mainly two-
constituent constructions in 1957, had moved away from this in
1965 (though never adequately explaining why).

Our construction *a new car* is thus one of many that can, but need
not, be analysed in binary terms. There are, however, a number of
constructions that seem to absolutely require a "multiple-
constituent" treatment. The best examples are provided by coordinative constructions such as *tea and coffee*, which seems to require the
analysis:

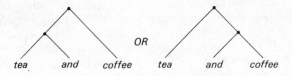

rather than either

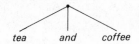

The *and* seems equally closely related to *tea* and to *coffee*; in fact,
the whole point of the *and* is to link the two coordinated nouns – *and*
only occurs when more than one noun is present. When more than
two nouns are coordinated, we need to posit an even larger construction, e.g.:

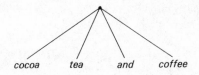

121

But in all of these coordinate constructions we are confronted by the problem that faced us above: while all the nouns play a similar part in the construction, the *and* obviously has a quite different function. Once again we must conclude that specifying the domain of a construction is only part of the story; we must also specify the nature of the constituents and the relations between them.

Our examples so far have had phrases or words as constituents, but, as we shall see in chapter 10, constituent analysis is also necessary within the word (for instance, to describe a word like *ungentlemanly*). We may get the impression that words may only form constructions with fellow-words, but this is far from true. If this were the case, the only possible analysis of *hard-liner* would be (a) rather than (b) in Figure 41,

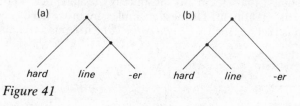

*Figure 41*

suggesting that it referred to a 'hard' kind of 'liner'; in actual fact, though, *hard-liner* should naturally be compared with *golfer* or *Londoner*, where the *-er* means 'person connected with X'. An analysis similar to (b) has to be envisaged for such sequences as *red-headed*, *left of centre-ish*, and *non-union member*. In a phrase like *my wife's brother's child*, we find this pattern recurring (see Figure 42, in which the parenthesized words indicate possible reductions). We may conclude that word status may not be taken as an overriding factor in determining construction boundaries. In

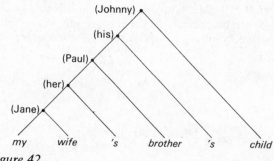

*Figure 42*

actual fact, the whole notion of "word" is somewhat unclear, and will be further examined later (chapter 10).

We earlier raised the question of "discontinuous constituents", in other words, cases where a construction involves elements that are not adjacent. This is a problem that everyone, whatever his grammatical model, has to face. There is no problem with a sequence like *take on more staff* (which might be a complete sentence). We could give its constituents as shown in Figure 43, *take on* being reducible

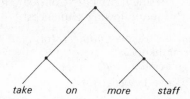

*Figure 43*

to *engage, retain, dismiss*, etc. and *more staff* reducing to *John* or simply *staff*; the first constituent-construction is a complex verb and the second a noun-phrase object, the over-all construction being a verb phrase. But what do we say of *take more staff on*? This seems totally equivalent, both semantically and grammatically, to our original sequence. To represent this equivalence, we would need to adopt a specially adapted tree diagram (Figure 44) along the lines we suggested above for *a new car* (Figure 40).

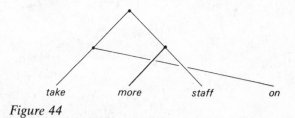

*Figure 44*

Discontinuous constructions require special diagrammatic conventions not only for tree diagrams but also for the equivalent formats of bracketing and Chinese box diagrams (as the reader can ascertain by trying these alternatives for the example just discussed).

As we saw in chapter 4, transformational-generative grammarians have reacted to this problem by giving such constructions a deep structure where the constituents are adjacent (but do not appear in their natural sequential order) and a surface structure where the constituents do not belong to an exclusive common construction (but do appear in their natural ordering). This does, however, seem an *ad hoc* solution, a solution that suggests there is something wrong with the basic framework and diagrammatic conventions.

The problem would be less serious if discontinuous constructions were rather rare; but they are not. Consider, for instance, the italicized portions of the following sequences:

(i) *Elizabeth* is unlikely *to object.* (cf. *That Elizabeth will object* is unlikely.)

(ii) John is *as* good *as Bill.*

(iii) England *have* beat*en* Brazil.

In each case there are clear syntactic and semantic grounds for treating the non-adjacent italicized elements as a single construction. The third example, moreover, is one of a set of verbal auxiliary constructions in English that are all discontinuous and may combine with each other, to give an effect something like that shown in Figure 45.

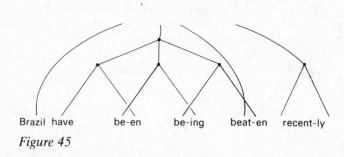

Brazil have    be-en    be-ing    beat-en    recent-ly

*Figure 45*

Discontinuity can be so woven into the fabric of a language that morphemes themselves can occur in a discontinuous form. We shall discuss cases of this, like the German *ge – t* of *gehabt* or Arabic triliteral roots, in chapter 10.

Links between non-adjacent morphemes are almost bound to occur, because of the one-dimensional nature of the speech chain in which linguistic utterances are sequenced. A morpheme may have only two morphemes actually adjacent to it (one preceding, one following); yet there is nothing to prevent it being grammatically linked to three (or more) other morphemes. Looking at it another way, a sequence ABC may exhibit links between A and B, B and C, and A and C, as is the case for a sentence like

Margaret hates herself,

where *Margaret* and *hates* have a concord relationship, *hates* and *herself* reduce to *suffers*, and *Margaret* and *herself* are anaphorically related, in that *herself* refers back to the individual identified by *Margaret* (see further chapter 12). A tree-diagram type of representation cannot adequately represent all of these relationships.

There is a further factor favouring the occurrence of discontinuous constructions. We have taken it as normal for items that exhibit "togetherness" to occur adjacent to each other, but this is a far from universal pattern. It is possible for closely linked words to be stationed at the extreme ends of a construction and thus act as markers ("structural signals") of the beginning and end of the construction. Sentential word order in German, for instance, is such that the closer an item belongs to the verb, the nearer the end of the clause it occurs; the verb itself occurs in final position in a subordinate clause, e.g.:

[Ich glaube, 'I believe']

| daß | Maria | morgen | in der Universität | ihr Examen | macht. |
|-----|-------|--------|--------------------|------------|--------|
| that | SUBJECT | ADV-TIME | ADV-PLACE | OBJECT | VERB |
| 'that' | 'Mary' | 'tomorrow' | 'in the university' | 'her exam' | 'takes' |

When the verb in question is the main verb, however, it occurs directly after the subject, giving the order:

| Maria | macht | morgen | in der Universität | ihr Examen. |
|-------|-------|--------|--------------------|-------------|
| SUBJECT | VERB | ADV-TIME | ADV-PLACE | OBJECT |

and the two most closely linked items in the verb phrase, viz. the verb and its (direct) object, occur at extreme ends of the construction. The occurrence of this word order may be said to have a demarcative function (see chapter 2), but it obviously gives rise to discontinuity in a construction.

## Relations of constituents within a construction

It seems evident, then, that, as we indicated earlier, it is necessary to describe not only the domain of a construction and the nature of its constituents, but also the relations that obtain between those constituents. These functional relationships may be and have been described from a number of different points of view.

Bloomfield introduced a distinction between ENDOCENTRIC and EXOCENTRIC constructions. The distinction is based on the question of an equivalence between the class of the construction as a whole and the class of any of its constituents. If there is such an equivalence, the equivalent constituent is the CENTRE (or HEAD) of the construction, and the construction is described as endocentric. An "uncentred" (or "headless"!) construction is exocentric. If we consider the reducibility of the constructions in

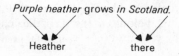

we find that, while both *purple heather* and *in Scotland* are reducible, only the former reduces to one of its constituents. Looking generally at the construction types (rather than this particular token), we may say that:

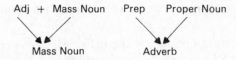

We have been careful here to refer to a particular subclass of noun, but difficulties of interpretation arise when different subclasses within a class pattern differently. We can appreciate this by considering the case of the DETERMINER + NOUN construction, where the noun may be subclassified as mass (e.g. *heather*), count singular (e.g. *plant*) or count plural (e.g. *plants*). In the context – *grow(s) in Scotland* – we may have

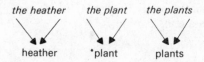

126

Thus, while the mass noun and plural-count noun may dispense with their determiner, the singular-count noun may not.

We find a somewhat similar state of affairs in VERB + OBJECT constructions. From the examples:

Jane was baking a cake.     Jane was making a cake.
→ Jane was baking.          → *Jane was making.

it can be seen that, whereas *bake a cake* allows omission of its object, *make a cake* does not. Speaking generally, we may say that the subclass of verbs that allow object-deletion occur in an endocentric construction, whereas those that do not, strictly speaking occur in an exocentric construction, since they only allow reduction to a different subclass of verb, object-deleting transitive (e.g. *bake*) or intransitive (e.g. *work*). It seems fair to conclude with Lyons (1968: 233) that "the concepts of endocentricity and exocentricity are therefore to be used with respect to some specified 'depth' of subclassification".

Endocentric constructions are traditionally subdivided into two types, SUBORDINATIVE and COORDINATIVE. Our previous examples of endocentric constructions have all been subordinative in the sense that the construction has had one centre and one other element subordinated to it, occurring as an optional extra, so to speak. In a coordinative construction, however, there are two (or more) independent centres with equal status, as in:

The total construction may be reduced to either one of its constituents, each of which is thus a centre. The above coordinative constructions are both "appositive"; but, in the more common type of coordinative construction, there is, in addition to the centres, a marker of coordination like *and* or *or*, as in:

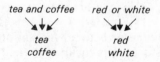

While the additive (*and*) type of construction may involve a change of subclass, in that the coordinative construction is plural but may include singular constituents, the alternative (*or*) type and·the appositive type maintain the subclass of their constituents, cf.:

> Agatha *is* here; Bertha and Cynthia *are* here; Deirdre or Eleanor *is* here; Frank Green *is* here.

As we saw above, the representation of coordinative constructions is problematic in that account needs to be taken of the difference in function between the coordinated elements and the marker of the coordination.

Coordinative and subordinative constructions are so different that it is probably better to regard them as independent types alongside exocentric constructions, rather than as varieties of endocentric construction. Our three types and the relations of their constituents (formulaically A, B) could be represented as in Table 3.

*Table 3*

| Construction type | Omission characteristics of constituents | Relationship between constituents |
|---|---|---|
| EXOCENTRIC | Both constituents obligatory, i.e. AB | Interdependence[b] (= mutual dependence) |
| SUBORDINATIVE | One obligatory constituent (= the centre), i.e. A(B) or (A)B | Dependence[b] (of modifier on centre) |
| COORDINATIVE | Neither constituent obligatory[a], i.e. (A)(B) | Independence[b] |

[a] A marker of coordination may be required when both constituents occur.
[b] Hjelmslev's terms INTERDEPENDENCE, DETERMINATION and CONSTELLATION are equivalent but have a more general value.

The syntactic relationship between the constituents of a construction gives each constituent a particular function, which can be made semantically explicit. In coordinative constructions, for example, the two (main) constituents are, as it were, joint heads of the construction, rather in the way of two clients sharing a joint bank account; the marker of coordination, normally a conjunction, obviously has a largely structural role, but also indicates whether the relation is appositive, additive or alternative.

In a subordinate construction there is a regular centre-plus-modifier relationship, but this may cover a range of different grammatical classes, e.g.:

  (i) *noun + adjective*: entity + differentiating quality
 (ii) *verb + adverb*: process/state + differentiating manner or degree
(iii) *adjective + intensifier*: quality + differentiating degree

The common strand, though, is the modification relationship between the central obligatory element and the optional element.

In exocentric constructions there would appear to be a more diverse set of possibilities. Exocentric constructions agree with coordinative constructions in that their constituents are equal in terms of occurrence (each is respectively dependent on or independent of the other), but exocentric constructions differ in that their constituents each make a different functional contribution to the construction. In most cases one exocentric constituent indicates a relational concept and the other constituent is an entity involved in that relation, in particular:

  (i) *verb + noun phrase*: process/state + participant
 (ii) *preposition (or postposition) + noun phrase*: spatio-temporal relation + point on axis/distance along axis
(iii) *subordinating conjunction + clause*: contingent/temporal (etc.) relation + proposition

In the latter two cases Tesnière would say that the first element had the function of converting (or "translating") the function of the second element: from nominal to adverbial, for instance, in (i); or from verbal to adverbial in (ii). Somewhat different are:

 (iv) *noun + determiner*
  (v) *verb + auxiliary*

which Chomsky (1970: 210) associates, calling the second element of each the "specifier". In these constructions the first element (the noun/verb) is clearly more central, but the second is equally necessary, although it simply specifies the "scope", so to speak, of the content word.

Our first type (*verb + noun phrase*) involves a much greater variety than the unitary label would suggest. The noun phrase associated with the verb may have the syntactic function of subject, or object or some other verbal complement, and its semantic role may be agent, experiencer, recipient, etc. The example *John's photograph* that we mentioned above (p. 118) indeed owes its ambiguity in part to the different functions which *John* may have relative to *photograph* in the phrase *take a photograph of* – did John photograph someone, or did someone photograph him? The third meaning would, of course, involve a different pattern: *John had/owned a photograph*, i.e. a difference in the understood verb.

Even when we know the syntactic function of a noun phrase, say as subject, we cannot be sure of its semantic role. Thus, while *John hurt himself* allows *John* to be understood as agent or experiencer:

> John hurt himself to show he was brave. (AGENT)
> John hurt himself through his own carelessness. (EXPERIENCER)

the sentence *John washed himself* has only an agentive interpretation.

The role of a constituent in a construction can obviously be stated with greater or less precision. The more precise the specification is, the more completely the semantic value of the constituent must be given. Grammar is thus enmeshed with semantics, and we shall discuss in chapter 11 just how "semanticky" the "deep" aspects of a grammar should become.

## Questions for study

1 Draw unlabelled tree diagrams to represent the constituent structure of the following sentences, noting any points where a decision is difficult and considering what factors should determine the choice. (Make words your smallest units, but treat possessive *'s* as a separate word.)
  (a) Bacon sold before the war tasted beautifully crisp.
  (b) The hut behind the church with stained-glass windows serves as a refuge for people without any money.
  (c) Those fairly large gains greatly increased the Liberal Party's electoral chances a few years ago.

2 Convert the tree diagrams of 1 (a) and 1 (b) into equivalent bracketed strings.

3 Consider the constituent structure of the following sentences, particularly in relation to: (i) assignment of problematic constituents; (ii) discontinuity of constituents; (iii) binary v. multiple constituents; (iv) constructional ambiguity.
  (a) My father and mother had gone by train despite my request.
  (b) They waited for help more patiently than John.
  (c) Between you and me I wanted to put our meeting off.

(d) Academic psychologists and philosophers are writing more interesting books.

4 The (imaginary) Gebra language contains the morphemes *a, b, c, d, e, f, i, p, s, t, u, v, x* and *z*. The following are the only permitted morpheme sequences in one type of Gebra sentence:

| | | | | | |
|---|---|---|---|---|---|
| a p s i | a p s u | e p s i | e p s u | p s i | p s u |
| a b z i | a b z u | e b z i | e b z u | b z i | b z u |
| a p f i | a p f u | e p f i | e p f u | p f i | p f u |
| a b v i | a b v u | e b v i | e b v u | b v i | b v u |
| a t s i | a t s u | e t s i | e t s u | t s i | t s u |
| a d z i | a d z u | e d z i | e d z u | d z i | d z u |
| a t f i | a t f u | e t f i | e t f u | t f i | t f u |
| a d v i | a d v u | e d v i | e d v u | d v i | d v u |
| a x i | a x u | e x i | e x u | x i | x u |
| a c i | a c u | e c i | e c u | c i | c u |

Every difference in form corresponds to an analogous difference in meaning, e.g. the difference in meaning between *a p s i* and *a p s u* is the same as between *a p s i* and *e p s u*. What constructions can you identify in the Gebra sentences? What is your evidence? What kinds of construction are they?

5 Consider how realistic are the word boundaries and hyphens in the following phrases as a representation of constituent structure:
(a) a red-haired student;
(b) a deputy headmastership.

6 Would you describe each of the following italicized constructions (of words) as endocentric-subordinative, endocentric-coordinative or exocentric? Are there some borderline cases?
(a) The boys may *start smoking*.
(b) The boys may *keep smoking*.
(c) *Take this* and *read it*.
(d) Come *back here*.
(e) *The teacher* was late.
(f) *Some teachers* are careless.

**Further reading**

On constructions and constituents: Bloomfield (1935), chapter 10; Hockett (1958), chapters 17 and 18; Lyons (1968), section 6.1. On the establishment of constructions: Wells (1947), sections 1–3; Glinz (1952), 85–98; Gleason (1961), chapter 10. On the analysis of constituent patterns: Wells (1947), section 5; Harris (1946), sections 1.0 to 3.8; Robins (1964), section 6.3; Longacre (1965). On relations of constituents within a construction: Hockett (1958), chapters 21, 22; Lyons (1968), section 6.4.

*Chapter 7*

# Grammatical class – the problem of "labelling"

---

### Class and subclass

We have seen in chapter 6 how the grammatical structure of a sentence needs to be described in terms of both the domain of the constructions involved in it and the relations between the constituents of those constructions. We now come to the question of what kinds of element those constituents are, or, more accurately, what CLASSES of element they are. In any kind of syntactic description we have to provide labels for the different kinds of element like PREDICATE, VERB, TRANSITIVE, etc. But how are these arrived at? What does the concept of "grammatical class" or "label" involve? How are classes identified? These questions need to be answered, whatever model of grammatical description we are working with. This means exploring the paradigmatic axis of grammar.

We are already familiar with the traditional word-classes, or "parts of speech" (nouns, verbs, adjectives, etc.). But the traditional definitions were a mixed bag of imprecise, though not value-less, notional ideas (e.g. VERB: ' word denoting an action') and of only partially adequate procedures (e.g. PRONOUN: 'a word that replaces a noun'). Something more comprehensive and systematic is needed.

We may define the notion of class by reference to the first (and most important) grammatical operation we discussed above: SUB-STITUTION (see pp. 98f). A grammatical class is: (a label assigned to) a set of substitution lists (of grammatical elements appearing in different contexts) that have identical or broadly similar members. The vagueness of the phrase "identical or broadly similar" is deliberate: it enables us to set up a small narrowly defined class at the one extreme, or a broad comprehensive class at the other. The generality of the phrase "grammatical element" means that we apply it to classes of morphemes, words, phrases, clauses (and even sentences), regardless of the size of the element: thus the class of deverbal noun-forming suffixes, the class of prepositions, the class of noun phrases, etc.

If we attempt to list the simple (i.e. single-morpheme) words that could complete the following sentential contexts in English:

$$\text{I noticed} \left\{ \begin{matrix} \text{the} \\ \text{his} \end{matrix} \right\} \left( \left\{ \begin{matrix} \text{empty} \\ \text{new} \end{matrix} \right\} \right) \text{ —— (yesterday).}$$

we find that broadly the same substitution list emerges whether we choose *the* or *his*, whether we include the adjective *empty*, the adjective *new*, or neither, and whether we include the adverb *yesterday* or not. It comprises COMMON NOUNS. The list would include words like:

> *book, boy, bread, child, cow, loaf, oil, plan, pride, space, vigour*

But the choice of adjective would make some difference to the list: after *empty* the word *bread* does not seem to fit; after *new* the word *sun* seems unusual. However, these differences are determined not so much by the grammatical potential of the words in question as by their lexical-semantic range or the state of those aspects of the external world they refer to. We do not need to stretch our imaginations too far to imagine uses for the concept of 'empty bread' or of 'new sun(s)'. So, broadly speaking, we disregard problems of semantic improbability when comparing substitution lists (cf. chapters 3 and 5).

Some restrictions on substitution, however, are clear-cut and must be regarded as grammatical restrictions on the cooccurrence of items. For example, suppose we modify our original sentence frame by replacing *the/his* with *little* or *(not) much* or unstressed *some*, 'a certain quantity' (=/səm/ not /sʌm/), to give:

$$\text{I noticed} \left\{ \begin{matrix} \text{little} \\ \text{some} \end{matrix} \right\} \left( \left\{ \begin{matrix} \text{empty} \\ \text{new} \end{matrix} \right\} \right) \text{ —— (yesterday).}$$

The contribution of these new DETERMINERS (as we call *the* and the various alternatives to it) is to strongly restrict our substitution list, affecting our sample list as follows:

> *\*book, \*boy, bread, \*child, \*cow, ice, \*loaf, oil, \*plan, pride, space, vigour*

In other words, if we wish to describe the class fully, we need to specify the SUBCLASS that appears in this limited context, viz. after the MASS determiners *little, (not) much* and *some.* We would have the scheme as shown in Figure 46.

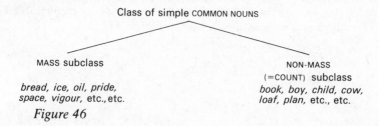

Class of simple COMMON NOUNS

MASS subclass

*bread, ice, oil, pride, space, vigour, etc., etc.*

NON-MASS (=COUNT) subclass

*book, boy, child, cow, loaf, plan,* etc., etc.

*Figure 46*

It happens that the same nouns that fail to occur with *little, (not) much, some* – the NON-MASS nouns – are all nouns that readily do occur with *a, one,* and in the plural, with or without the numerals *two, three,* etc., all with the meaning 'a discrete quantity/discrete item (of the class)', e.g. *a book, one cow, two loaves,* but *\*a bread, \*one oil, \*two vigours* (except in the meaning 'a/one/two kinds of'). (But notice that two items in the MASS noun list do have a COUNT use, viz. *one ice,* 'one icecream', *one space,* 'one discrete portion of space'. These nouns may be said to have "multiple class membership", see below, pp. 146–7).

Grammatical classes almost invariably subdivide into subclasses, and very often the subclasses further divide into sub-subclasses, and so on. If we take as an example the class of English verbs, a typical context like the following would produce a list of verbs including those given below (allowing for individual differences in the realization of *-ed*):

Probably his sister —— ed {the doll
clean {the car. )
cough
like
retreat
skate
sleep[1]
take[1]
watch

Now, out of this over-all representative list of verbs, some – the intransitive ones *cough, retreat, skate, sleep* – do not occur at all with a following noun-phrase object (like those given). Of the

---

[1] The combinations *sleep + -ed* and *take + -ed* are, of course, realized as *slept* and *took* respectively. See further chapter 10.

remainder that do, some – *like, take* – cannot occur without their
object and the others – *clean, watch* – allow omission (or "deletion") of their object, in the case of *clean* where the object is left
indefinite, in the case of *watch* where it is contextually recoverable.
This suggests a subclassification as in Figure 47.

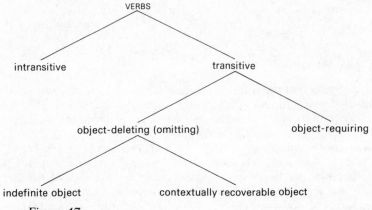

*Figure 47*

If we adopted such a (sub)classification, it would be possible to
describe "transitive" as a subclass, "object-deleting" as a sub-
subclass and "indefinite object" as a sub-sub-subclass; but such a
cumbersome terminology tends to be avoided, and the word "subclass" is used throughout.

The more subtle a subclassification becomes, the more the classes
seem to have a semantic coherence. In a simplified account, English
non-sentence adverbials, for instance, could be divided up on the
basis of syntactic criteria, as shown in Figure 48.

Adverbials as a whole are characterized by certain properties,
and, within the group, non-sentence adverbials, sometimes called
ADJUNCTS, are identified by various syntactic criteria, such as their
inability to occur initially in a negative sentence (Quirk *et al.*, 1972:
421f.), e.g.:

    *Carefully, he didn't open the door.
    (cf. Wisely, he didn't open the door.)

On the other hand, as we proceed (from left to right) through our
subclassification, the subclasses become more and more semantically based, and the tests tend to be more semantic in nature, e.g. for
TIME adverbials, the kind of question they answer – "When?",
"How long (for)?", etc.

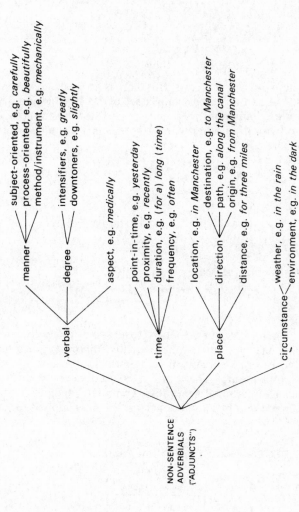

*Figure 48*

## Syntactic features

Quite frequently a hierarchical organization of classes and subclasses does not give the best description of the data under scrutiny. Considering the following partial system of subject personal pronoun forms:

|  | SINGULAR | PLURAL |
|---|---|---|
| 1ST PERSON | I | we |
| 3RD PERSON | he/she | they |

we find a system of $2\times 2$ contrasts. But there is no special reason to regard SINGULAR and PLURAL as subclasses of 1ST PERSON and 3RD PERSON any more than there is reason to regard SINGULAR v. PLURAL as the major division. In other words, there is no reason to favour either of the classifications in Figure 49.

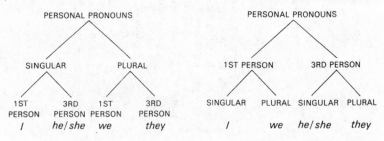

*Figure 49*

What we need here is a schema that gives the two distinctions equal status, making the pairs of features equally important; in other words, a kind of cross-classification. For this purpose a MATRIX seems most appropriate. The concept is used by such diverse schools as transformational-generative grammar, tagmemics and systemic grammar and by all phoneticians. We may apply it to our own example thus:

SUBJECT PERSONAL PRONOUNS

|  |  | NUMBER | |
|---|---|---|---|
|  |  | SINGULAR | PLURAL |
| PERSON | 1ST | I | we |
|  | 3RD | he/she | they |

*Figure 50*

138

Here each box contains the item that has the particular combination of values given by the matrix.

In such representation, where we previously had subclasses, we now have distinctions in terms of SYNTACTIC FEATURES. Each feature distinction is given in a different dimension, both dimensions being regarded as of equal importance. It is quite common for us to need to represent a third dimension (and even a fourth, fifth, and so on), i.e. to have other independent bases for classifying our element; in the present case we have the SUBJECT v. NON-SUBJECT distinction, giving *I* v. *me*, etc. However, although it is not possible to display a third feature in a two-dimensional diagram, using the above format, that does not mean it is not desirable, in fact necessary, to envisage three- and multi-dimensional matrices. They are a commonplace in mathematics.

As a matter of fact, if we recast our diagram to represent not so much the total range of possibilities for the system but rather the specification of individual items, the problem of displaying more than two features disappears (cf. Table 4).

*Table 4*

$$X_{mnp}$$

|  | Number | Person | Case form |
|---|---|---|---|
|  | $X_m$ | $X_n$ | $X_p$ |
| I | SING | 1ST | SUBJECT |
| he | SING | 3RD | SUBJECT |
| we | PLUR | 1ST | SUBJECT |
| ⋮ etc. | ⋮ | ⋮ | ⋮ |
| me | SING | 1ST | NON-SUBJECT |

Here each box contains the specification for a particular variable given at the head of its column, for the item given at the left of its row.

But if we just read off the specification for one (e.g. the first one, *I*), we have no information to tell us what SINGULAR is opposed to in the system; and similarly with NON-SUBJECT, except, of course, that the names suggest they are counterparts of PLURAL and SUBJECT, respectively. As such they participate in a BINARY opposition, an opposition of two features. It has been assumed in some circles, e.g. transformational-generative ones, that ALL linguistic distinctions are ultimately binary. This position is certainly defensible (in terms of language being stored electrochemically in the brain and thus subject to the yes–no choice of a particular electric circuit being turned on or off); but the view is by no means universally accepted. Many genuine three-way (and four-way, etc.) distinctions seem to operate within the grammatical systems of natural languages, e.g. PRESENT – PAST – FUTURE in French, Spanish, etc., or MASCULINE – FEMININE – NEUTER in German, Russian, etc., and although any three-way system may be broken down to two two-way ones (e.g. grouping together PRESENT and FUTURE as "NON-PAST"), this is far from a necessary step.

If we do accept a binary specification of syntactic features, and if we specify the features as positive and negative on a polarity basis, we can provide readings as in Table 5.

*Table 5*

|     | Plural | 1st person | Subject |
|-----|--------|------------|---------|
| I   | −      | +          | +       |
| he  | −      | −          | +       |
| we  | +      | +          | +       |
| ⋮   | ⋮      | ⋮          | ⋮       |
| me  | −      | +          | −       |

If we extend such a matrix specification to cover cases where a hierarchical subclassification appears more appropriate, we feel the need of a symbol "0" to indicate neither 'positive' nor 'negative' but 'not applicable'. We may illustrate this point with a recasting of our previous example of transitivity in verbs. Given the binary features TRANSITIVE [+,−], OBJECT-DELETING [+,−], and CONTEXTUALLY RECOVERABLE OBJECT [+,−], we would need to specify the types of verb as in Table 6.

The 0 is a way of saying that the distinction referred to does not apply, but it does not say so very clearly.

Since neither a fully hierarchical nor a fully matrix representation of class is entirely appropriate for all cases, Halliday and others use a more sophisticated notation. In Halliday (1967/8), for example, the "system network" for English verb transitivity is given as in Figure 51.

In such schemes, which are read from left to right, a simple choice (between syntactic features) is represented by →[( or →[ for three-way choices); at the extreme left of the chart, for instance,

*Table 6*

|         | TRANSITIVE | OBJECT-DELETING | CONTEXTUALLY RECOVERABLE OBJECT |
|---------|------------|-----------------|---------------------------------|
| cough   | –          | 0               | 0                               |
| like    | +          | –               | 0                               |
| clean   | +          | +               | –                               |
| watch   | +          | +               | +                               |

verbs are divided into two classes according to whether they are "extensive" or "intensive". A simultaneous pair of choices are joined by an opening brace {, thus indicating a matrix situation; for instance, the "extensive" class is further characterized by two syntactic features, one chosen from "effective" v. "descriptive", and the other simultaneously chosen from "operative" v. "middle" v. "receptive". A closing brace } is used, in conjunction with linking

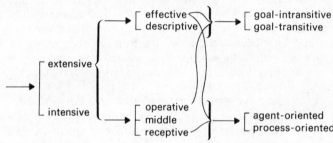

*Figure 51*

lines, to indicate that a choice is only made in the event of a particular combination of previous choices having been selected: for example, "goal-intransitive" v. "goal-transitive" only applies if both "effective" and "operative" have been selected. The partial scheme given here specifies nine possibilities. These are as follows, each given with Halliday's own example:

(1) extensive, effective, operative, goal-intransitive:
    *She washed* (sc. *the clothes*).
(2) extensive, effective, operative, goal-transitive:
    *She washed the clothes.*
(3) extensive, effective, middle:
    *She washed* (sc. *herself*).

(4) extensive, effective, receptive, agent-oriented:
*The clothes were washed.*
(5) extensive, effective, receptive, process-oriented:
*The clothes washed.*
(6) extensive, descriptive, operative:
*He marched the prisoners.*
(7) extensive, descriptive, middle:
*The prisoners marched.*
(8) extensive, descriptive, receptive:
*The prisoners were marched.*
(9) intensive:
*She looked happy.*

It is of course quite possible to find this theory and its representation attractive without assenting to the descriptive analysis given in the example.

An idea that is important in a binary matrix system, but appears less so in systemic grammar, is the notion of MARKED and UNMARKED members in a contrast. We presumably need some basis for deciding which item is [+] and which [−], i.e. which item represents a positive choice and which simply abstention from that choice. This decision may be made on the basis of a number of factors:

  (i) MORPHO-PHONEMIC REALIZATION: the marked item may be rendered by the presence of a morpheme v. its absence, e.g. present *wait* – past *waited*.

 (ii) OCCURRENCE IN NEUTRALIZED POSITION (see below): the unmarked item should be the one to occur when the category involved is lacking, e.g. *I want to wait, where the tense-less infinitive is identical in form to the present.*

(iii) THE ORGANIZATION OF THE SYSTEM: unmarked items will generally be expected to participate in a fuller range of subdistinctions, e.g. only the present tense of a verb like *wait* having a special 3rd person singular form (*waits*) or Latin indicative mood being unmarked, with more tenses, as against the subjunctive mood with fewer tenses.

These points lead us on to our next topic within the field of class.

**Neutralization**

Whatever our way of representing class (hierarchies, matrices or system networks), we must have a means of presenting the fact that a (sub-)distinction between syntactic features does not operate in certain cases. By this we mean that, in combination with certain other features applying to the same segment, a particular syntactic feature does not apply. The feature of object-deletion is non-applicable in respect of intransitive verbs, virtually by definition. Consider further the way gender works together with number in German: there are three clearly distinguished genders in the singular, but a common form for all genders in the plural. This is true for all grammatical cases, but we shall illustrate with the accusative:

| MASC. | FEM. | NEUT. |
|---|---|---|
| d*en* ar*men* Bruder | d*ie* arm*e* Tochter | d*as* arm*e* Mädchen |
| 'the poor brother' | 'the poor daughter' | 'the poor girl' |
| | | |
| d*ie* arm*en* Brüder | d*ie* arm*en* Töchter | d*ie* arm*en* Mädchen |
| 'the poor brothers' | 'the poor daughters' | 'the poor girls' |

In such a case, it is not so much that the syntactic feature of gender does not apply in the plural, but rather that whether it applies or not it is never expressed: we may say the syntactic feature is NEUTRAL-IZED.

Syntactic neutralization is akin to phonological neutralization and, like the latter, may be used either in a purely paradigmatic sense (when it is SYSTEM-determined) or in a partially syntagmatic sense (when it is CONTEXT-determined). The phonological feature of VOICE, which applies in many languages to plosives and fricatives, is often described as being neutralized for nasals, in the sense that it is non-applicable for this part of the system. This is comparable in the syntactic field to German gender, and they might be displayed as in Figure 52.

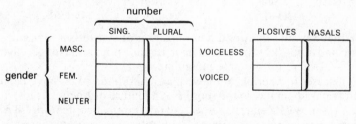

*Figure 52*

This sense of NEUTRALIZATION is a purely paradigmatic one: it simply refers to the options or choices available in the system at a particular point in the text, being unaffected by what precedes or follows. It is sometimes called SYNCRETISM.

Further examples of this kind of neutralization or syncretism may be taken from Latin and Russian. In Latin there is a regular CASE distinction of nominative v. accusative for all masculine and feminine nouns, e.g.:

| MASC. | Nom. | *mūrus* (pl. mūrī) 'wall' |
| | Acc. | *mūrum* (pl. *mūrōs*) |
| FEM. | Nom. | *fenestra* (pl. *fenestrae*) 'window' |
| | Acc. | *fenestram* (pl. *fenestrās*) |

In the case of neuter nouns, on the other hand, no such distinction is made:

NEUT. Nom.⎫
⎬ *ātrium* (pl. *ātria*) 'reception-room'
Acc. ⎭

Further, this applies to ALL neuter nouns. There is, then, a neutralization or syncretism of the nominative and accusative cases for neuter nouns in Latin.

Something similar, but slightly more complicated, takes place with masculine nouns in Russian. Most Russian feminine and neuter nouns distinguish (amongst others) the three cases, nominative, accusative and genitive. Russian masculine nouns ending in a consonant – which is the norm – have a different system, however: inanimate ones have an accusative form identical with the nominative, while animate ones have an accusative form identical with the genitive. For example:

| | MASC. INANIM. | FEMININE | MASC. ANIM. |
| NOM. | stul | ⎰'knjigǝ | stu'djent |
| ACC. | | ⎱'knjigu⎱ | |
| GEN. | 'stulǝ | 'knjigi ⎱ | stu'djentǝ |
| | 'chair' | 'book' | 'student' |

We may say that there is a neutralization or syncretism of nominative and accusative for inanimate masculine nouns, and of genitive and accusative for animate masculine nouns.

The cases of neutralization we have considered so far have been purely paradigmatic, in the sense that a feature distinction is lost in the presence of a simultaneous second grammatical feature. Syntagmatic or context-determined neutralization operates in cases where a distinction is lost when another grammatical feature is present in the preceding or following context. This is the type of neutralization Trubetzkoy (1958: 206–18) originally envisaged. We might instance the loss of the nominative-accusative contrast in Latin for the subject and object in a so-called "accusative and infinitive" type of embedded sentence:

| | |
|---|---|
| Nauta puellam amat. | 'The sailor loves the girl.' |
| (NOM.) (ACC.) | |
| Dixi nautam puellam amāre. | 'I said that the sailor loves |
| (ACC.) (ACC.) | the girl.' |

A further instance that might be cited is the restriction on occurrence in French of the future tense in clauses with *quand, lorsque,* etc., cf.:

| | | |
|---|---|---|
| PRESENT | Nous partons demain. | 'We leave/are leaving tomorrow.' |
| FUTURE | Nous partirons demain. | 'We shall leave tomorrow.' |

| | | |
|---|---|---|
| PRESENT | *Quand nous partons demain, . . . | |
| FUTURE | Quand nous partirons demain, . . . | 'When we leave tomorrow,' . . . |

These examples may all be compared with phonological neutralization according to context, as in the loss of the voiceless- voiced distinction for plosive and fricative consonants (/p/ v. /b/, /f/ v. /v/, etc.) in final position in languages like German and Russian.

A third kind of grammatical neutralization may be termed "accidental" or LEXICALLY determined neutralization. In such cases the grammatical distinction is only lost in respect of individual lexical items. It is, for instance, an accidental fact of English verbs like *cut, hit, shut,* etc. that they have no differentiation in their forms for present and past tense (except for third person singular, where the *-(e)s* of the present acts as a marker). This loss of distinction is in no way systematic and seems to be a fact of lexis and phonology rather than of grammar. The same would apply to those English nouns that have a common singular-plural form, e.g. *sheep, deer.*

We have thus observed three kinds of grammatical neutralization:

(i) system-determined
(ii) context-determined
(iii) lexically determined

and the question arises: in which cases should the neutralization be thought of as giving rise to a genuine ambiguity, and in which is it a matter simply of non-specification or vagueness? Putting the matter differently, does the speaker using a neutralized form intend a distinct item and merely fail to make clear which, or does he actually refrain from making a choice? We have suggested that all cases of lexically determined neutralization involve mere failure to make clear a distinction that the speaker nevertheless has in mind. When saying, for instance,

145

> The sheep grazed in this field.

he is surely clear about whether the sheep are more than one in number. The same probably applies to many examples of the other two types of neutralization, e.g. gender in German plurals, case in Latin; but consider the English sentence:

> I was told he'd left.

from which must be reconstructed one of the following:

(1) "He's left."
(2) "He left."
(3) "He'd left."

Clearly one of these must be the original words reported, but does the speaker always clearly have in mind which? The boundary between ambiguity and vagueness is not so clear-cut as we might like it to be.


## Class membership

We may have given the impression so far that classes (or major classes, at least) are quite distinct from each other in terms of the contexts in which they occur, and in their contribution to the sentence or other construction they participate in; but in reality things are more complex. We quite normally find major classes occurring in the same kind of context as each other, and as a result ambiguity may arise according to which class the word in question is interpreted as belonging to, e.g.:

> I saw the book *open*  1. 'ADJECTIVE'
> 2. 'VERB'

> He made the car *fast*  1. 'ADJECTIVE'
> 2. 'ADVERB'

Of course the class membership of the word is not the only factor involved in the ambiguity – each class participates in a different kind of construction – but all we are noting here is that contextual frames are often not unique to one class, and that one item can apparently belong to more than one class. This is usually referred to as CLASS CLEAVAGE or as MULTIPLE CLASS MEMBERSHIP.

Consider the different environments in which the item(s) *open* occur(s), relative to ordinary adjectives like *big* and to ordinary verbs like *write*:

146

|  | *big*, etc. | *write*, etc. | *open*, etc. |
|---|---|---|---|
| He is ——ing a book. | × | √ | √ |
| The book is ——. | √ | × | √ |
| I saw the book ——. | × | × | √ |

Now, as Harris (1946: footnote 8) pointed out long ago, such a state of affairs as we have observed with *open* can in theory be described in at least three different ways:

(i) We may insist that each item belongs to only one class and be forced to recognize three separate classes:

| VERBS | ADJECTIVES | "VECTS" |
|---|---|---|
| write | big | open |
| locate | nice | shut |
| operate | beautiful | clean |
| etc. | etc. | etc. |

(ii) We may accept the two classes of ADJECTIVE and VERB, but allow any item to be a member of more than one class. This is generally described as CLASS CLEAVAGE (Bloomfield, 1935: 206–8) or as DUAL/MULTIPLE MEMBERSHIP of the classes.

(iii) Again accepting the two classes, we may follow a suggestion of Bloch's (1946: section 1.6) and dissociate *open*, 'VERB', and *open*, 'ADJECTIVE', as separate lexical items.

The second solution seems the obvious one. The last solution would presumably entail either a syntactic kind of homonymy or the use of "zero morphemes" (see chapter 10).

The first solution has failed to take account of the ambiguity of *open* in *I saw the book open* and would therefore be inappropriate in this instance. In other cases though, where no ambiguity arises, it might be preferable, e.g. for attributive and predicative adjectives, where a distribution like the following presents itself:

|  | *big, nice* etc. | *major, utter* etc. | *ill, awake* etc. |
|---|---|---|---|
| The N is ——. | √ | × | √ |
| The —— N ... | √ | √ | × |

e.g. *The city is big./The big city ...*
*The reason is major./The major reason ...*
*The student is awake./The awake student ...*

## Class markers

We saw earlier (chapter 5) how a particular kind of construction may be marked as such by factors like the class of the elements, their sequence and so on. We must now ask: how is membership of a particular class marked?

Of course in a sense we were previously asking how a particular class of construction was marked, but now we are faced with a slightly different question, in that we are concerned with classes of words and morphemes. Words of a single morpheme do not have any internal structure as such. So how is their class determined? How does the native listener identify a word or morpheme as belonging to a particular class (and therefore as having the potential to participate in certain kinds of construction – thus giving him a strategy for comprehending an utterance)?

Following Whorf (1956: 88f.) we say that a class may be marked overtly or covertly. OVERT marking of a class only applies completely to complex items (complex words, phrases, etc.) and not to single morphemes, since it means that one constituent of the item functions as clear marker of the class. We may observe, for example, that the English suffix *-est* is an automatic marker whenever it occurs (e.g. *biggest, nicest, fullest*) of the word-class ADJECTIVE, and in particular of the subclass SUPERLATIVE. We may say that an English suffix of the form *-ly* (where it is a true suffix with morphemic status) has at least a 95 per cent chance of being a marker of the word-class ADVERB (the only exceptions being adjectives like *friendly, princely, lowly, kindly*). In some cases a word-class has a marker that is not a morpheme but merely a kind of phonological pattern such as initial stress.

When the marking of a word-class is COVERT, as it has to be where only one morpheme is involved, there are three kinds of marking:

    (i)  IDENTITY OF ITEM. The very identity of the item marks the class. Except for cases of class cleavage, each word is assigned to a particular class and, particularly if it is a common item, will be recognized by the listener as a member of that class. Thus, English *window* is inherently a noun and is instantly recognized as such by a speaker of the language – just as easily as if it had been marked as a noun with an affix like *radiat-or*.

   (ii)  CO-OCCURRENCE RELATIONS. An adjectival modifier like English *very* cannot occur without the presence of an adjective in the immediate context (possibly in a preceding sentence). We can say, then, that *very* determines and thus marks the occurrence of such an adjective. Similar syntagmatic restrictions – referred to as "colligational" by followers of Firth, e.g. Mitchell (1975: 156–60) – require us to expect a noun (as part of a noun phrase) on each side of a verb such as *like*. These examples concern the co-occurrence of major word-classes, but equally important is the role of co-occurrence restrictions between subclasses – what is generally termed AGREEMENT (Bloomfield, 1935: 190–4). This is discussed below as a phenomenon in its own right, but its role in marking word-classes may be exemplified by the French third-person plural present tense form *ont*, 'have', which determines the occurrence of a third-person plural subject in a sentential frame like —— *ont faim*.

(iii) SEQUENCE OF ELEMENTS. For predicting the occurrence of a particular class of word, its position relative to its neighbours is obviously just as important as the actual identity of those neighbours. Thus in English within the noun phrase proper there is no necessity to have any word preceding the determiners (*that, my*, etc.), but, if there is one, it must be a member of the predeterminer class (which includes, *all, both*) as in *(all) those big heavy suitcases*. Or again, the occurrence of an English adverbial initially in a sentence followed by auxiliary and subject in inverted order marks the adverbial as negative or interrogative, e.g.:

Never
At no time
Where ⎬ have I seen a flower like that. (?)
*Somewhere
*Here

## Agreement between subclasses (= subcategories)

When we have described the constructions that make up sentences and specified the classes – with their relevant subclasses – that participate in these constructions, we have still left unsaid what the rules are for combining subclasses or syntactic features of different classes with each other. The choice of a syntactic subcategory is most commonly made with reference to the other categories or subcategories present in the context, for example, singular determiner with singular noun, or transitive verb with a following object. This is within the domain of context-sensitive rules in a generative grammar (see above, pp. 81f.). We say that there is grammatical AGREEMENT whenever context-sensitivity requires that a particular subclass or syntactic feature should be chosen by reference to another subclass or syntactic feature elsewhere, but NOT in cases where the choice of subclass (e.g. transitive v. intransitive verb) depends simply on the presence v. absence of a structural element (in this case, a noun phrase). The subclassification will generally involve what is normally called a grammatical CATEGORY like number, case, gender, voice, aspect, etc. (see chapter 10).

By AGREEMENT, then, we mean that there is a kind of "harmony" between the elements in question. Two different kinds of agreement are traditionally distinguished, CONCORD and GOVERNMENT, but a third, CROSS-REFERENCE, was added by Bloomfield (1935: 193–4) and we must consider whether this really constitutes an independent type. As Lyons (1968: 239–43) points out, the difference between concord and government is made in terms of "surface structure", i.e. the way in which the categories are phonologically marked: whereas in concord both of the items in agreement are marked for the shared category, in cases of government it is only the one "governed" item that is so marked. Despite the apparent simplicity of this division, agreement can involve more complex relationships.

We may illustrate CONCORD with examples from either the determiner-adjective-noun construction or the subject-predicate construction in a whole range of languages (e.g. Spanish, Russian, Latin, Arabic, Swahili, etc.). We shall choose English, where it is straightforward and purely a matter of NUMBER. Thus, in the demonstrative-noun construction we may have, for instance:

(He bought) this book.     (He bought) these books.
(He bought) *this books.   (He bought) *these book.

i.e. an all-singular or an all-plural construction. Similarly with subject and predicate, e.g.:

He walks (a lot).     They walk (a lot).
*He walk (a lot).     *They walks (a lot).

If we say all-singular or all-plural, we do not necessarily accept that the two elements in each construction are on a par with respect to number; in some sense the noun element is the primary domain of number in each case, even though the other element may become crucial if the noun loses its distinction (is subject to neutralization) as in:

This/these sheep (looked tired).
The sheep grazes/graze (all day).

The other languages mentioned have more complex concord relations because other categories are involved, such as gender (commonly) or definiteness (in Arabic). (See further, chapter 10.)

GOVERNMENT is involved where only one element in the construction is marked for the category in question, the other element governing or requiring it. The classic examples are of verbal and prepositional objects in a particular CASE. Thus the German verb *helfen*, 'help', takes a dative object, while *unterstützen*, 'support', takes an accusative, giving, for example:

Wir helfen *den* Arbeitern.    'We help the workers.'
Wir unterstützen *die* Arbeiter. 'We support the workers.'

In Russian the preposition до /do/ ('up to') governs the genitive, /k/ ('towards') the dative, and в /v/ (in the sense of 'into') the accusative. In such cases we do not normally say that the verb or preposition *is* accusative or dative (etc.) but that it governs or takes that particular case.

Things are slightly different for gender. French nouns are not usually marked for a particular gender, but we normally say that *livre*, 'book', IS masculine and *table*, 'table', IS feminine, and this means no more than that they require one or the other gender to be marked in related determiners and adjectives. Is this case any different in principle from that of verbs or prepositions governing a particular case? Hockett (1958: 214–17) wants to say it is, because of the kind of construction involved: preposition-object or verb-object combinations form exocentric constructions, while the kind of gender agreement we have referred to operates within endocentric constructions and across construction boundaries from subject to predicative attribute (e.g. *la grande table, la table est grande*). Such a distinction is worth making, and may be important, but it does not remove such gender agreement from the scope of government, as defined above (Hockett wants to call it "governmental concord").

We cannot deny, however, that in some cases government and concord operate simultaneously, each for a different grammatical category. In many combinations of determiner/adjective + noun, for instance, the noun may be said to govern the gender of the determiner/adjective, but the noun and determiner/adjective are in concord in respect of number. We may cite the following examples:

| Spanish: | SING. | *el color hermoso* | *la piel hermosa* |
|---|---|---|---|
| | PL. | *los colores hermosos* | *las pieles hermosas* |
| | | 'the colour(s) | 'the skin(s) |
| | | beautiful' | beautiful' |

| Swahili: | SING. | *mtu mkubwa yule* | *kitu kikubwa kile* |
|---|---|---|---|
| | | 'man large this' | 'thing large this' |
| | PL. | *watu wakubwa wale* | *vitu vikubwa vile* |
| | | 'men large these' | 'things large these' |

Bloomfield applied the term CROSS-REFERENCE to cases where one element in the combination "contains a mention" of its fellow. This applies particularly to the agreement between nouns on the one side and pronouns or genitive-type affixes on the other. Consider, for example, the English sentences:

> The boy scraped his leg and hurt himself when he fell.
> The girl scraped her leg and hurt herself when she fell.
> The dog scraped its leg and hurt itself when it fell.

or the Finnish:

| minun kirjani | 'of-me my-book' |
| hänen kirjansa | 'of-him/her his/her-book' |

In each example we may say the linked items – in English agreeing in gender, in Finnish in person – mention or refer to the same item at different points in the sentences. Both would fall under Bloomfield's category of cross-reference, but there is a difference. Whereas the Finnish example involves strict grammatical agreement and qualifies as concord, the English involves a looser kind of agreement – because gender is a looser category in English. The conventions for the use of proforms (or "substitutes" as Bloomfield called them) may be purely grammatical or purely referential or, more likely, a blend of the two. Thus in any gender classification of English, words like *teacher, neighbour, adolescent* would have to have dual membership of masculine and feminine, rather than have "common" gender, since in any particular instance they are either one or the other. As we saw in chapter 3, while *neighbour* is indeterminate for sex, *buxom neighbour* or *pregnant neighbour* is very clearly marked!

In some languages a conflict arises between grammatical gender and natural gender (or sex) and in cases of pronominal reference it tends to be resolved in favour of natural gender. Thus German would have

> *Sie* war schön, das Mädchen.   'She was beautiful, the girl.'
> *Es war schön, das Mädchen.

i.e. while the determiner *das* is neuter, for the relatively distant pronoun feminine *sie* is preferred to neuter *es*; relative pronouns are more problematical. If we are to speak of CROSS-REFERENCE at all as a kind of agreement, we might reserve it for the looser kind of harmony obtaining for proforms relative to their antecedent (or "postcedent").

**Questions for study**

1 Consider again the Gebra data given at the end of chapter 6 (question 4). What grammatical classes of morphemes need to be set up, what subclasses, and so on?

2 We have seen in this chapter that, in order to account for the occurrence of English nouns with determiners and with the plural morpheme, we must divide them into count nouns and mass nouns. Look now at determiners and see how many classes of them need to be set up to account for their occurrence with singular count nouns (like *loaf*), with plural count nouns (like *loaves*), or with mass nouns (like *bread*). (You will find that not all determiners are limited to just one type of noun.) Consider the following determiners: *a(n), each, enough, his, little, more, (not) much, some, several, that, the, these, this, those.*

3 Say which member of the following contrasts you would regard as the unmarked one, and why:
   (a) English tense: present v. past
   (b) French gender: masculine v. feminine
   (c) German (or Latin, Russian, etc.) case: nominative v. accusative v. genitive v. dative (v. ablative/instrumental, etc.)

4 Recall the discussion of the neutralization of the French present v. future distinction after *quand* and *lorsque*. How does the pattern after French *si* compare? And how does English differ from French in this area?

5 Each of the following English words has multiple class membership ("class cleavage"): *rise, dark, over, since, one.* Name the different classes each word belongs to, and give some words with which it would contrast in that use.

6 Consider the choice of infinitive v. gerund in the following:
   I enjoyed playing.     I succeeded in passing.
   I hoped to play.      I managed to pass.
   Would you regard this as a case of government or of concord? Why?

**Further reading**

On class and subclass: Harris (1951), chapter 15; Bolinger (1975), 142–56. On syntactic features: Chomsky (1965), 75–84; Cook (1969), 49–54, 69–71; Halliday (1969). On neutralization: Bazell (1949a); Lyons (1968), 253–5. On class membership: Bloomfield (1935), 204–6, 265–6; Hockett (1958), chapter 26. On class markers: Fries (1952), chapter 7. On agreement between subclasses: Bloomfield (1935), 190–4; Hockett (1958), chapter 25; Lyons (1968), subsection 6.5.4.

*Chapter 8*

# Transformations

## The raison d'être of transformations

The notion of TRANSFORMATION has been implicit in linguistic studies for centuries, but the term itself is relatively new. It was first used by Harris in the early 1950s, and later considerably extended by (his pupil) Chomsky. Basically, it has been used to refer to situations where there is a complex relationship between the expression aspect of a linguistic element and its meaning or function. In a linguist's paradise every linguistic element would have a separate single meaning and its position in the sentence would make its contribution to the meaning unequivocal; in practice, language is so complex that a single meaning may have multiple realization, a single grammatical pattern may have variant meanings, grammatically linked items are not always adjacent to each other (recall our discussion of discontinuous constituents in chapter 6), and in general grammatical complexity cannot always be accommodated simply in terms of bracketed constructions with labelled constituents.

Although the meaning of the term "transformation" is, in general, clear, it has, like many new words, been used with some flexibility. The word has, for example, had slightly differing interpretations in early generative grammar (e.g. Chomsky, 1957), in the so-called "standard theory" (e.g. Katz and Postal, 1964), in generative semantics (e.g. Lakoff, 1971a; McCawley, 1968) and in non-generative grammar (e.g. Harris, 1957). These differences in interpretation stem from the different over-all conceptions of grammar that linguists have had, and the different parts they have felt transformations should play within them. We might begin our study of the subject, then, by considering the different motivations there have been for introducing transformations into a grammar.

Harris's notion of transformation arose from his work on co-occurrence restrictions. He believed that a grammar needed to account for all the restrictions on co-occurrence of individual mem-

bers of the grammatical classes in a construction; so that for an
ADJECTIVE + NOUN sequence in a noun phrase, for example, restrictions such as the following would be evident. (As semantically
determined restrictions, these involve different degrees of likelihood, and even the asterisk only denotes a sequence that is
extremely unlikely.)

|                   |                   |                 |
| ----------------- | ----------------- | --------------- |
| careful drivers   | *abridged drivers | ?damp drivers   |
| ?careful poems    | abridged poems    | *damp poems     |
| *careful houses   | ?abridged houses  | damp houses     |

But he found precisely the same co-occurrence restrictions applying
between the two grammatical classes in patterns such as NOUN +*be*
+ ADJECTIVE and *make* + NOUN + ADJECTIVE, e.g.:

Drivers are careful.     Make drivers careful.
?Poems are careful.      etc.

Harris therefore postulated a transformational relationship between these structures, saying that one structure may be derived
from another. This meant that the co-occurrence restrictions
could be stated once and for all for the basic (or "kernel") structure
and then automatically carried over to the others.

Perhaps the most central use of the notion of transformation is for
cases where complex differences in form correspond to a simple
difference in meaning or function. The standard example of this,
which has been discussed since ancient times, was used in Harris
(1952) and was discussed in chapter 4, is the active-passive relationship in languages which distinguish two (or more) different voices.
Comparing the sentences:

The gardener mows the lawns.               (ACTIVE)
The lawns are mown by the gardener.        (PASSIVE)

we find that they differ from each other formally in a number of
different aspects:
  (i) *the gardener* occurs now initially without a preposition, now
      finally preceded by *by*;
 (ii) *the lawns* occurs now in post-verb position, now in initial
      position;
(iii) the verb *mow* occurs now in the simple present form, now
      in a present passive form entailing the insertion of auxiliary
      *be* before it and the suffix *-n* after it;
 (iv) the number of the verb is indicated in the first verb word
      (*mows* or *are*), but this is now singular (to agree with *the
      gardener*), now plural (to agree with *the lawns*).
Despite the multiplicity of the differences between these two sen-

tences, they are semantically very close, and we may well want to say that they differ in only one syntactic feature. We may do this by saying that they are directly related by transformation. Such a relationship may be stated in the form of a rewrite rule, of which a provisional form might be:

$$NP_1 + Aux + V + NP_2 \rightarrow NP_2 + Aux + be + V + -en + by + NP_1$$

(The problem of descriptive adequacy will be discussed below.)

In a similar way other sentences may be related to our original active sentence, including:

> The gardener doesn't mow the lawns.
> It is the lawns that the gardener mows.
> Does the gardener mow the lawns?

In each case there is a complex of differences between the "transformed" sentence (or TRANSFORM) and the original (or KERNEL[1]) sentence, and yet only a simple difference in its value; in other words, a transformational relationship is involved.

A second motivation for including transformations in a grammar is to provide a way of dealing with variant forms of a structure. Consider, for example, the following three sentence patterns:

| | |
|---|---|
| Frequency Adverbial + NP Subject + VP: | *Occasionally I walk home.* |
| NP Subject + Frequency Adverbial + VP: | *I occasionally walk home.* |
| NP Subject + VP + Frequency Adverbial: | *I walk home occasionally.* |

It would be possible to say that each of these represented a different grammatical pattern; but such a view would be unrealistic, because every native speaker will feel they are in some sense "the same", and therefore uneconomic in the sense that we would be duplicating (actually triplicating) our account of the pattern. Generative grammarians have generally set up one of these patterns as basic (usually the third), and derived the others from it by transformational rules. An alternative (rather neglected) approach is to consider that the elements participate in a single construction, in which the constituents are unordered relative to each other.

A third reason for introducing a transformational component into a grammar is to be found in the study of complex sentences. This was another one of the areas that prompted Harris (1952) to

---

[1]  This latter notion is now rejected by most transformationalists.

introduce the notion of transformation. Comparing sets of sentences like:

(a) Casals stopped performing after the fascist victory.
Casals/he is self-exiled.

(b) Casals, who is self-exiled, stopped performing after the fascist victory.

he found that the complex sentence pattern of (b) could only be adequately explained by relating it to the pair of sentences in (a). The relationship involves setting up an equivalence between *Casals* and *who* (also *he*) and rules for embedding the one sentence within the other. (They can, of course, be embedded the other way round.) In this way the vast array of possible complex sentence structures, many involving multiple embedding, can be reduced to a limited number of basic sentence types. Transformations can thus be used to link two sentences by downgrading one of them to make it a subpart of the other, within which it is "embedded". (We shall discuss this notion more fully in chapter 9.) They may also be used to "conjoin" sentences on a more equal footing in a coordinate structure, cf.:

Casals left Spain. Picasso left Spain.
Casals left Spain, and Picasso left Spain.
Casals left Spain, and so did Picasso.
Casals and Picasso (both) left Spain.

There are, however, some serious difficulties involved in the application of transformational rules to such structures.

The three motivations we have so far considered have all involved using transformations to relate sentences that have a complex relationship to each other. These three uses of transformations are those proposed by Harris; but there is an important fourth use within generative grammar, proposed by Chomsky (1964, 1965). As we saw earlier (at the end of chapter 4), phrase-structure grammar with a limitation to continuous constituents is inadequate, and, if we are to work within a rewrite-rule constituent structure framework, it becomes necessary to set up a system of binary or multiple phrase markers (in the form of tree diagrams) for each sentence. These deep (and intermediate) and surface structures need to be related by rule, and, since a conventional phrase-structure rule is incapable of doing this, it is proposed that a transformational one may accomplish it. Such rules can be obligatory, and when they are, they seem to relate not one sentence with another, but merely two stages in the development of the same sentence. These obligatory rules can have the effect of inserting meaningless elements (like *do*, below), deleting non-occurrent items (like *for* below), and reordering deep structure patterns to conform to their surface, e.g.:

* -ed you smoke? → Did you smoke?
* I hope for to go. → I hope to go.
* I have -en be -ing wait. → I have been waiting.

In general terms, then, obligatory transformations serve the purpose of generally tidying up the deep structure (determined by its deep syntactic-semantic relations) to conform to the surface structure (determined by the actual format of the sentence as actually pronounced).

These different motivations for introducing transformations have some degree of independence from each other. We might, for example, wish to accept transformations based on the first two, but reject the third and the fourth. The fourth in particular would seem to have a function only within a grammar with deep and surface levels of description. However, since it is generative grammarians that have done the most important work on transformations, it will be useful to consider next the way in which they have integrated transformations into their grammar.

## Transformations in generative grammar

Transformational rules, to sum up, are required in a generative grammar to deal with both simple and complex sentences. For simple sentences they are needed: to link transformationally related structures (one of which is normally equated with deep structure); to link variant forms of a structure (one of which again is equated with deep structure); and to link deep and surface structures of a single sentence (where complexities of realization and sequencing prevent a simple phrase-structure account). For complex sentences they are needed in accounting for embedded and conjoined structures.

Why are phrase-structure rules incapable of accomplishing these tasks? The answer is that phrase-structure rules, with their conventions to ensure the correct assignment of structural descriptions, were designed purely for the purpose of developing phrase markers, in other words, extending tree diagrams until they are complete down to the last terminal symbol. The role that we now envisage for transformations, however, is not one of developing a single phrase marker, but that of linking one phrase marker (the deep(er)) with another (the(more)surface); this applies whether the deep and surface structures are needed for a single sentence or for linking two different structures.

The following (algebraic) examples should elucidate the difference between the two kinds of rule. (We indicate a phrase-structure rule with a normal arrow (→) and a transformational rule with a double-shafted arrow ( ⇒ ).) We shall consider the effect of the rules on the tree structure in Figure 53. It will be noted that, in the new, transformationally derived, phrase marker, one of the symbols in the old phrase marker has disappeared, something that was excluded for phrase-structure rules. The symbol is, however, only absent from the derived phrase marker, and this phrase marker is integrally linked to its underlying form.

**Phrase-structure rule**

$a \rightarrow p + q$

**Transformational rule**

$a \Rightarrow p + q$

Effect of rule: extension of phrase marker to:

Effect of rule: derivation of new (surface) phrase marker from old (deep):

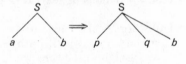

*Figure 53*

The format of a simple rewrite rule, as we have used it in this illustration, is, however, not entirely suitable for transformations. Although in our illustration only one of the elements in the underlying structure was affected by the rule, it is possible for a wholesale restructuring to take place through a transformation, as in passivization. In such cases, we may find the same symbol recurring at different points in the structure (e.g. NP, Det, N), and a different format is necessary to make the precise effect of the rule clear. The standard format for transformations would therefore present our above illustration as follows, where SD = structural description (a common variant of SD is SA = structural analysis) and SC = structural change:

*Sample transformation*
SD: $X - b - Y$ (where $X$ and $Y$, either of which may have a
SC: 1   2   3   null value, provide the context)
$$\Rightarrow$$
1 $p + q$ 3

In this representation of the rule each item affected by the rule, including the context, is numbered (either with 1, 2, 3, etc. or with $X_1, X_2, X_3$, etc.) and the derived structure is given in terms of these numbered items.

Two other items of information are necessary for the full specification of a transformational rule:

(i) A note of whether it is optional (abbreviated as op.) or obligatory (abbreviated as ob.). Optional rules relate two different structures; obligatory rules relate deep and surface forms of the same structure. (Phrase-structure rules do not need any such indication, because they always apply whenever they are applicable, so as to ensure full development of a phrase marker.)

(ii) Any special conditions required for the application of the rule must be stated, e.g. if referential identity of two of the affected NP's is required.

Figures 54 and 55 show two possible examples from English of the working of transformational rules. Note that dashes separate the elements which the numbers refer to.

SD:   $X$ — Adv — $Y$
SC:   1    2    3
$$\Rightarrow^{\text{op}}$$
3 1    2    0

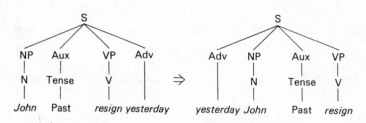

*Figure 54 Adverbial-fronting transformation*

161

SD: $X -_{pp}[P - S]_{pp} - Y$
SC: 1   2   3   4
$\Rightarrow^{ob}$
    1   0   3   4

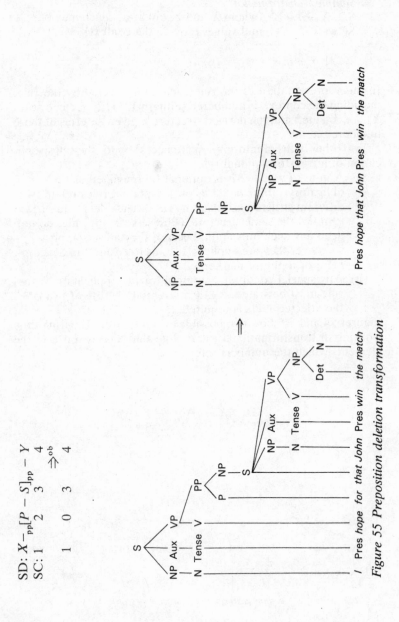

*Figure 55 Preposition deletion transformation*

162

Since the left-hand phrase marker fulfils the structural description requirement of the above rule, the rule is applied and the phrase marker is obligatorily replaced (in all cases) by the new phrase marker on the right-hand side.

So much for the mechanics of transformational rules; but what of the part they play in a transformational-generative grammar? It is difficult to answer this question in a straightforward way, because this is an issue on which views have changed and diverged most dramatically. Our answer, in fact, will have to be partly historical.

We saw in our preliminary discussion that transformations were advocated for a number of different purposes, and we can distinguish five different kinds of transformational rule in the kind of grammar proposed by Chomsky (1957):

(1) *single-based, optional, stylistic ( = meaning-preserving)*, e.g. adverbial-fronting
(2) *single-based, optional, non-stylistic ( = meaning-changing)*, e.g. negation, question formation
(3) *single-based, obligatory*, e.g. preposition deletion, number concord
(4) *double-based, embedding*, e.g. relative-clause formation
(5) *double-based, conjoining*, to account for the formation of coordinate sentences

Of these, all but the third were evident in Harris (1952, 1957). It is the third (obligatory, single-based) type of transformation that is crucial to the development of generative theory. While optional (single-based) transformations link one sentence with a transparent syntactic structure to a related sentence with a more complex one, sentences generated by using obligatory transformations involve two (or more) different phrase markers for the one sentence, an underlying one showing its syntactic-semantic relations and a derived one indicating the shapes and sequence of the words and morphemes. Figure 56 represents the two processes diagrammati-

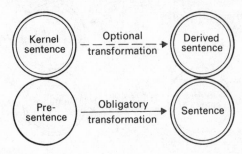

*Figure 56*

cally. This figure does not, however, take account of the possibility that one or more obligatory transformations may apply to all sentences. If this is the case, and if the obligatory transformations are applied last of all, then optional transformations will relate different pre-sentences to each other (related pre-sentences that are destined to become different sentences). This point applies equally to the diagrams illustrating deep- and surface-structure relations. The sentence involving an obligatory transformation was, following Hockett (1958), said to have a DEEP STRUCTURE (equivalent to the pre-sentence) and a SURFACE STRUCTURE (as we saw in chapter 4).

Now it was always the generativists' programme to provide a complete account of the grammar of the language, and thus of the native speaker's competence. While Chomsky, Halle and others worked on generative phonology, Foder and Katz worked on the semantic component of the grammar. Both of these components had to be linked with the syntax.

It is clear that the phonological component of the grammar must link up with surface structure; and equally clear that the semantic component must link up with deep structure. Now we have seen that sentences involving obligatory transformations were seen as having a hypothetical structure as their deep structure, but those involving optional transformations were seen as deriving from another actual sentence. This kernel sentence must obviously be regarded as representing the deep structure, both of itself and of its derived form. This is shown diagrammatically in Figure 57.

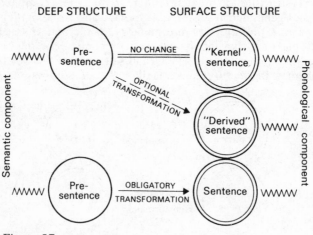

*Figure 57*

The terms "kernel" and "derived" are put in quotes in the figure because they are no longer significant in generative theory. These former "kernel" sentences are said to have a deep structure which is identical to their surface structure (unless other transformations have affected them). The deep structure will distinguish for us ambiguous phrases like *the shooting of the hunters*, which we could diagram as in Figure 58.

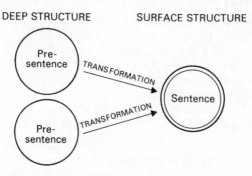

*Figure 58*

We now meet a problem, however, the one faced by Katz and Postal (1964). It concerns those optional transformations that are non-stylistic, i.e. meaning-changing, such as negation and question formation. If the deep structure of a negative sentence is more or less that of the corresponding affirmative one, then it is missing a vital part of the meaning. The answer which Katz and Postal suggested was to locate a negative element NEG or *not* (or interrogative Q, imperative I, etc.) in the deep structure and make the transformation affecting it obligatory. The effect is to transfer choices like affirmative-negative, or declarative-interrogative, from the transformational component to the phrase-structure component, or "base" as Chomsky (1965) renames it.

Similar reasons are adduced for making the choice of embedded sentence in the phrase-structure rules, and for making the dependent transformations operate obligatorily. The net result of all these changes is to reduce transformational rules to two types – obligatory and optional, both of which preserve the meaning of the sentence intact. (The status of conjoining transformations is problematic and will be discussed further in our next chapter.) We have thus reached the position of the so-called "standard theory", according to which transformations simply have the function of relating each deep structure with one or more synonymous surface structures.

But just how different may surface structures be when linked to the same deep structure? It is all very well to pair off the following:

1 (a) John looked up the number.
   (b) John looked the number up.
2 (a) John arrived last night.
   (b) Last night John arrived.

But what about those given below?

3 (a) John drove carefully.
   (b) John drove in a careful manner.
4 (a) John opened the door.
   (b) John made the door open.
5 (a) John killed the duckling.
   (b) John made the duckling die.
6 (a) John sliced the salami with a knife.
   (b) John used a knife to slice the salami.

Generative semanticists, committed to the principle that each set of synonymous sentences (even 5 and 6) should be related to one deep structure, came to set up more and more abstract deep structures. Taking things to their limit, we may find ourselves saying that the "simple" sentence 4(a) has the same kind of complex structure as that which 4(c) below must be given:

4 (c) I declare to you that it is the case that it happened that John caused it to come about that the door became open.

If every semantic relationship is to be accounted for syntactically, it means that there is no longer a distinction between deep syntax and semantics. In fact, generative semanticists explicitly reject deep structure as a redundant intermediate stage for which they see no justification.

It may be useful, at this stage, to represent the over-all view of grammar taken by three transformational-generative theories we have touched on (Figures 59 to 61). It will be seen that the generative-semantic scheme (Figure 61) shows not only a simplification but also a change in directionality: the starting point for each sentence is no longer an abstract initial symbol that eventually acquires both phonetic form and meaning, but instead a meaning which is given a surface syntactic, and eventually phonetic, form. Such a view seems unjustifiably slanted towards the speaker rather than the hearer (though it can be argued that generative grammar is a model for competence, while speaking and hearing are a matter of performance).

166

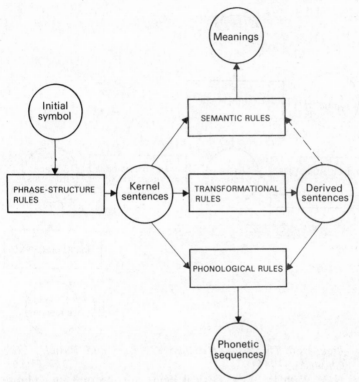

*Figure 59 Early generative grammar (Chomsky, 1957; Lees, 1960)*

Chomsky did not follow the generative semantic path but instead modified the "standard theory" to an "extended standard theory" (Chomsky, 1971a). The chief feature of this was a new link between surface structures and the semantic rules. This was required in Chomsky's view because certain linguistic features, including quantifiers, co-reference, some adverbials, and topic-comment, seem to vary in their interpretation according to whether particular transformations, like passivization, have applied or not. Yet the transformation itself is required to be meaning-preserving. Consider:

A lot of people like few politicans.
– Few politicians are liked by a lot of people.
John washed his own socks.
– ?* His own socks were washed by John.
John unwittingly kissed Mary.
– Mary was unwittingly kissed by John.

167

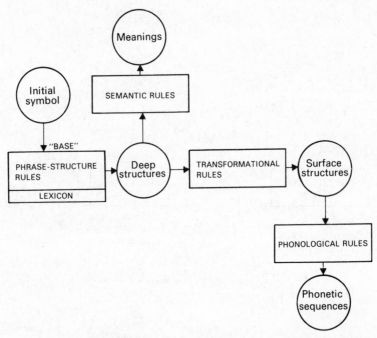

*Figure 60 The "standard theory" (Katz and Postal, 1965; Chomsky, 1965)*

N.B. With the base, lexical items are inserted into phrase markers by (lexical) transformation. Deep structures thus have all lexical items fully specified.

In each case the effect of the passivization is not to preserve the basic meaning intact but rather to change the value of, respectively, the quantifiers, the anaphoric determiner *his own* and the adverb *unwittingly*. Such semantic features, Chomsky felt, needed to be interpreted with reference to surface structure. More recently he goes even further and suggests that ALL rules of semantic interpretation relate to "a suitably enriched notion of surface structure" (1976: 83); he consequently abandons the term "deep structure" in favour of "initial phrase marker(s)".

Despite all these differences of viewpoint, two points of agreement seem to be shared by all those attempting to integrate transformations within a generative grammar:

(1) Within a grammar, transformations have as their input more abstract, semantically revealing, initial structures and, as

168

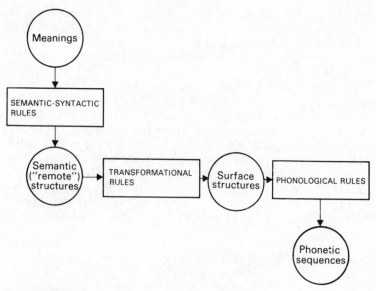

*Figure 61 Generative semantics (McCawley, 1968; Lakoff, 1971a; Postal, 1970)*

their output, surface structures that relate directly to phonetic form.

(2) Transformational rules with syntactic import are all located within one transformational component of the grammar.

We must now ask what the nature of this transformational component is, and how the different rules are arranged within it.

For any generation of a sentence, the rules must be applied sequentially, i.e. one after the other (simultaneous application, though a theoretical possibility, is rarely advocated), but how is the sequence determined? It is possible for the rules to be applied in a random sequence – in which case they are often described as UNORDERED – but more commonly some relations of precedence obtain – in which case they are described as ORDERED. Ordering of rules is of two kinds, INTRINSIC, stemming from the inherent nature of the rules themselves, and EXTRINSIC, imposed by a separately stated explicit order.

To return, for a moment, to phrase-structure rules, it is clear that, in the derivation of a particular sentence, a rule NP → Det + N would have to be preceded by one or more rules introducing NP, such as VP → V Q NP, S → NP + Aux + VP. Phrase-structure rules will therefore always involve intrinsic ordering; but nothing beyond this, no extrinsic ordering, is required, or even permitted. For transformational rules, however, the situation is different. Despite some dissenters, it is generally agreed that not only are some transformations intrinsically ordered but also that others are extrinsically ordered.

There are some transformational rules that are not even intrinsically ordered relative to each other; this applies particularly when the two rules affect quite different parts of the sentential structure. For instance, it has been maintained (e.g. by Burt, 1971) that REFLEXIVE and THERE-INSERTION transformations are unordered. This means that whichever one may apply first it will not prevent the other from applying where it should, nor will it stop the other transformation producing the correct output. An example of the operation of these two transformations, assuming that the optional THERE-INSERTION had been chosen, would be:

(a) REFLEXIVE *first:*
A youth was scratching a youth.
→ A youth was scratching himself.
→ There was a youth scratching himself.

(b) THERE INSERTION *first:*
A youth was scratching a youth.
→ There was a youth scratching a youth.
→ There was a youth scratching himself.

The sequence in which the two transformations are applied is thus immaterial (assuming also that the two occurrences of *the youth* are co-referential).

Consider now as an example of intrinsic ordering two further transformations from Burt (1971), PASSIVE and AGENT DELETION. The first would operate on the noun immediately following the verb, moving it to subject position, and make the other necessary changes, including introduction of the preposition *by*, to produce a passive sentence, e.g.:

$$\left\{ \begin{array}{l} \text{The professor} \\ \text{Someone} \end{array} \right\} \text{painted the door}$$

$$\to \text{The door was painted by} \left\{ \begin{array}{l} \text{the professor} \\ \text{someone.} \end{array} \right\}$$

The second transformation would delete a final *by* + indefinite NP to produce a sentence with a passive verb, e.g.:

The door was painted by someone.
→ The door was painted.

Clearly agent deletion can only operate if the sentence is already passive; otherwise the conditions for its application cannot be met. Thus there is no need for any ordering to be stated. This part of the grammar will work anyway (or at least so long as the opposite order is not prescribed!).

But now let us compare the situation with PASSIVE and DATIVE. The dative transformation is an optional one, which takes a structure like the one underlying *John gave me the book* and converts it to *John gave the book to me*; the structural description it operates on is a sequence of V + NP + NP (with no intervening preposition). The passive transformation is obligatory once the element "Pass" has been selected in the phrase-structure rules (we must assume Burt considers this to be a meaningful choice). Taking this into account we have four possible sentences to account for, which we can display in Table 7. If we consider the critical case, where both

*Table 7*

|  | "Pass" not selected | "Pass" selected |
|---|---|---|
| Dative transformation not applied | *John gave me the book* | *I was given the book by John* |
| Dative transformation applied | *John gave the book to me.* | *The book was given to me by John.* |

transformations have applied, we find that the right structural description is met for the passive to be applied; i.e. *John gave the book to me* has an NP + Aux + V + NP structure, so that the passive can happily follow the dative. On the other hand, if we imagine the passive applying first and look at the structure of *I was given the book by John*, we find the conditions for the dative are no longer met; it would then be impossible to generate *The book was given to me by John*. It is therefore essential for the passive to follow the dative transformation.

The examples of rule ordering we have considered so far have all related to simple sentences. In a complex sentence most transformations have the possibility of operating independently in each clause (or even in each nominalization). Thus in a sentence like

I expected Liverpool to beat Manchester United.

both the main verb *expect* and the embedded verb *beat* may be involved in passivization. In actual fact, the sentences discussed here also involve the transformation of (OBJECT) RAISING, but for simplicity's sake we leave that out of account here, cf. Bach (1974: 120–5). If the subordinate verb undergoes the passive transformation first, we get:

I expected Manchester United to be beaten by Liverpool.

This sentence still has a suitable structure[1] for the passive transformation to apply to the main verb *expect*, which now has *Manchester United* as a following NP. Passivization of the NP thus gives:

Manchester United were expected by me to be beaten by Liverpool.

On the other hand, once we have passivized the main-clause verb to give:

Liverpool were expected by me to beat Manchester United.

it proves impossible to go on and passivize the embedded verb without getting something like:

*Liverpool were expected by Manchester United to be beaten by me.

In other words, it is necessary to apply transformations in a complex sentence so that they apply to the embedded clause first. This applies as a more general principle, known as the transformational CYCLE, according to which (i) transformations are applied, however complex the sentence, from the innermost (i.e. most deeply embedded) clause, working outwards; and (ii) within the cycle for each clause transformations are applied in the same sequence.

A diagrammatic representation of the ordering of transformations according to the cyclic principle would look something like Figure 62.

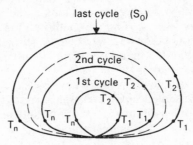

*Figure 62*

[1] Assuming that *Manchester United* has been "raised" to be object of the main (matrix)-clause verb *expect*.

172

Thus a schematic deep structure like Figure 63.

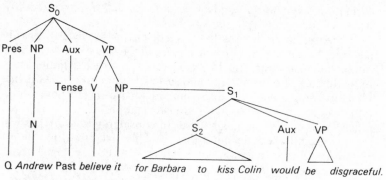

*Figure 63*

would have transformations applied in the required order to $S_2$, then in the same order to $S_1$, and then similarly to $S_0$. (Perhaps ending up with a sentence like *Was it Andrew that believed that it would be disgraceful for Colin to be kissed by Barbara?* with transformations operating on all three cycles. The reader may consider precisely which.)

The cyclic ordering of transformations within a generative grammar is not, however, a principle that has been universally accepted in its purest form. Different scholars have presented evidence for PRECYCLIC rules (Lakoff, 1968), POSTCYCLIC rules (Bresnan, 1971) and FINAL CYCLIC rules (Lakoff, 1968). The whole area has, in fact, presented rather a confusing picture with series of suggestions, rejections and counter-suggestions. The problem is a familiar one: to make transformations powerful enough to account for the wide range of linguistic data, and yet to limit them in such a way that they reflect the known characteristics of human language *vis-à-vis* other systems. We now turn to the question of the precise powers of individual transformations.

**The powers of transformations**

Having considered why and for what transformations are needed, and how they fit into a generative scheme of grammar, we are now in a position to assess the contribution different individual transformations make. It will be recalled that a transformational rule links two phrase markers that share some characteristic(s) but differ

173

from each other in some clearly defined way. It will be useful, then, to examine precisely what differences in structure a transformation may "bridge" and what kinds of relationships it thereby accounts for.

In theory, the transformation, as a device, is so powerful that it can bring about any conceivable change in the shape of a structure; but certain restrictions need to be observed, if we are to limit its use to the linking of realistic deep and surface structures. The possible kinds of transformation can be limited to five or six elementary types, although more complex transformations may need to be regarded as combinations of these. In considering these types we must constantly bear in mind the principle that transformations should not change meaning, a principle recognized by Chomsky and generative semanticists alike as we saw above (p. 165).

DELETION of an element is one effect that a transformation may have. Deletion transformations have a format like:

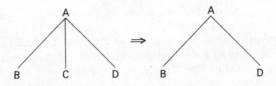

Like other transformations such deletions may be either obligatory or optional, and they vary in their function accordingly. Earlier in this chapter (p. 162) we saw an example of an obligatory transformation of this type, preposition deletion. The effect of the rule was simply to erase a preposition before the complementizers *that* and *to* in a sentence like:

> I hope (*for) that John will win the match.
> I hope (*for) to win the match.

In these cases we could say that the point of the deletion was to avoid a totally forbidden sequence (preposition + *that/to* complementizer), but in other cases the purpose seems to be avoidance of duplication, e.g.:

> I offered (*me/*myself) to go,

where the subject of the second, embedded, verb (*go*) is compulsorily deleted, being identical to the main-clause subject. The status of the embedded subject (*me/myself*) is actually a bit suspect. Since no contrast is possible, i.e. the two subjects are obligatorily co-referential, it seems more realistic to speak of a "shared subject". A related phenomenon is to be observed in a sentence like

I persuaded John to go,

where *John* represents both the object of *persuade* and the subject of *go*.

Optional deletion is of a different order. Transformations of this kind relate a sentence containing a particular item with a sentence that is identical except that the item is absent. If the meaning-preserving nature of transformations is to be maintained, then the reduced sentence must be no more than stylistically different from its full form. We may distinguish two motives for optional deletion, two reasons why an item sometimes goes unmentioned: it may be irrelevant and of no interest to the speaker and therefore left indefinite; or it may be definite enough but so clear from the context that it needs no mention. The first, indefinite, type of optional deletion is illustrated by:

John is reading.
= John is reading something (or other).

The second, contextually definite, type is illustrated by:

John is watching.
= John is watching you (/the cricket/ etc.).

Optional deletion thus takes care of the irrelevant and the redundant.

SUBSTITUTION, i.e. replacement of an item with a different item, is also a possible kind of transformational rule. Substitution transformations have a format like (a) or (b) below:

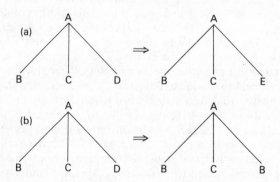

If, however, changes of meaning are to be prohibited, the use of substitution transformations is as good as limited to two cases:
(i) sentences where a lexical item is optionally replaced by a word with the same grammatical class but pronominal in

nature, a PROFORM (see chapter 12), which carries the same meaning in this context;

(ii) sentences where a word is obligatorily changed to agree with an item already present in the sentence.

Optional substitution of a proform morpheme for a word may be exemplified by:

John met Mary at the party.
= He met her at the party.

Similar optional use of proforms occurs where the proform replaces a whole construction, i.e. a node dominating a sequence of constituents, e.g.:

John met Mary at the party.
= John met Mary there.

Such cases might be termed "proform reduction", although they can also be regarded as cases of substitution. Proform reduction obviously has a similar function to (contextual) optional deletion.

In earlier generative grammar (e.g. Chomsky, 1957, 1964; Koutsoudas, 1966) grammatical agreement was achieved through an obligatory substitution transformation that converted a category into the appropriate subcategory, e.g. Present Tense $\Rightarrow$ -s or ø, respectively. Such changes have been effected more recently, however, through the use of transformations involving syntactic features (see below).

If an item is introduced without replacing any element in particular, it is preferable to describe it as ADJUNCTION (additon or insertion). Again, we must guard against the introduction of additional meanings, and we must therefore expect that no new nodes will ever be added. We are therefore limited to the adjoining of terminal elements, i.e. morphemes. Since languages very rarely use optional additional morphemes that are meaningless, the majority of adjunction transformations will be obligatory. This means that they will be used to ensure that we correctly insert required grammatical elements like *do* or *there* in sentences like *Do you smoke? There is a match on today.* (The *there*-insertion transformation is sometimes formulated so as to replace a noun phrase with *there* as subject, which would thus count as a substitution transformation.) When *do* is adjoined, it is added to join another element under the Tense node, to effect a change like that in Figure 64. This kind of adjunction, where the new element is added to join fellow-morphemes under a common node, is termed SISTER-ADJUNCTION.

PERMUTATION transformations, when they are obligatory, have a similar function to that of sister-adjunction, that of providing the

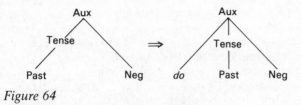

*Figure 64*

correct format for the surface structure. In the case of permutation, however, it is not a question of introducing anything, but of re-ordering elements under the same node, to convert a deep(er) structure to a surface one. Very often such re-orderings will have the effect of erasing a deep-structure relationship in surface structure (this being one of the reasons why surface structure is insufficient alone), as in Figure 65. For this reason permutation is not always

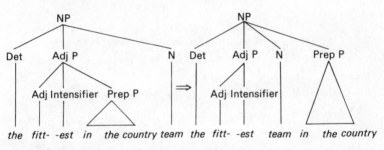

*Figure 65*

regarded as an elementary transformation, but instead is seen as a combination of (sister-)adjunction and deletion. Permutations can also be optional, in which case both the underlying and the transformed version of the structure occur as surface structures, e.g.

    John arrived last night.
    = Last night John arrived.

In such cases the transformation, like all optional ones, has the function of bringing together stylistic variants (= bringing stylistic variants together!).

So-called CHOMSKY-ADJUNCTION differs from sister-adjunction in that, instead of simply adding an empty morpheme to an existing node, we actually create a new node. Normally this would be inadmissible because a new node would add a new meaning, but it is acceptable in Chomsky-adjunction because the "new" node is only a copy of a node already present. An example of a structure involv-

177

ing Chomsky-adjunction appears in Figure 66. In early generative grammar such a structure would have been produced by a transformation of the double-based ("generalized") type. Later theory, however, requires such recursive rules to be incorporated in the "base component", although they remain transformational in nature (cf. Chomsky, 1965: 133–7). The structure of Figure 66, for example, would have been generated using a base rule NP→NP (S). (The lower NP would be "pruned" if S were not selected, i.e. when there is no relative clause. But the validity of tree representations like this is debatable.)

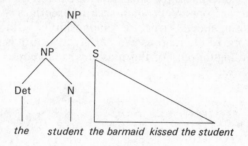

= 'the student (that) the barmaid kissed'

*Figure 66*

The transformations we have discussed so far have all involved operating with grammatical segments, but it is often necessary, as we saw in chapter 7, to break down elements into their constituent features. This means using FEATURE SPECIFICATIONS. These are of two types: those that convert segments to features, introducing what Chomsky (1965) terms "complex symbols", e.g. [count], [common], etc. for nouns; and those that ensure agreement between the feature specifications of items at different points in a structure, e.g. the [singular] feature of a subject NP being passed on to the verb. Since such agreement is required for the sake of full grammaticality, feature-specification transformations are normally obligatory.

In our survey of types of transformational rule it has appeared that, although transformations are in theory all-powerful, attempts are made to limit their power. The requirement of preservation of meaning means that any new elements that are introduced must be (relatively) meaningless terminal elements, i.e. morphemes like *do*, and that the only new nodes permitted are copies of ones already present (as in Chomsky-adjunction).

As regards the elements that are lost by transformational rules, some restrictions are again prompted by a desire for meaning preservation. Deletion would thus ideally be limited to cases where either the transformation regularly deletes the same item e.g. *you* in imperative sentences, or (under so-called "identity conditions") the element deleted is present elsewhere in the sentence. The latter case can, however, give rise to difficulties. Although transformational rules are often provided with a condition of identity restriction (e.g. 2 = 4, where 2 and 4 are both NP's), this is not adequate. In a sentence that undergoes pronominalization, the affected NP may be:

(a) co-referential with an NP in the same sentence, e.g. *John left early because he felt tired*;
(b) co-referential with an NP in a neighbouring sentence in the text, e.g. [*John left early.*] *I know he felt tired*;
(c) identified purely from the situational context, e.g. *He's staying at home today* [sc. the man who usually works (etc.) here].

In the case of (b) and (c) it is difficult to see how a pronominalizing transformation can operate without deleting some semantic information. Cases like (c) prompted Chomsky (1971a) and Jackendoff (1972) to generate pronouns directly in the base and make their semantic interpretation dependent on surface structure.

Limitations on the power of transformations have been proposed not only for the sake of meaning preservation but also to prevent transformational-generative grammar becoming as powerful as an unrestricted rewrite-rule grammar (see chapter 4). Ross (1967) proposed universal constraints on permutation (or "movement") transformations affecting noun phrases (see Bach, 1974: 208–13). Emonds (1972) suggested that, with the exception of "root transformations" which are limited to non-embedded clauses (see below, p. 189f.) no transformations should be allowed to produce a structure of a type not already provided for in the base rules.

On the other hand, other work has suggested that transformational rules, as traditionally restricted, may not be powerful enough. Perlmutter (1971) finds that the ungrammaticality of certain combinations of Spanish clitic pronouns (*\*se se lo, \*se le lo*) makes it necessary to impose restrictions on the regular operation of transformations by imposing surface (or "output") restraints. Lakoff (1970b) suggests the need for "global" ( or "transderivational") rules which scan the transformational history of a string, to account for phenomena relating to quantifiers such as *all, many, few,* etc. Finally, in the grammatical model proposed in Chomsky (1965) a filtering device is proposed, whereby strings that fail to have sentential boundary signals deleted by transformation (e.g. an impossible relative clause where the pronoun was not co-referential with any antecedent) would be filtered out as ungrammatical. For example, the string *The baker # the baker was happy # arrived early* would simply have the #s removed as part of the relative clause-formation transformation, to give *The baker who was happy arrived early*, whereas the string *The baker # the butcher was happy # arrived early* would fail to meet the conditions of this transformation and be filtered out as ungrammatical because of its internal sentence-boundary markers. All of the above proposals, whether they are necessary or not, serve to further extend the power of a transformational grammar in the direction of unrestricted rewrite-rule grammars.

Substantial differences of opinion have thus arisen amongst generative grammarians over the precise role of transformations in a grammar. The difficulty is that all of the data that might resolve the issue seem to be interpretable in various ways. The same applies to the data relating to the dispute about the function of the transformational component between the proponents of generative semantics and generative syntax/interpretive semantics. Indeed Bach (1974: 225) reckons the theories to be strongly equivalent.

In the face of these unsettled problems, it is as well to remind ourselves that it is not at all clear that generative grammar itself is a viable proposition. If, in addition, we find that the major problems with transformations arise through incorporating them into a generative grammar, we might be excused for wondering if it is not preferable to consider transformations as worthwhile in their own right. We should therefore recall that the transformations supported by non-generativists and generativists alike are those of the optional single-based variety (whether they involve meaning differences or not) and embedding transformations. These, of course, are the types that Harris (1957) originally concentrated on. We have already seen something of the single-based variety, and in our next chapter we shall be considering the question of embedding in some more detail.

## Questions for study

1 Examine the "kernel" sentence (a); then work out the transformations that have affected the sentences (b) to (e), describing the changes in form and in meaning/stylistic value that are involved in each case. (Some sentences have undergone more than one transformation.)
(a) That student kissed our waitress in the bar last night.

(b) It was our waitress that that student kissed in the bar last night.

(c) That student didn't kiss our waitress in the bar last night.

(d) He kissed her in the bar, didn't he?

(e) Who was she kissed by there last night?

2 Each of the following sentences will need to be given a tree diagram for its "deep structure" that differs from its "surface structure" in a number of different respects. What kinds of change will obligatory transformations need to perform to "tidy up" the deep structure?

(a) John did not agree to play.

(b) John was unlikely to play.

3 Construct underlying and derived partial phrase markers (in the form of tree diagrams) to illustrate the application of the following transformational rules:

(a) *Relative-clause formation:*

```
SD:   W  [      NP [ X  NP  Y  ]    ]      Z
         NP      S              S   NP
      1          2    3   4   5          6    ⇒ob

SC:   1          2 that 3  0   5          6
```

(b) *Indirect-object formation:*

```
SD:   X  V  NP  [   to    NP  ]   Y
                PP  for        PP
      1  2  3       4     5    6       ⇒op
SC:   1  2  5       0     4    6
```

4 Classify the following transformations as either non-stylistic (= meaning-changing) or stylistic (= meaning-preserving): clefting, negation, question formation, adverbial fronting.

5 Consider the three transformations, passivization, tag formation (to account for sentence-final *isn't he, have you,* etc.) and *there*-insertion (to derive *There were two girls in the library* from *Two girls were in the library,* etc.). What would the following data suggest about their ordering?

The girl was arrested by the policeman, wasn't she? (*wasn't he?)

There are two girls in the library, aren't there? (*aren't they?)

There was a girl arrested by the policeman.

6 Which kind of transformational change (substitution, adjunction, permutation, deletion or some combination of these) is involved in the following transformations?
 (a) adverbial fronting
 (b) tag formation
 (c) indirect-object formation (as described in question 3 above)
 (d) relative-clause formation

**Further reading**

On the raison d'être of transformations: Harris (1957), sections 1 to 3; Chomsky (1957), chapters 7, 8. On transformations in generative grammar: Chomsky (1965), chapter 3; Matthews (1967); Jacobs and Rosenbaum (1968), chapters 4, 9, 11; McCawley (1968); Lyons (1970b), chapter 7; Bach (1974), chapters 5, 6. On the powers of transformations: Jackendoff (1972), chapter 1; Bach (1974), chapter 9.

*Chapter 9*

# "Rank" – the size units of grammar

### The rank scale and other scales

At the beginning of chapter 6 we saw how a sentence can be broken down into its ultimate constituents, morphemes, through a number of intermediate stages of immediate constituents. In chapter 7 we discussed the problems of labelling the different classes of elements that can act as constituents. As a result, we are able to make statements like: a sentence consists of a noun phrase, an auxiliary structure and a verb phrase, etc. The notion CONSISTS OF is important here, in that it implies that at each stage we may exhaustively analyse the construction into a number of discrete constituents, i.e. the constituents neither leave any remainder nor overlap each other.

In labelling the constructions and constituents, we traditionally use terms like sentence, noun phrase, adjective (word), that imply a certain size of unit. Traditional grammar, in fact, seems to assume a size relationship as follows:

sentence > clause > phrase > word (> morpheme)

i.e. every sentence may be divided into clauses, every clause into phrases, every phrase into words. (Traditionally the word was not broken down further, but from a modern linguistic point of view such an analysis is essential.) As an illustration, the sentence

Old people may work even after the job is finished.

can be analysed as shown in Figure 67. This seems nice and straightforward. Each size unit seems to be on a definite "level" or have a definite RANK compared with the units higher or lower than it on the scale, and to link automatically with the next element on the scale. This is a point which both systemic and tagmemic grammar have constantly emphasized.

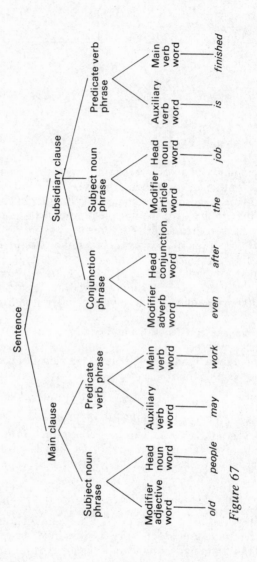

*Figure 67*

Unfortunately, things are not quite so simple as this. For one thing, the predicate phrase will most commonly divide up not directly into words but rather into further phrases, of which one will itself be the verb phrase, but the other will be an adverbial phrase, adjective phrase or noun phrase (e.g. an object). For example, if instead of *may work* we had had *may live in very large houses* for our predicate phrase, one of its constituents would have been *live in very large houses*, itself a phrase; and this pattern would repeat itself to give a structure that we might represent in Figure 68. There is

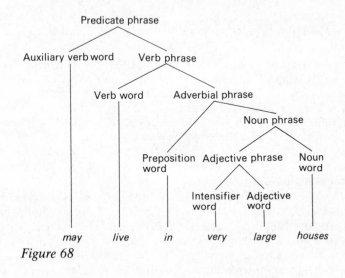

*Figure 68*

nothing unusual about this patterning: no special process like embedding or coordination is involved (though, in actual fact, tag-memicists, who limit each of their "levels" to one construction under "normal mapping", would describe our example as a case of "non-recursive layering"). It is just as normal, for example, for the second constituent of an adverbial phrase to be a noun phrase as it is for the subject of a sentence to be a noun phrase. We simply seem to be faced with larger (= "higher rank") and smaller (= "lower rank") phrases. Somehow, at the top end, phrases are constituents of clauses, while at the bottom end phrases have words as their constituents. In traditional grammar the transition to clause is held to occur when a subject-predicate construction is involved, and to word when only a single word remains; but we shall discuss the validity of these criteria later.

Systemic grammar more or less takes over the traditional view of

185

rank, though preferring the term "group" for the traditional "phrase". However, it introduces the concept of "rank shift". This concept is employed to account for cases of embedding, i.e. where an element has its natural rank shifted downwards. An element, for example, that has the internal structure of a clause may nevertheless function as a constituent of the "group" (phrase), i.e. in a place normally occupied by words. An example from Scott *et al*. (1968: 144) (which uses a Hallidayan model) is:

> M   H        Q
> The letter [[which he gave me]] was posted last week.

The capital letters M, H, Q, represent different structural places within the nominal group (= noun phrase), and Q, which could have been a word (e.g. *upstairs*), is a clause shifted downwards to word rank. Tagmemicists would describe such a pattern in a similar way but refer to it as a "loopback" when, as above, a unit is a constituent of a unit lower than itself (e.g. a clause within a phrase) or as a "layering" when a unit is a constituent of a unit of the same rank (or "level") as itself (e.g. a phrase within a phrase). We shall use the term EMBEDDING throughout.

A rather different problem in the study of rank is provided by cases in which there is no extra complexity (as with embedding) but rather extra simplicity! Instead of finding at each rank a construction of constituents of the next lower rank, we may just find a single element – which may simply be the natural reduced form of that construction. In our sentence above, for example, the subject *old people* may be reduced to *they*: is it then, as Halliday would say, a phrase of a single word? In the same way sentences may break down directly into phrases (in the case of one-clause sentences); and phrases may have morphemes as direct constituents. In the ultimate case we may have a sentence consisting of a single morpheme like *Run!* Halliday would describe this as a sentence consisting of one clause, consisting of one phrase, consisting of one word, consisting of one morpheme. Although this position is ridiculed by, for instance, Matthews (1966), the item *run* does have the required attributes at least of sentence, clause, word and morpheme, if not of phrase (we shall discuss their defining characteristics below).

Tagmemicists use the concept of "level-skipping", by which "a filler from a lower level construction is used in a higher level construction" (Cook, 1969: 31). Such a definition would appear to cover cases of the sort we have just considered. In practice, however, tagmemicists seem to limit the application of "skipping" to

so-called "bound relaters" (also termed "phrase clitics") such as the
*ed* and *'s* of:

the red-hair*ed* girl
the girl*'s* hair

each of which, in other uses, acts as subword morpheme but in the
cited examples acts directly as a phrase constituent.

Rank (or "level") must be seen as a scale, or, more strictly, as a
gradation, since there are a number of discrete steps from one end
to the other. It is worth distinguishing the rank scale from two other
important scales that relate to language:

(a) the scale of REALIZATION (also termed "exponence" by
     Halliday)
(b) The scale of DELICACY (the term is owed originally to A.
     McIntosh)

since occasionally the scales are partly or wholly conflated.

The scale of REALIZATION is a scale of abstraction extending from
the relatively concrete sequences of phonologically specified
morphs to the underlying grammatical meanings. In the sentence
*These dogs run fast*, for example, we might detect at least three
stages in the realization of the plurality (Figure 69). The abstract-
concrete scale thus corresponds to a scale running from meaning
through grammar and lexis to phonology.

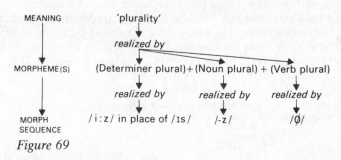

*Figure 69*

The scale of realization can also, however, be seen as running
through grammar itself. At the concrete end of the scale grammatical patterns are simply sequences of morphemes. Each sequence
represents a pattern in so far as the morphemes represent (=
realize, manifest) particular grammatical patterns; see for instance
Figure 70.

Even such a scheme involves an oversimplification. In a sense we
are conflating two variables under the heading of "realization": the
path from meaning through linguistic form to phonetic manifesta-

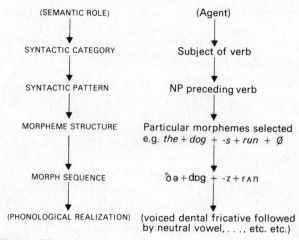

*Figure 70*

tion; and the scale from the general linguistic description of patterns to the specific or concrete manifestation of those patterns in particular cases, e.g. word – noun word – the word *table*. The first kind of realization relates closely to the deepness or surfaceness of a grammatical characterization (see chapter 11); the second comes close to (but is not identical with) our other scale, that of delicacy.

The scale of DELICACY refers to the depth of detail recorded in a structure or classification. This degree of subtlety used in describing linguistic data could be illustrated by the subcategorization of different kinds of verbal complements or objects in English (Figure 71). Consider the following examples:

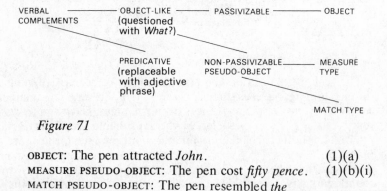

*Figure 71*

| | |
|---|---|
| OBJECT: The pen attracted *John*. | (1)(a) |
| MEASURE PSEUDO-OBJECT: The pen cost *fifty pence*. | (1)(b)(i) |
| MATCH PSEUDO-OBJECT: The pen resembled *the pencil*. | (1)(b)(ii) |

188

PREDICATIVE COMPLEMENT: The pen was *a luxury*.             (2)

At one level of detail all the italicized elements share the characteristic of being noun-phrase complements to the verb; at a second level (1)(a) and (1)(b)(i) and (ii) are the same in being purely nominal completions of the verb, as against (2) which is an attribute predicated of the verb, and as such may have an adjective phrase such as *(very) luxurious* substituted for it; at a third level of delicacy (1)(a) is a passivizable object (*John was attracted by the pen*), while (1)(b)(i) and (1)(b)(ii) are not (*\*Fifty pence were cost by the pen. \*The pencil was resembled by the pen*); finally, even (1)(b)(i) and (1)(b)(ii) differ, at least in the semantic functions of the noun phrase.

The scale of rank differs from both the scales of realization and delicacy in that it involves size units, and also in that it has the devices of embedding and coordination, which allow recursive structures to develop. The three scales should therefore be clearly distinct.

Stratificationalists, however, propose a number of different strata for the linguistic description of an utterance. The precise number of strata proposed has varied; and in some accounts each level is subdivided into a description involving -EME units (e.g. morpheme) and a description involving -ON units (e.g. lexon). The strata of Lamb (1966) are:

> hypersememic-sememic-lexemic-morphemic-phonemic-
> hyperphonemic

and they are said to run from meaning through grammar to phonology. They thus follow a scale of realization. At the same time the step from the lexemic stratum to the morphemic involves a difference in size unit, i.e. rank: for instance, a lexeme like *afternoon* is analysed into a morpheme sequence *after + noon*. (Strictly speaking, the lexeme *afternoon* consists of two lexons, which are realized respectively by the morphemes *after* and *noon*.) Apart from this, differences in rank are accounted for in the separate "tactic" (or structural) account given for each stratum.

It is most useful, however, to examine grammatical rank as an independent variable. Before examining the separate units of the rank scale, though, it is necessary to understand the part that embedding and coordination play in it.

## Embedding

As we have already indicated, embedding involves the downgrading of an element from a higher to a lower status. A good analogy for an embedded structure is that of building structures, which we referred to in chapter 1. We can compare a house to a sentence, with each room corresponding to a sentence constituent at the next rank down. Consider, however, the status of an annexe to the house, built perhaps for an elderly grandparent (a so-called "granny's flat"). Such an annexe, which might well contain a bed-sitting room plus a kitchenette and small bathroom, is in one sense a complete house in miniature, but, at the same time, it is a constituent of the total house in the same way that other rooms are. We may say that it is a house embedded within a house.

Embedding takes place, then, when at a particular point in a linguistic structure we find not a typical straightforward constituent, but rather an element that might have occurred with a higher status. In the case under review this element has been downgraded to a constituent of the construction of which it is a specimen, or alternatively a constituent of a constituent of such a construction. In other words, the element $X$ where it is circled in Figure 72 would be said to be embedded.

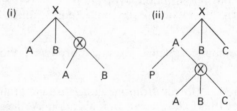

*Figure 72*

A linguistic example will clarify matters further. If we consider the structure of the English noun phrase, we observe that besides the core elements determiner and noun, it may also contain, *inter alia*, a single-word adverbial (i.e. an adverb) as postmodifier, e.g. *the house nearby*. This structure may be represented thus:

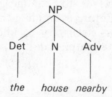

Instead of a single-word adverbial, however, the postmodifier might have been an adverbial phrase, typically consisting of a preposition plus noun phrase, e.g. *the house near the pub*. The phrase *near the pub* identifies the intended house in the same way as the word *nearby*. This larger noun phrase may therefore be represented as in Figure 73. It is clear that this tree diagram adheres to the format of our second embedding schema: the noun phrase *the pub* has been downgraded to act as a constituent of a construction that is itself a constituent of a noun phrase.

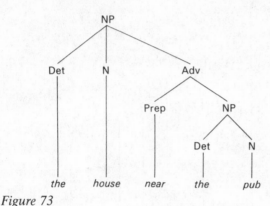

*Figure 73*

A pattern like this could be generated by a pair of phrase-structure rules:

(1) NP → Det + N ( + Adv)
(2) Adv → Prep + NP

In practice generative grammarians generally prefer to derive postmodifiers from relative clauses such as *(the house) that is near to the pub*. This also involves embedding, but of a sentence rather than a noun phrase. Obviously the pattern can give rise to recursion, and, grammatically speaking, there is no limit on the number of noun phrases that may be embedded with adverbial phrases within noun phrases, e.g. *the house near the pub behind the church opposite the shops next to.* . . . Each additional embedding adds to the complexity of the associated tree diagram (Figure 74), whereas in coordination, as we shall see below, an extra conjoined element does not necessarily increase the complexity of the structure.

The above example can be described as a case of noun-phrase embedding. A further example is illustrated by *her sister's husband's uncle's friend's daughter's house*, where the embedding takes place in the determiner position (*her* could be expanded to *Mary's* or to *my fiancée's*). Such cases are sometimes described as left-

191

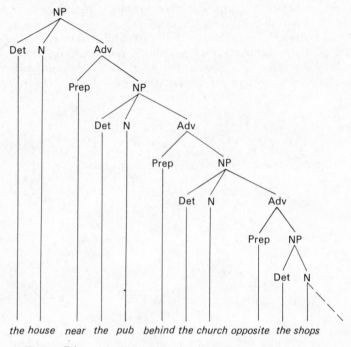

*Figure 74*

branching, since the tree is developed repeatedly from the left-hand (= earlier) constituent, whereas our previous example involving adverbial postmodifiers was right-branching.

An even more common kind of embedding is sentence-embedding. In this case a sequence that could have acted as a sentence in its own right is relegated to the position of constituent within a superior (or "matrix") sentence. Consider the sentence

Alan said that Bill thought that Catherine regretted that David discovered that Edward had leaked the phonetics papers.

The verb *say*, instead of taking a simple object like *a few words*, is complemented by the *that*-clause which continues till the end of the sentence. Within the *that*-clause, however, the verb *thought* is complemented by a further *that*-clause which includes the verb *regretted*; and so on until the verb *leak* which has a plain object. The structure could be given after the form of Figure 75. This figure does not accommodate the conjunction *that*, which may be thought of either as co-constituent with the embedded S or as one of its subconstituents; in any case it should be regarded as a marker of embedding (see below). The embedded sentence would be described in traditional grammar (and by tagmemicists and systemicists) as a subordinate clause, and we shall later have to decide whether the use of the term "clause" here involves some duplication.

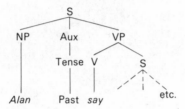

*Figure 75*

If a sentence is embedded in subject position, it may be said to follow our first schema for embedding in the sense that the embedded sentence is a direct constituent of the matrix sentence. Compare, for example, the sentences in Figure 76, (a) without, and (b) with embedding (we assume *that* to be a subconstituent of the embedded S). If, in such a case, we allow a further sentence-embedding to take place in subject position, i.e. to replace the noun phrase *the thought*, we meet the problem that the *that* of the first embedded sentence is left stranded on the left-hand side of the second embedded sentence, thus giving two *that*'s in a row and hence a doubtful sentence:

?That that the decision pleased Hughes, annoyed Smith, surprised Callaghan.

If yet a further embedding takes place, the sequence becomes totally unacceptable:

*That that that the goal was credited to Heighway, pleased Hughes, annoyed Smith, surprised Callaghan.

The acceptability of such sentences is not noticeably improved if we use an abstract noun phrase with the *that*, e.g. *The idea that the thought that the decision that the goal was credited to. . . .* All of these sentences are of course far more natural in alternative forms with extraposition, e.g. *It surprised Callaghan that the thought annoyed Smith*, or with passivization, e.g. *Callaghan was surprised that Smith was annoyed that Hughes was pleased that the goal was credited to*

193

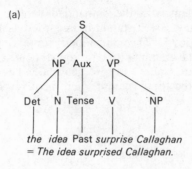

(a)

the idea Past surprise Callaghan
= The idea surprised Callaghan.

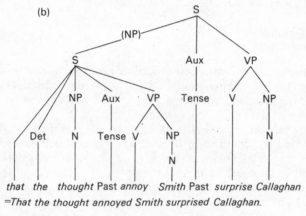

(b)

that the thought Past annoy Smith Past surprise Callaghan
=That the thought annoyed Smith surprised Callaghan.

*Figure 76*

*Heighway.* The fact is that, when an embedding takes place in the middle of a structure, it causes discontinuity in a construction, of a kind that is referred to as "nesting", or, where, as here, the embedding is in the place of a direct constituent of a similar construction, as "self-embedding" (cf. Chomsky, 1965: 12–13). Such constructions are only tolerable to a very limited extent.

Most embeddings are of noun phrases or of sentences. One common type, nominalization, involves downgrading a sentence so thoroughly that it has all the characteristics of a noun phrase, cf.:

Cromwell defended the castle.
Cromwell's defence of the castle . . .

where the verb corresponds to a deverbal noun, the subject noun phrase corresponds to a possessive determiner and the object noun phrase corresponds to a postmodifying noun phrase.

There are also some minor types of embedding. At a morphological level, within compound nouns (see further chapter 10), it is possible to have a preceding noun modifying a following one, and for the modifier itself to be such a compound. This can give rise to a compound like that shown in Figure 77. A rather different kind of embedding is seen in *much*, *too much*, *much too much*, *too much too much*, etc.

pork sausage róll salad

*Figure 77*

We have seen that embedding normally gives rise to recursive structures; but in some cases the recursion is blocked. In a sentence with a relative clause, it is required that there be co-reference between a noun phrase in the matrix sentence and a noun phrase in the embedded sentence (relative clause), the latter noun phrase being rendered with a relative pronoun, e.g.:

The porter, who (= the porter) arrived, was sneezing.

Since a relative pronoun cannot have a relative clause dependent on it, no further embedding is possible, e.g.:

*The porter, who, who had the key, arrived, was sneezing.

However, if the relative clause includes a noun phrase in some non-subject position, recursion becomes possible, e.g.:

This is the cat that caught the rat that . . .

Thus, in principle at least, all embedding is recursive.

We noted above that the conjunction *that* may act as a marker of an embedded sentence, i.e. of a subordinate clause. In fact it is very normal for embedding to be marked in some way; such marking will make it clear to the listener (or reader) that the structure is being used with its downgraded rather than its full value. The following are examples:

| FULL STRUCTURE | EMBEDDED STRUCTURE |
|---|---|
| (I saw) the medical student. | (I saw) the medical student's (work). |
| John has arrived. | (I believe) *that* John has arrived. |
| Has John arrived? | (I wonder) *whether* (/*if*) John has arrived. |
| Where has John gone? | (I wonder) where *John has gone.* |

In the first example the noun phrase *the medical student* is embedded (in determiner position) in a larger noun phrase of which the noun *work* is the head. The marker of the embedding is the particle *'s* (which is attached to the preceding noun phrase, not just to the noun *student*). In an alternative structure *the medical student* can act as postmodifier, with *of* acting as marker of the embedding, in *the work of the medical student*.

In the other three examples it is a sentence that is embedded. When the sentence is a statement, the conjunction *that* (optionally deleted) acts as a marker of embedding; when a *yes-no* question is involved, the conjunction *whether* or *if* is used; when a *wh*-question is embedded, this is marked by the word order, the finite verb following the subject instead of preceding it, as in a full question.

The optionality of the conjunction *that* in the second example highlights the fact that there is wide variation in the degree to which embedding is marked. A cross-language comparison of the same structure brings this point out. Translating the phrase *the little man's house* (= *the house of a little man*) into Welsh and Turkish, we find Welsh not marking the embedding at all and Turkish marking it doubly:

| | | | | |
|---|---|---|---|---|
| *Welsh*: | ⎰tŷ | dyn | bach⎱ | ZERO |
| | ⎱'house' | 'man' | 'little'⎰ | MARKING |
| | | | | SINGLE |
| *English*: | a little man's house | | | MARKING |
| *Turkish*: | ⎰küçük | adam*ın* | ev*i* ⎱ | DOUBLE |
| | ⎱'little' | 'man's' | 'house-*his*'⎰ | MARKING |

Presumably such wide divergence in the degree of marking of embedding is possible because languages with zero grammatical marking either use phonological markers such as intonation patterns, tempo and rhythm or simply leave more to the detective skill of the listener. (This point applies to the marking of grammatical

196

structures in general, of course.) Embedded structures that are marked are therefore identified by grammatical words (prepositions/postpositions, conjunctions), grammatical categories (case, mood), word order, and/or prosodic phenomena.

Embedding has always been handled in generative grammar through transformations. In the earlier model (e.g. Chomsky, 1957) there was a special embedding type of transformation which simply placed one sentence at a particular point (e.g. subject, complement position) within another, the "matrix" sentence, e.g.:

> The secretary – we appointed the secretary yesterday – arrived late this morning.

Obligatory single-sentence transformations then converted the overlapping noun phrase in the embedded sentence into a relative pronoun. In later theory, however, it is assumed that the embedding must take place in the base component of the grammar, which therefore includes rules like:

$$NP \rightarrow (Det) \ N \ (S)$$

which embeds a sentence within a noun phrase. This means, of course, that one of the motivations for including transformations within a generative grammar has been removed.

## Coordination

In introducing embedding, we drew on the analogy of the structure of a house, and we can extend that analogy for coordination. Whereas embedding involved downgrading a house to be a mere annexe and, as such, a constituent of the house alongside other constituents, coordination would be equivalent to the division of a house into two or more flats (or apartments). Each flat is in effect an independent dwelling with all the requisites of a full house, but a number of flats are housed together in one building, all of them having equal status.

The basic notion of coordination – also termed "conjoining" or "conjunction" – is one of a parallel grouping of equals: no element is downgraded; all coordinated elements are on a par with each other. A general formula for coordinations would therefore be

$$X = X \ \& \ X \ (\& \ X)^n$$

where & stands for a coordinator such as *and* or *or*, and where $n \geq 1$. Not only are the coordinated elements equal in status, they must also be alike in their category and/or function. Nouns are

197

coordinated with nouns, adjectives with adjectives and so on, e.g.:

| | |
|---|---|
| NOUN (PHRASE): | (We bought) bread and milk. |
| ADJECTIVE (PHRASE): | (Vincent was) tall, dark and handsome. |
| ADVERBIAL: | (I'll go) by bus or on foot. |
| VERB PHRASE: | (Jim) saw the place, thought over the offer, but decided against it. |

Chomsky (1957: 36) goes so far as to make conjoinability in a coordinate construction a criterion for class identity. Dik (1968: 27–9), however, suggests that the equivalence between the members of a coordinate construction is one of function rather than class or category, citing examples like:

I saw him and the man who was late yesterday.

In this sentence there is a coordination of a pronoun and a noun phrase including a relative clause, items that differ in internal structure and, to some extent, in external relations, e.g. *him* must be converted to *he* to appear in subject position (as in a passive transformation), but *the man who was late yesterday* remains unchanged.

A further point arising from our general formula is the identity of function or class between the constituents and the construction as a whole. In the above example both coordinates might have been described as noun phrases, and the total is a noun phrase, but, whereas the constituents are each singular, the construction is plural (cf. Lyons, 1968: 233). It should, however, be noted that these limitations seem only to apply to coordinations involving nouns and noun phrases.

Although, then, broad identity of function and class is required within a coordinate construction, the actual class of such constructions, as we saw above, has a wide range of possibilities. As a result, syntactic ambiguity, of the type Dik (1968: 236–41) terms "relational", can arise when the precise domain of the coordination is unclear, e.g. Wells's classic *old men and women* (1947: section 3). Here the ambiguity arises because the coordination can be of noun phrases as in (a) or of nouns as in (b) of Figure 78. Of a similar nature is the ambiguity of *John read and answered letters*, where the coordination may be either of two verbs *read* and *answered*, the two jointly forming a verb phrase with their object *letters*, or of two verb phrases *read* (with unspecified object) and *answered letters*.

Coordinate constructions vary not only in their grammatical class but in their length. They do this by extending a single construction rather than by complicating the structure with further construc-

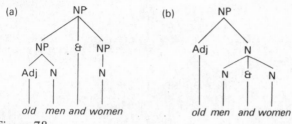

*Figure 78*

tions. There is no general linguistic limit on the number of co-ordinated elements (though there are, of course, psychological and physiological ones):

(At the bar they had) whisky and brandy and gin . . .

However, particular coordinators do place their own semantically determined restrictions, cf.:

John was (tall,) dark and handsome.
John was (tall,) dark or handsome.          [I forget which.]
John was (*tall,) dark but handsome.

The conjunction *but* may thus coordinate only two items. Some speakers of English also feel uncomfortable about using *both . . . and* and even *either . . . or* with more than two elements, e.g.:

? both England and Scotland and Wales
(?) either England or Scotland or Wales.

The pattern otherwise is to have two or more members in a co-ordinate construction.

In longer constructions a further complexity arises: the possibility of layered or hierarchical coordination, i.e. coordinations of elements that are themselves coordinated. For example, a waitress given an order for *bacon and egg and fish and chips* would, it is to be hoped, interpret the order as in Figure 79 rather than as including a combination of *egg and fish* or as four separate dishes. (Custom would obviously help here in her interpretation.) Higher groupings are possible, as when the waitress passes on the above order to the kitchen staff, along with another order for a different table, . . . *and steak and mushrooms and tripe and onions*. Genuine ambiguity could arise, however, when there are few contextual clues, as in a sentence like:

I've written to Jim and David and Margaret,

where David could be grouped with Jim or with Margaret or with

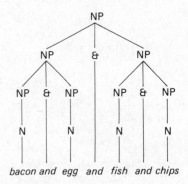

Figure 79

neither. In spoken language, such factors as intonation, rhythm and tempo will generally make it clear which interpretation is intended.

Coordinate constructions are thus unlimited both in length and in depth, and this has made them something of a problem for generative grammarians. It would be theoretically possible to generate coordinate structures with a (recursive) rule of the type:

NP → NP' (NP).

The difficulty is, though, that even assuming that structural descriptions could be assigned without problems (but see chapter 4), the tree diagram developed would be of the format of Figure 80, which hardly represents the correct structure of a coordination – where all

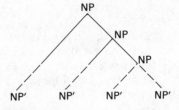

Figure 80

constituents are equally closely related. It was therefore assumed from the beginning in generative grammar that coordinate constructions would be derived transformationally. Since, however, it would be duplicative to have a separate rule for each kind of coordination (noun phrase, verb, verb phrase, etc.), and since a coordination of constituents like *John and Mary came* was thought always to be equivalent to a sentence coordination like *John came, and Mary came*, it was believed that all other coordinates should be

200

derived from sentence coordinations. However, as Dik (1968: 78) pointed out, a relatively simple sentence like:

> Noah and his wife gave the elephants, lions and tigers food and drink at sunrise, noon and sunset.

would have to be derived from thirty-six ($2 \times 3 \times 2 \times 3$) different underlying sentences. Even more significantly, the sentence does not seem to refer to thirty-six different events (*Noah gave the elephants food at sunrise/His wife gave the elephants food at sunrise/*etc.). This point comes out clearly when we contrast

> John and Mary kissed.
> John and Mary failed.

The first sentence certainly refers to a single event, and does not resolve into \**John kissed, and Mary kissed.* In the second sentence, on the other hand, John and Mary may be understood as acting either as a group or separately, in which case the sentence corresponds to *John failed, and Mary failed.* This kind of ambiguity comes about because a coordination may either be a close-knit unit, forming what Dik calls a coordination of members, or a loose-knit combination with each element contracting a separate but parallel relationship to the rest of the sentence.

Because of the inherent difficulties of the transformational analysis, generative grammarians have come to prefer "rule schemata" for coordination. These are essentially abbreviatory devices for (possibly infinite) sets of phrase-structure rules that generate coordinate structures directly. Unfortunately they rather belie the generative aim of producing an infinite range of data with finite means, since the schemata are basically non-finite in nature.

A final issue for generativists and non-generativists alike is the question of the markers of coordination (or coordinators). The first point is how obligatory or optional their occurrence is. In some languages, e.g. Chinese, Malay, it is normal for the coordination to remain unmarked, and it even happens in English, when the co-ordinated elements are given in an exemplificatory kind of list, cf.:

> (What does the shop sell?)
> They sell household articles, tools, gardening accessories . . .
> (that sort of thing).

Alternatively *and* might have been used between each coordinate; or again it might have been used only before the final one. We might represent the three patterns thus:

> (i) A, B, C, D, e.g. *beef, pork, lamb, chicken*

    (ii)  A & B & C & D, e.g. *beef and pork and lamb and chicken*

    (iii)  A, B, C & D, e.g. *beef, pork, lamb and chicken.*

In the case of correlative coordinators like *both. . . and, either. . . or,* there is in addition a proclitic item that precedes the whole co-ordination, or, in the case of verb-final languages like Japanese, follows it.

    Because coordinators are grammatical in value, they are some-times described as semantically empty. This is obviously inaccurate, since they may have at least the following different values:

    (a)  additive (or "combinatory"), e.g. *and,*
    (b)  alternative, e.g. *or,*
    (c)  adversative, e.g. *but.*

The last may be regarded as a variant (a), since *but* can be inter-preted as roughly 'and surprisingly' in *I liked it but John didn't* or as '(and) instead' in *I don't want margarine but (I do want) butter.*

    Finally let us remind ourselves of the paradox of coordination. It brings together two equivalent items to form a construction that is (more or less) equivalent to either of them on its own. This is proved by the fact that the coordination may itself be coordinated (and so on, *ad infinitum*). How can the whole be the same as part of itself? This is a problem that will face us as we proceed to examine the different units of the rank scale in detail.

## A critical view of rank

It was apparent in our examination of the tagmemic and systemic view of rank at the beginning of this chapter that the traditional rank units of sentence, clause, phrase, and word had simply been sup-plemented by the new minimum unit of morpheme and that the modern view of embedding and coordination were accommodated as auxiliary devices. On closer scrutiny, however, we may find, in the light of our knowledge of embedding and coordination, that the traditional rank scale needs revision. A straightforward way of assessing the problem will be to scrutinize the units of the scale in turn, starting at the top.

    The sentence, as a unit of written language, is of course relatively easy to define – as any sequence of words bounded by full stop or beginning of the text on the one side and by full stop or end of the text on the other. "Full stop" is taken here to include exclamation mark and question mark. There is, however, a difficulty with colons, semi-colons and dashes – which seem to be different levels of compromise between full stop and comma. (I have preferred the traditional British term "full stop" to the technical and/or American "period".) But the real problem is: how do writers decide where to put their full stops? The answer is partly a matter of how they were trained in reading and writing; but we can safely assume that writers would not be able to use full stops with even their current standard of accuracy if these did not correspond to some kind of boundary for which they have at least an intuitive feeling. What we need not assume is that this intuitive sentence (of our linguistic competence) corresponds precisely to the prescriptions of traditional grammar.

Traditional attempts to define the sentence were generally either psychological or logical-analytic in nature: the former type spoke of "a complete thought" or some other inaccessible psychological phenomenon; the latter type, following Aristotle, expected to find every sentence made up of a logical subject and logical predicate, units that themselves rely on the sentence for their definition. A more fruitful approach is that of Jespersen (1924: 307), who suggests testing the completeness and independence of a sentence, by assessing its potential for occurring alone, as a complete utterance.

The criterion of potential for independent occurrence as an utterance, though crucial, is not, however, sufficient. Consider the problem of punctuating the following word sequences:

(1) I warned Tom I was late
(2) Bill taught linguistics in Manchester he also taught phonetics.

In (1) we are unable to say whether the sequence forms one sentence or two; and in (2) we have two sentences but are unable to say whether the dependent adverbial *in Manchester* belongs to the first or to the second. In each case, therefore, we need to know the intonation pattern and/or the meaning before we can come to a decision. The essential criteria for dividing up a text into sentences are therefore: that the sequences selected as sentences should be the minimum units capable of occurring elsewhere as complete utterances without any change in form, accentual pattern or meaning; and that the sequences shall be so selected as to leave no remainder of non-sentences. This amounts to applying an extraction or omission test.

Most sequences identified in the above manner will correspond to traditional sentences, but we meet a problem in "response sentences", i.e. either answers to *wh*-questions or completive com-meats appended to statements, for instance, the items italicized below:

> A: When did John arrive? B: *At 3 o'clock.*
> A: John's coming this afternoon. B: *At 3 o'clock.*

Such "response sentences" are elliptical in the sense that they require a preceding context for their interpretation, and, while they form separate sentences when used by a new speaker, they would be reckoned as part of the same sentence in, for instance,

> John arrived this afternoon – at 3 o'clock.

Coordinate sentences present a different kind of problem. Consider first the sequence:

> The men walked too fast – the women walked too slowly.

This would undoubtedly fulfil the criteria for two separate sentences (though it is surprising how often writers use a comma when the sentences have such strong semantic links as this). But what is the effect of inserting a coordinator like *and, or, but, so* (and perhaps *though*)? The traditionalists are rather inconsistent here, forbidding a separate sentence with *and*, frowning on one with *but*, preferring one with *so*, etc. But does the coordinator do any more than mark a relationship that in our case may already be there? If the constituents of coordinate noun phrases are merely simple noun phrases, why are not the constituents of coordinate sentences themselves just simple sentences, rather than clauses?

This brings us on naturally to a consideration of the clause itself. If coordinate clauses can be regarded as no more than a coordination of two sentences, then certainly subordinate clauses can be regarded as no more than sentences embedded at some point within another (outer or "matrix") sentence. It goes without saying that different kinds of subordinate clause represent embeddings at different points in the structure of a sentence, either as direct constituents or as constituents of constituents, etc. Take the following italicized clauses:

> (1) Margaret regretted *that she had been unkind to Jim.*
> (2) *When she came back*, he was smoking a pipe.
> (3) The girl *who lives next door* speaks Breton.

In (1) the sentence has been embedded as an object, in (2) as a time adverbial, and in (3) as a postmodifier within the subject noun phrase.

Every subordinate clause may thus be described in terms of embedding, a mechanism that is already required for grammatical description in any case. It is therefore perfectly possible to forgo the clause as a grammatical unit; it is not essential in the same way as the sentence. In fact, if we do try to treat the clause as a necessary step along the rank scale, we run into difficulties when we attempt to exhaustively analyse into clauses a sentence like the following:

Whatever he does – is interesting.

In this sentence our second, or "main", clause has no subject, and, if we ask what the subject is, it is the first clause. In other words, we do not have two clauses side by side and simply added together to form a sentence (as tagmemics and systemic grammar give the impression) but rather one sentence occurring (embedded) within the other; and the label "clause" only seems appropriate for the inner sentence, not for a mere sentence remainder, which is all the "main clause" is.

Some cases of sentence-embedding are not traditionally described as clauses, cf.:

I intended *that John should start the meeting early.*
I intended *John to start the meeting early.*
I intended *to start the meeting early.*

Whereas the first sentence contains a straightforward clause as its object, the second and third contain what are sometimes referred to as "non-finite clauses" (strictly a contradiction, since a finite verb is one criterion for clause status) or perhaps better "clausoids". The embedded sentence in the second example, though having a non-finite verb and therefore no subject-verb concord, has otherwise all the normal attributes of a sentence, subject, verb, object, adverbial, etc. The third sentence-embedding additionally lacks an overt subject (we are required to interpret the "main-clause" subject as doing double duty) but has all the other attributes. If we use the label "clause", we must probably extend it to cover these cases. But how far can we go along the following scale:

The train *which is now arriving at platform three* . . .
The train *now arriving at platform three* . . .
The train *now at platform three* . . .
The train *at platform three*
The train *nearby* . . .

At some stage we shade over from sentence-embedding to noun-phrase embedding within an adverbial postmodifier of a noun phrase. But where?

The phrase is no easier a unit to delimit than the clause, but for different reasons. We saw at the beginning of this chapter that the phrase does not constitute a single point on the rank scale, since a whole series of different size units are traditionally labelled as phrases. We noted how an adjective phrase can be regarded as a constituent of the noun phrase, and so on. In any such series of different sizes of phrase, each occurring within a larger one, the largest will of course be a direct constituent of the sentence, and the smallest will be a minimum construction of words.

The word itself is far from being a clear-cut unit. As we shall see in our next chapter, the written language provides no clear answer to the question "What is a word?" (cf. the inconsistent spellings *matchbox, horse-box, telephone box*), and phonological factors such as stress are also inconclusive. Basically, word status is a matter of syntactic and semantic freedom of occurrence; we have much greater freedom to use the word *star* than the root *astr(o)-*, for instance. But the grounds for defining the word as a particular size of unit are unsure. A word can be just as big as a corresponding phrase: compare *un-success-ful-ness* with *lack of success*. It may therefore be possible to regard the word as a special kind of phrase, one in which the members are close-knit, both grammatically and semantically. We recognize this status of affairs by describing combinations of morphemes within a word as morphological, but combinations outside the word as syntactic. Perhaps the word should be thought of as a lexical rather than a grammatical unit.

Having detached the clause and the word from the rank scale, because they each involve more than simple constituency relations, we are left with a simple three-term system:

sentence > (phrase >) morpheme.

In this simplified schema we have a maximum unit, the sentence, an independent speech-act, which has as its constituents either morphemes directly or some kind of construction; this construction in turn may have as its constituents either morphemes or some lower construction; and so on. Each of these intermediate constructions is a phrase, and obviously there are phrases of different rank, depending on how directly they are sentence constituents.

We may represent this alternative view of rank in a diagram (Figure 81). In this alternative view, then, the extreme units are sentence and morpheme, while all the intermediate units are different kinds of phrases. All that is then needed to complete the picture is: coordination, which allows structuring at one particular rank without changing the rank; and embedding, which allows a possibly recursive loopback to a higher rank; and perhaps also the tagmemic concept of "skipping" to give a direct route to the morpheme in particular structural positions. The only point not adequately catered for here is the relationship between the morpheme and the word, and that is the question we turn to now in the next chapter.

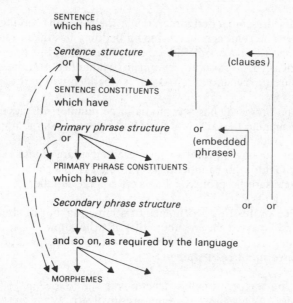

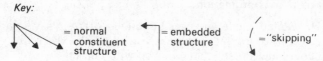

*Figure 81 An alternative view of rank*

## Questions for study

1 Make a traditional analysis of the following sentences into clauses, then phrases, then words, then morphemes, noting any difficulties:
   (a) Soon after the boys had left, their mother put on the kettle.
   (b) If the bowler touches the ball before it hits the wicket and the batsman is out of his crease the umpire will declare him out.

2 List all the linguistic scales and their subvarieties that were discussed in the first section of this chapter, providing each with an alternative name you find apposite and an example you find illuminating.

3 Identify the embedded structures in the following, noting the point in the sentence where the embedding has taken place. Sentence (a) is a simple unembedded sentence, but in sentences (b) to (f) it either appears embedded in some other structure or has another structure embedded within it (or both).
   (a) The professor has accepted a large number of students.
   (b) I imagine that the professor has accepted a large number of students.
   (c) My nephew's professor has accepted a large number of students who cannot speak a foreign language.
   (d) I caused the professor to accept a large number of students.
   (e) The professor's acceptance of a large number of students embarrassed the members of staff who knew about it.
   (f) I regret that the professor agreed to consider accepting a large number of students.

4 What are the coordinated structures in the following sentence? What classes of item are involved? What are the markers of coordination?

   He wanted bacon and eggs but either forgot to say so or came down too late for breakfast, and so he was both hungry and thirsty, and annoyed with himself.

5 Divide the following unpunctuated text into sentences, noting alternative divisions where they exist. Can these be marked in spoken language (through intonation, rhythm, etc.)?

   Mary reminded John about the arrangement she would write home if the weather deteriorated he would leave early even though he had forgotten he was on duty.

6 Describe the sentences given under (1)(a) and (1)(b) in terms of the "alternative view of rank" suggested in the last section of the chapter.

**Further reading**

On the rank scale and other scales: Halliday (1961), especially section 7; Cook (1969), chapter 1; Berry (1975), chapters 8, 9; Berry (1977), chapter 2. On embedding: Chomsky (1965), chapter 1, section 2; Koutsoudas (1966), chapter 8; Fowler (1974), chapter 7 (also covers coordination). On coordination: Koutsoudas (1966), chapter 7; Dik (1968); Cook (1969), 99–106; Halliday and Hasan (1976), chapter 5. On a critical view of rank: Jespersen (1924), 305–12; Lyons (1968), chapter 5; Allerton (1969).

## Chapter 10
# Morphological structure

---

### Words and morphemes

In chapter 3 we described the morpheme as the basic unit of grammar. We saw how words like *boys, inexpensive* and *fire-engine* break down into morphemes. Although we met problems in the case of unique morphemes like *cran-* and of pseudo-morphemes like the *-appoint* of *disappoint*, we worked with the idea of a morpheme as a minimum meaningful unit. We were, however, aware that morphemes are lacking in precision, definition and independence compared with words. It is easy to assert that the element *milit-* has morphemic status in the words *military, militant, militate, militia* but equally easy to see that the meaning of the morpheme is not so definite that it totally predicts the meaning of the word.

The word, itself, may be thought of as the minimum lexical unit, in the sense of the minimum unit with an independently usable meaning. But this will not quite do, since it leaves out of account the problem of idioms, such as *catch a crab*, 'jam oars when rowing', *(run) hell for leather*, 'very fast, hurriedly'. Here we find that our minimum semantic unit is even larger than the word. So there must be more than just semantic factors at stake in the notion of WORD.

The word (like the sentence) is apparently defined for us by the written language – at least for languages that have a written form. Writing systems are, however, generally not especially systematic in their traditional conventions for putting spaces between words. Consider, for instance, the following sets from English:

     matchbox      firewood
     horse-box     fire-engine
     telephone box  fire insurance

Every item is a compounding of two elements that could have been words in their own right but are here merged to give a compound which has a meaning that is more than just the sum of its parts. A *telephone box*, for example, is not just any box with a telephone in it, but rather a box-like building specially constructed for making telephone calls. All the above items agree in being noun compounds; yet three different modes of spelling are used, suggesting they are one, one-and-a-half or two words, respectively.

If, then, we are to find an additional criterion to our lexical one for word status, it must be other than orthographic. We described the word as an independent unit, and it has syntactic as well as semantic independence. This independence or "freedom" is sometimes, following Bloomfield (1935: 177f.), seen as a question of the item's ability to occur as a complete sentence. This is too strong a requirement: it will not be met by a host of words like *the, is, of.* A more practical method is to use two of our operational tests (see chapter 5), viz. insertion and permutation. If, for example, we compare the Spanish verb form *habl-o* 'speak-I' (which is one word) with the English two-word phrase *I speak*, we find that, whereas Spanish allows absolutely nothing to intervene between the *habl-* and the *-o* and never allows the order of the sequence to be changed, English, on the other hand, allows both insertion and permutation, cf.:

>    *Insertion:*   I usually speak French.
>                   fortunately
>                   etc.
> *Permutation*:   (I said I'd speak and . . .)
>                   speak I will.

Compare also Lyons's tests of "interruptibility" and "positional mobility" (1968: 202).

Such tests, then, give us an indication of the syntactic independence of two morphemes, and thus of whether they should be written together as one word or not. Unfortunately, though, the problem often extends beyond two adjacent morphemes and involves matters of constituent structure. Imagine we have a sequence (. . . $X'''$) $X''$ $X'$ $Y$, with the constituent structure shown in Figure 82. Now it may be the case that $X''$ and $X'$ are clearly separable as separate words but $X'$ and $Y$ are bound together in one word. Examples from English would be *a hundred and six-th*, *the*

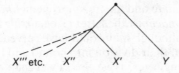

*Figure 82*

211

*King of England's hat, left of centre-ish*. In one sense *a*, *hundred*, *and* and *six* are separate words; but in another the *-th* is attached to an item to form a single word.

The problem is not, of course, confined to English. The Turkish suffix *-li*, for instance, is normally added to a noun to form a derived adjective (rather like English *-ly* or *-ish*), e.g. *rutubet*, 'moisture', beside *rutubetli*, 'moist'; *ev*, 'house', beside *evli*, 'married'. But the suffix may also be appended to a whole phrase (Figure 83). Similar phenomena are found in many languages.

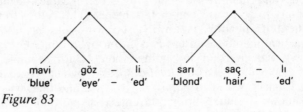

*Figure 83*

In Eskimo and a number of Amerindian languages the morphology of the verb requires a mention not only of the subject but also of the object (for transitive verbs). As a result a word like

taku  -  b  -  a  -  ŋa
'see'  -  pres.  -  'he'  -  'me'  =  'he sees me'

in Eskimo incorporates a whole transitive sentence within itself, bringing the word closer to the sentence.

Given the notion of 'word', a BOUND morpheme is then defined as a morpheme that only ever occurs as part of a word, never as a word in its own right; a FREE (or perhaps better "separable") morpheme, on the other hand, is one that may do precisely that. (Strictly speaking, we should speak of a bound MORPH, since it is possible , as we shall see below, to have variant forms of a morpheme, i.e. allomorphs, one or more of which is bound and one or more of which is free, e.g. *wive-* (as in *wives*) beside *wife*.) Bound and free morphemes are thus distinguished in terms of their POTENTIAL for independent occurrence as a word. Our examples in chapter 3 (*boys, loved, inexpensive, dentist, fire-engine, washing machine*) provided us with the bound morphemes *-(e)s* 'noun Plural', *-(e)d* 'past tense', *in-, -ive, dent-, -ist, -ing* and the free morphemes *boy, love, expense, fire, engine, wash, machine*, the latter all occurring as parts of words in our examples, although they could have served as entire words.

Independently of their division into bound and free, morphemes in apparently all languages, as we also saw in chapter 3, fall into one of two major classes, those with primarily lexical value, so-called

ROOTS, and those with primarily grammatical value, which we may term NON-ROOTS, or simply "grammatical morphemes". Roots may be illustrated by *boy, love, expense, dent-, econom-*; non-roots by *in-, -ive, -ing, -(e)s, the, of.* Roots give an independent specification of meaning; they also have an open class membership, which is easily extended through borrowing from other dialects or languages. Non-roots, on the other hand, make a semantic contribution that is subsidiary to that of lexical items, either modifying the meaning of the latter or organizing the relationship between different lexical items.

Roots may be either bound or free. In English the vast majority of all roots are free, but there are a reasonable number of bound roots, e.g. *dent-* (cf. *dental, dentist*), *econom-* (cf. *economy, economic*), *matern-* (cf. *maternal, maternity*). In inflecting languages, on the other hand, bound roots are in the majority, since the major categories of word at least (i.e. nouns, adjectives, verbs and possibly adverbs) require some kind of inflection whenever they occur. In Latin, for instance, a noun stem like *amīc-*'friend' occurs in words like *amīcus, amīcum, amīcī*, where it has a companion bound morpheme indicating its number and case. The situation is similar for nouns in Russian and other Slavonic languages; even though certain feminine and neuter nouns (e.g. кни́га/'knigə/, 'book'; чу́вство /'tʃufstvo/, 'feeling') occur apparently without an inflection in the genitive plural form, we are possibly justified in setting up a zero morpheme (see below).

Non-roots, also, may be either bound or free. When they are free, they of course constitute grammatical words in their own right, and are often referred to as PARTICLES. (An alternative term is "marker", used, for instance, by Hockett (1958: 209). This has the disadvantage that some writers use it in the more general sense of 'structural signal', thus making it cover affixes as well.) Examples from English are *the, than, of,* infinitival *to.* Languages of the so-called isolating type, such as Chinese and Vietnamese, make extensive use of such particles, since they do the work that is accomplished by bound grammatical morphemes in other languages.

Bound non-roots, where they do occur, are generally referred to as AFFIXES. The relationship between roots, affixes and particles may thus be given as follows:

|  | BOUND | FREE |
|---|---|---|
| GRAMMATICAL | affixes | particles |
| LEXICAL | bound roots | free roots |

Affixes may not normally be added to each other, cf. *\*un-ish, \*re-ation*. Being both bound and non-lexical they normally have to

213

be added to a lexical element to form a word, e.g. *un(real), (tempt)ation, (book)s*.

The lexical element to which an affix is added is in the simplest cases just a lexical morpheme, i.e. a root, as in the examples above. However, an affix may also be added to a combination of morphemes, as in *un-gentlemanly, football-er, revisionist-s*. This complex or compound element to which an affix is added is termed a STEM, and the word formed is a COMPLEX WORD. A stem is not specified for size, and a root may be thought of as simply a minimum stem. For example, although each of the words *boy-s, worker-s, footballer-s* and *revisionist-s* consists of a noun stem plus the plural affix *-(e)s*, only *boy* is a minimum stem, and therefore a root. The other stems all include roots (as does every stem); *footballer*, in fact, includes two.

Amongst affixes two fundamentally different kinds need to be distinguished, giving two different kinds of complex word: DERIVATIONAL affixes, which form DERIVED words; and INFLECTIONAL affixes, which form INFLECTED words. Derived words or stems may, in all contexts where they appear, be replaced by a simple word or stem to give a sentence of the same type. For example, in the sentence:

The florist ordered those beautiful flowers.

we find two derived words *florist* (from the bound root *flor-*, cf. *floral*) and *beautiful*, each of which can have as substitutions a whole range of simple words, e.g. *man, girl, thief*, etc. and *nice, pretty, dear*, etc. respectively. In the same sentence we find two inflected words *ordered* and *flowers* which may only be replaced by words which are inflected in a similar way, e.g. *orders, expected, expects*, etc. and *plants, vegetables, fruit*, etc. respectively. An inflected word, then, in at least some of the contexts where it occurs, may have its place taken only by a word of similar structure: this is because inflectional affixes play a part in expressing syntactic relations between words, such as concord and government, while derivational affixes do not. Thus while derivational affixes like *un-, re-, ish, -ation, -al* may determine the major syntactic class of the word they form, inflectional affixes like noun plural *-(e)s*, verb past *-(e)d*, verbal *-ing* leave the major class unchanged, but do determine the subcategory, such as past or plural, which may have to agree with another word in the sentence. On the formal side, derivational affixes tend to occur nearer to the root, inflectional ones nearer to the outside of a word, as in *flor-ist-s*.

Since inflectional affixes thus work more at the level of phrase or sentence, they are not usually thought of as forming new words but rather as giving variant forms of an already existing one. No one, for example, would expect to find separate explanations in a dictionary for *consult, consults, consulted, consulting*; if anything we would expect such matters to be dealt with in a grammar. On the other hand, we would expect to find separate entries for *consult, consultant, consultation* and *consulting room*. In a way these are all different words in more than just the obvious sense; they are different lexical items or LEXEMES.

Our set of *consult, consults, consulted, consulting* could, however, be said to be variant forms of the same lexeme – we might even call them "allolexes". There are still other senses of the word "word" to distinguish: (1) "word-form" v. "word" in the sense that two homonyms like *bat* are the same word (-form) yet not the same word; (2) "word-type" v. "word-token" (see chapter 2), in the sense that different occurrences of the same "word" constitute different "words" (cf. Matthews, 1974: 20f.; Lyons, 1968: 68–70, 196–8).

The study of the production of new lexical items, i.e. lexical morphology, is generally termed WORD-FORMATION and involves one of two processes, DERIVATION and COMPOUNDING. Derivation, as we have seen, is the process by which derivational affixes are added to stems (including simple roots) to form a derived word. Compounding, the second process, means combining two stems (either or both of which may be single roots) to give COMPOUND words, e.g. *mad-* + *-man, foot-* + *-ball, washing* + *football* + *player*.

The rather complicated relationship between the different kinds of non-simple word and the processes by which they are formed is displayed in Figure 84.

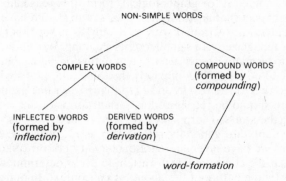

*Figure 84*

Compound words present us with the same kind of paradox as do coordinate constructions (which we examined in chapter 9). By "compound word" we mean a word made up of two stems, each of which, if they are free stems, could have occurred as a word in its own right. If we apply the tests described above (insertion and permutation), how can both the compound word (e.g. *darkroom*) and the component words (e.g. *dark* and *room*) simultaneously fulfil our criteria for a minimum separable unit?

The resolution of this paradox lies partly in the fact that the word-status applies to particular occurrences (or "tokens") of morphemes and morpheme sequences rather than to the morphemes as types. Moreover, in those particular occurrences we must check not only for syntactic limitations (non-insertion and non-permutation) but also for specialization of meaning. For example, *darkroom* not only refuses to be expanded to *\*very-darkroom* or *\*dark-blue-room*, but it also limits the meaning of *dark* to '(potentially) totally light-excluding' and adds to the meaning of the whole word 'used for photographic or similar purposes'. Similarly, it is one of the facts of English word-formation that a *spaceship* is a ship for travelling through space, but that *airship* and *cargo ship* are to be interpreted differently. This specialization of interpretation is sometimes referred to as the lexicalization of a compound. We shall find something very similar for derived words, when we discuss lexical morphology in more detail later in this chapter.

## Morphology and phonology

We have so far considered morphemes without any reference to their phonological (or graphological) form. It is reasonable, however, to expect that any morpheme we set up should have a fairly consistent form associated with it, if only to ensure that it is efficiently recognized as a signaller of its meaning. We require a morpheme to be manifested by a particular phonological segment, then; but it need not always be precisely the same one. It is obvious, for example, that the items *a* /ə/ and *an* /ən/ carry the same meaning and therefore should be recognized as variant forms of the same morpheme (the stressed forms /eɪ/ and /æn/ respectively also occur). Such variants are generally referred to as ALLOMORPHS; and the examples we have given are PHONOLOGICALLY CONDITIONED, in the sense that the choice of which variant to use is determined for the speaker by the nature of the phonological context. In our example /ə/ occurs before consonants and /ən/ before vowels. There is a similar distribution for the two allomorphs of the English definite article *the*, viz. /ðə/ before consonants, /ðɪ/ before vowels, e.g. /ðə pɛə/ *the pear*, but /ðɪ ˈæpl̩/ *the apple*. We should note that, although these variants are phonologically conditioned, it is not possible, with a knowledge of the phonology of English, to predict that the allomorphs will take the particular form they do. We might compare with them *either pear* (/'aɪðə/) and *either apple* ('aɪðər/) and see the pattern:

|  | BEFORE CONSONANT | BEFORE VOWEL |
|---|---|---|
| *a(n)* | ə | ən |
| *the* | ðə | ðɪ |
| *either* | 'aɪðə | 'aɪðər |

(Alternative pronunciations for *either* are /i:ðə/ and /i:ðər/ respectively. In some styles of English pronunciation, e.g. S. W. English, Scots English, most American English, both occurrences of *either* will be pronounced identically, with /r/.)

Other cases of phonological variation in the form of a morpheme, however, may be explained purely in terms of phonological patterning. Consider, for instance, the English regular noun plural and verb past-tense affixes, which we might term /-Z/ and /-D/ respectively:

| /-Z/ | | /-D/ | |
|---|---|---|---|
| (1) | /–ɪz/ after sibilants and affricates (viz. /s,z,ʃ,ʒ,tʃ,dʒ/), e.g. *horses* | (1) | /–ɪd/ after alveolar plosives (viz. /t,d/), e.g. *lifted* |
| (2) | /–s/ after other voiceless consonants, e.g. *cats* | (2) | /–t/ after other voiceless consonants, e.g. *pushed* |
| (3) | /–z/ in all other cases, i.e. after all other voiced sounds, e.g. *dogs* | (3) | /–d/ in all other cases, i.e. after all other voiced sounds, e.g. *pulled* |

These are not simply cases of phonologically conditioned allomorphs. For each morpheme, one allomorph (/-z/ or /-d/ respectively) occurs whenever it gives a sequence that accords with English phonology. Thus after *pen* /pen/, for instance, either /-ɪz/ or /-s/ would be phonologically acceptable (they give us the actual English words *pennies* and *pence*), but only /-z/ is the accepted form of noun plural morpheme. On the other hand, /-z/ would be impossible in the contexts where /-ɪz/ and /-s/ occur, cf. */'hɔːsz/, */kætz/. We may conclude that /-z/ is the preferred, basic or underlying form of the morpheme, and that the other allomorphs are quite automatic phonological variants, /-s/ occurring to ensure that consonant clusters are, if not all voiced, then all voiceless, and /-ɪz/ occurring to prevent a sequence of two sibilant consonants. Everything is thus

phonologically predictable except for the precise quality of the
inserted vowel /ɪ/, but this has /ə/ as a variant in any case. The same
applies to /-d/ *vis-à-vis* the verb past-tense morpheme. Such matters
as these, then, are better taken care of in the phonology rather than
the grammar of a language; they are sometimes accounted for under
the heading of "sandhi" (cf. Bloomfield, 1935: 186–9; Matthews,
1974: chapter 6).

Even more strictly phonological variation takes place in languages which have vowel harmony, like Turkish. Almost all Turkish
suffixes have vocalic elements that vary according to the last vowel
of the stem to which they are added. Suffixes with a close vowel have
four variants (using the vowels *i, ı, ü, u*), while suffixes with an open
vowel have two variants (using the vowels *e, a*). The following
examples, translating 'in my NOUN', make the matter clear:

| ev | - | im | - | de | kitab | - | ım | - | da |
|----|---|----|---|----|-------|---|----|---|-----|
| 'house' | - | 'my' | - | 'in' | 'book' | - | 'my' | - | 'in' |

| göz | - | üm | - | de | yol | - | um | - | da |
|-----|---|----|---|----|-----|---|----|---|-----|
| 'eye' | - | 'my' | - | 'in' | 'road' | - | 'my' | - | 'in' |

The suffix for 'my' thus has four "allomorphs" and the suffix for 'in'
(also 'on', etc.) has two; but the rules of Turkish vowel harmony
require this to be so. The variation is not therefore just in individual
morphemes but in all such morphemes, and should thus be
described outside morphology. The same applies to the pronunciation of final written *-s* in European Portuguese, which is pronounced either /z/,/ʃ/,/ʒ/ or ø, thus giving four different
"allomorphs" for each word like *mais* 'more', *os/as* 'the' (plural).
It is better then to reserve the label "allomorph" for phonologically
unpredictable variants of morphemes.

The variants we have discussed so far have all been phonologically conditioned, but it has also been proposed that MORPHOLOGI-
CALLY CONDITIONED ALLOMORPHS be set up. Within the English
plural morpheme, for instance, we might find not only the regular
(phonologically determined) allomorphs /-s/,-z/,/ɪz/ but also the
/-ən/ of *ox-en* and the /-rən/ of *child-ren* (this latter word would also
have allomorphy in its stem (i.e. root), /tʃaɪld/ v. /tʃɪld-/ or /tʃ ɪld-/).
Similarly, the forms *good* /gʊd/, *bett-er* /'bet-ə/ and *be-st* /be-st/
exhibit morphologically conditioned allomorphy of the root compared with the regular *cold, cold-er, cold-est*. The difficulty with
such cases is that the so-called variant, associated as it is with a
particular morphological context, partly has the function of signalling that context. When hearing /'ɒks-ən/ or seeing *oxen*, for
instance, a listener/reader partly uses the /-ən/-*en* to recognize the

word *oxen* as opposed to, say, *boxes*. Similarly the *bett-* of *better* is not only a variant of *good* but also a clear marker of comparative (probably a clearer marker than the murmured vowel of *-er*). Describing these cases purely in terms of allomorphic variation is therefore not fully realistic, although it has been standard practice for those working within this grammatical framework.

Conditioned allomorphs are conventionally distinguished from NON-CONDITIONED ALLOMORPHS (also termed "free variant allomorphs"). These are variant forms of a morpheme that may be used regardless of the context in which they occur. In English, pairs like /plæk/ = /plɑːk/ *plaque*, /skɒn/ = /skəʊn/ *scone*, show variation between totally equivalent forms which may be freely substituted for each other. It may be that a non-conditioned allomorph is characteristic of a group of speakers within a speech community, i.e. it is dialectally marked; or it may be a characteristic of the individual speaker; there may even be variation within one speaker's idiolect, either random or according to social situation (his "style" or "register").

Whatever variation there may be in the form of morphemes, we generally assume that they are realized or represented by some phonological sequence or other. There are cases, however, where we are tempted to make a morphemic analysis but where there is no basis for choosing morphemic segments. We found it relatively easy to recognize an *-er*, 'more (comparative)', element in *better*, and were thus able to postulate an element *bett-*/ bet-/ as a variant, an allomorph, of *good*, despite the total lack of common phonological form. With *worse* /wɜːs/, however, the case is different, since we cannot even recognize an *-er* element. What are we to do? Make an arbitrary division into, say, /wɜː-/ plus /-s/? Or follow Lyons (1968: 183–4) in saying that the morpheme is not a segment at all, that sometimes each morpheme corresponds to a morph but sometimes is "represented in the substance of the language in other ways"? Neither solution seems perfect, and the trouble is that not only are there other examples like this[1] (e.g. French *au* /o/ = *à + le*, corresponding to *à la*) but that, once we free our morpheme of its bond to phonological form, we open the way to any kind of lexical or grammatical feature being elevated to morpheme status (e.g. *bull* = two morphemes, 'male' + 'bovine'; Latin *-us*, of *bonus* = three morphemes, 'masculine' + 'nominative' + 'singular'). We shall see, too, that the phonological analysis of affixes, generally, presents

---

[1]  Hockett (1947: 334) refers to them as PORTMANTEAU MORPHS. As a kind of affixation the process is sometimes referred to as SUPPLETION. But these seem no more than "escape labels".

considerable difficulties for a theory of morphemes and allomorphs.

Affixes are conventionally classified according to the place in
which they are attached to their stem. Languages that use affixes
may have either PREFIXES placed before the stem, or SUFFIXES placed
after the stem, or INFIXES interrupting the stem. English prefixes
include *en-* *(enlarge)*, *mis-* *(misjudge)*, *un-* *(unkind)*; note that they
are all derivational. English has dozens of derivational suffixes
including *-en (widen) -ish (biggish)*, and ten or twelve inflectional
ones including *-s, -ed, -ing*. To illustrate infixes we must go outside
English to a language like Tagalog (the official language of the
Philippines) or Cambodian. We may cite Bloomfield's (1935: 218)
examples from Tagalog: *-um-* and *-un-* occurring in the words
/su'mu:lat/, 'one who wrote', and /si'nu:lat/, 'that which was written', compared with the root /'su:lat/, 'write'. It should be noted that
infixation has the effect of making the stem or root morph(eme)
into a discontinuous phonological sequence.

In some languages we find what appears to be a combination of
prefix and suffix operating as a unit. For instance, in Malay the
discontinuous affix *pĕ*———*an* is added to verbal roots like *rasa*,
'feel', and *kĕrja*, 'work', to form the abstract nouns *pĕrasaan* and
*pĕkĕrjaan*, 'work' respectively. Such affixes may be termed CIRCUM-
FIXES. A further example is the affix *ge*———*(e)t* which forms
regular past participles in German, e.g. *ge-leb-t*, 'lived', *ge-töt-et*,
'killed' (there was a similar circumfix for past participles in Old and
Middle English).

We have seen how either a root morpheme or an affix may be
discontinuous. In the Semitic languages it is normal for both to be!
Typically there is a root morpheme consisting of three consonants
(hence "triliteral root") to which (discontinuous) infixes or infix-
cum-suffix or infix-cum-prefix are added. The Arabic root *k-t-b*,
'write', has, for instance, the following words formed from it:

| | | | |
|---|---|---|---|
| *kita:b* | 'book' | *kataba* | 'he wrote' |
| *yaktubu* | 'he writes' | *katabtu* | 'I wrote' |

Discontinuity is thus built into the morphophonemic system of the
language.

Affixes differ, then, in the precise location they are given relative
to their stem. They also differ in the degree to which they harmonize
phonologically with their stem. Although some affixes, e.g. English
*dis-*, *-less*, are invariable in form, other affixes, as we have already
seen, have phonologically conditioned variants, either on an individual basis like English *a/an* or following a general phonological
rule like Turkish vowel harmony. Most "harmonization" serves

simply to ease the pronunciation of the transition from one morpheme to the other, either by avoiding an uncomfortable vowel
sequence or consonant cluster, or by assimilating some phonological features of the affix (such as voicing, place of articulation) to
those of the stem. Sometimes matters go further than the mere
modification of the affix to the stem: in REDUPLICATION the affix is a
segment that is partly or wholly copied from the stem. For instance,
in Gothic a whole class of verbs formed their past (preterite) tense
by prefixing the initial consonant of the stem plus the vowel /e/,
written *aí*, e.g. *slêp-an*, 'to sleep', beside *saí-slêp*, 'slept'. In the San
Blas language of Panama, as reported by Nida (1949: 69), things go
a stage further, in that the whole stem may be repeated, e.g. /mu:a/,
'to rise and fall', beside /mu:amu:a/, 'to rise and fall successively (as
of large waves)', and even /mu:amu:amu:a/, 'to rise and fall successively (as of little ripples)'. This repetition has gone so far as to
become non-arbitrary symbolization.

So far we have tended to assume that all our morphemes, or at
least the morphs that represent them, will be concrete segments that
are simply added together to produce words, as when *-ure* /-jə(r)/ is
added to *fail* /feɪ/ to give *failure* /'feɪljə(r)/. But how do we analyse
such words as *closure* /'kləʊʒə(r)/, where the /j/ of *-ure* has, so to
speak, blended with the /z/ of *close* to give /ʒ/? Or how should we
describe the set of words like *shelf* v. *shelve, sheath* v. *sheathe, house*
(NOUN) . . . (VERB), where a noun with a final voiceless fricative /f,θ,s/
corresponds to a verb with a final voiced fricative /v,ð,z/? The only
way of bringing out the regular pattern involved in such phenomena
is to allow morphs with a phonological form partly or wholly composed of phonetic features like /PALATAL/, /VOICED/. Affixes like this,
sometimes referred to as SIMULFIXES, cannot be regarded as simply
being added on to the stem, like other affixes.

The same problem arises with the so-called SUPERFIXES, i.e.
affixes represented by feature patterns extending not over a single
phoneme but over whole syllables or words. English accentual
patterns could be regarded as affixes of this kind, when they dif-
ferentiate nouns from verbs, e.g. /'ɪnsʌlt/ beside /ɪn'sʌlt/, *insult*;
sometimes simultaneous change in the phonemic sequence is
involved, e.g. /'rebl̩/ beside /rɪ'bel/, *rebel*. Depending on which we
take as the root, either /'−−/ 'noun' or /−'−/ 'verb' could be regarded
as a superfix.

Perhaps even more problematical is the practice, first indulged in
by Sanskrit grammarians, of positing ZERO morphs. A zero morph of
the English plural morpheme is often proposed for words like *sheep,
deer, (air)craft*, that have identical singular and plural forms; or for
the past-tense form of verbs like *hit, shut*; or even for the plural

221

present form of all verbs. Scrutinizing, for instance, the sentences:

(1) The sheep is grazing in the meadow.
(2) The sheep are grazing in the meadow.
(3) The sheep must be grazing in the meadow.

we would find a zero allomorph of the noun plural morpheme in the first sentence, but not in the second; while in the third it would depend on the meaning intended. Because of this difficulty some linguists would prefer to say that the plural morpheme just does not occur with such roots, and that the singular-plural distinction is neutralized (see chapter 7).

Zero morphs are at least normally members of a morpheme with some positive manifestation.[1] Zero morphemes, on the other hand, if accepted, would have a much more shadowy existence, never being overtly realized at all. We may well be happy to set up a zero morpheme for 'genitive plural' in Russian and other Slavonic languages, where this case-number category is a term in a close-knit system of otherwise overt morphemes (see above). On the other hand, we would presumably not wish to set up a zero singular morpheme for all English nouns; yet English derivation does present some plausible examples. Words like *shame* and *fall* have identity of form between their use as noun and as verb; and many cases can be cited of overt suffixes being used to form nouns from verbs, e.g. *betray-al*, or verbs from nouns, e.g. *fright-en*. But that precisely is the difficulty: how, apart from at best semi-relevant historical considerations, are we to decide whether *shame*, for instance, is a verb and a zero-derived noun or a noun and zero-derived verb? (For further discussion, see Haas (1957).)

So far we have thought in terms of an affix, albeit zero in some cases, being added to a stem. Bloomfield (1935: 217), however, suggested the possibility of SUBTRACTIVE morphs (his term was "minus-feature"). Considering French adjective gender pairs like:

| MASCULINE | | FEMININE | |
|-----------|------|----------|--------|
| *plat* | /pla/ | *platte* | /plat/ |
| *laid* | /lɛ/ | *laide* | /lɛd/ |
| *long* | /lɔ̃/ | *longue* | /lɔ̃g/ |
| *gris* | /gri/ | *grise* | /griz/ |

---

[1] Though the positive manifestation may be minimal. An interesting example is seen in Welsh words like *plentyn*, 'child' – *plant*, 'children', which go against the normal Welsh pattern of an unmarked singular form but a plural formed by suffixation. Since *plentyn* and a few other words have a suffix for the singular, shall we set up a singular morpheme for all other words, saying that they have a zero allomorph?

he pointed out that it is simpler to form the phonological patterns of the masculine from the feminine than vice versa (the traditional way): we simply state that the final consonant (or consonants) is (are) subtracted. This would be a subtractive affix, and it would have the advantage of avoiding the apparent irregularity of any proposed feminine suffix. Although generative grammarians, such as Schane (1968: 1–17), would deal with such matters differently (by positing an underlying form with a final vowel in the feminine form), Bloomfield's proposal remains an important contribution in that it tests how far morpheme-allomorph theory may be extended.

The data that stretch this descriptive framework to the limit, however, are those exemplified by such English word-pairs as *foot – feet, dig – dug*, and *heat – hot*. The words *foot* and *feet*, for instance, are clearly related in both semantic value and phonological form. The most obvious analysis is to regard /f—t/ as a (discontinuous) root with two possible infixes /-ʊ-/ 'singular' and /i:-/ 'plural'. However, it is not normal in English to have an affix for the singular form – this is normally unmarked – and so it is probably preferable to consider /fʊt/ as a single morpheme in the singular, but one which has the root allomorph /f—t/ in the plural, where there is an infix /-i:-/ for the plural morpheme.

Both of the above analyses nevertheless depend on the acceptance of infixation and a discontinuous morph /f—t/ in the plural, two phenomena which are unknown in English outside this type of word-pair. Gleason (1961: 74–5) and others therefore proposed REPLACIVES as morphs, e.g. *feet* /fi:t/ = /fʊt/ + /i:←(ʊ)/ (to be read as '/i:/ replaces /ʊ/'). It is clear, however, that replacement is an operation not a segment, and we cannot "add" replacement to a stem; rather, we just replace the stem. In other words, replacement, and subtraction for that matter, are not things to be added, but are alternative processes to addition. If this view is accepted, we have moved to a different view of morphological (or at least morphophonemic) description, where we see things not in terms of ITEM AND ARRANGEMENT (IA) but ITEM AND PROCESS (IP).

The disadvantages of IP model are that it presents data in an apparently historical account, and that it sometimes requires arbitrary choices about which of two forms is basic and which derived. Nevertheless it has won renewed favour in recent years, particularly amongst generative grammarians, for whom each rewrite rule can be viewed as a process. Hockett (1954), who first suggested the labels IA and IP, saw an IP treatment of the verbs *bake* and *take* as stating that, instead of consisting of root plus affix morphemes (as in IA), they have a root morpheme subjected to a process, which he terms "past-tense formation"; the difference between the two verbs comes out not in differing allomorphs (as in IA) but in that the process has different "markers", *bake* simply a suffixed segment /t/, *take* replacement of its vowel with /ʊ/.

The IP model is preferred to various reasons. It is seen as simpler (Palmer, 1971: 122), in that it avoids the problem of specifying which phonological segments correspond to which bits of meaning (but is this perhaps avoiding the issue?) IP also appeals to our native speaker's feeling that some word-forms, e.g. present tense, are more basic and others "derived" (but, as we have seen, sometimes the choice is difficult). The difficulty of the IP model is precisely the difficulty of unrestricted rewrite-rule grammar that we discussed in chapter 4: such lack of discipline leaves little guidance for the grammarian. In Chomsky (1964) and Chomsky and Halle (1968), for instance, we find rules deriving *presidential* [prezɪ'denʃl] from [prezɪdent] + [i] + [æl], or assuming that *right* includes an underlying velar fricative [x] before the [t]. Such rules start from deep, abstract, often highly debatable, representations of roots and affixes, which have a whole series of rules applied to them, gradually reshaping their form till it matches the required phonetic representation. More recent work by Aronoff (1976) suggests that generally applicable phonological rules should be retained in the phonological component, but that a generative morphology should contain word-formation rules and adjustment rules that apply to only limited parts of the lexicon.

A third morphological model, WORD-AND-PARADIGM (WP), has also been proposed by Robins (1959) and Matthews (1970, 1974). This model views the word as a more fundamental unit than the morpheme (or formative), and is even less inclined than I.P. to bring out phonetic-semantic links. Influenced by the difficult problems of interpretation presented by inflectional morphology in particular (see below), the proponents of this model are content to specify the phonetic form of a word alongside its lexical meaning and grammatical characteristics, making clear which parts of the total phonological segment realize which categories. Figure 85 represents one of

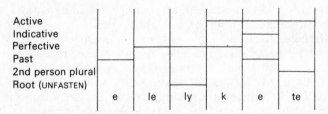

*Figure 85*

Matthews's own examples (1974: 143) from Greek, *elelýkete*, 'you (plur.) had unfastened'. Such a description at least recognizes the problems of segmentation.


## Lexical and inflectional morphology

Earlier in this chapter we equated lexical morphology, i.e. the study of the formation of new lexical items, with word-formation and distinguished this from inflectional morphology, through which a single lexical item, a lexeme, can be inflected for a variety of grammatical subcategories, such as number, case, tense. Lexical morphology subdivided into compounding, which gave new lexemes by combining two stems (e.g. *darkroom, football*), and derivation, which did so by affixation to a stem (e.g. *unkind, florist*). But both branches of lexical morphology agree in making a contribution to the vocabulary or lexicon of a language. As such they are more "particularistic", dealing with individual words, whereas inflection is of general applicability and integrates with general syntactic patterns.

The "particularistic" quality of word-formation comes out in a number of ways. We expect an inflectional affix to be usable with any appropriate lexeme in the language: so that all English common nouns, for instance, must have a plural form, even though some have irregular forms, and some would have a zero allomorph – at least they can all occur in the plural. Even MASS nouns have a plural with the meaning 'kinds of', e.g. *We are talking about two different milks*. Derivational affixes, on the other hand, are rarely so predictable. Take, for example, the English suffix *-eer*, which forms animate nouns from noun stems, e.g. *mountaineer, engineer, profiteer* (which have also become verbs by zero-derivation); it is unable to produce words like *\*hilleer, \*motoreer, \*advantageer*. Similarly, although it is perfectly acceptable English to say

I disbelieved what he said,

it is not acceptable to say

\*I disaccepted what he said.

The lexical distribution of the affixes *-eer* and *dis-* is thus defective in a way in which inflectional affixes are not. Compound formations are equally defective. A common type of noun-plus-noun $(Y+Z)$ compound in English has the meaning 'Z for making/holding/etc. Y', e.g. *cotton mill, cotton reel*; but we find that some other plausible combinations just do not occur, e.g. *\*wool mill; \*nylon mill; \*string reel*.

225

A·related aspect of the "particularism" of lexical morphology is the fact that the meanings of lexical patterns (whether derived or compound) tend to be much vaguer and more diffuse than their inflectional fellows (noun plural is noun plural, no more, no less). As a result of their semantic diffuseness, derivational affixes and compound patterns tend to come into competition with each other, and it is impossible to give watertight rules for the selection of a particular affix. In the field of English nouns denoting persons engaged in an occupation, we find words like *conservation-ist, petition-er, grammar-ian*, all alike in having abstract noun stems, and yet each with a different affix. A comparable set of abstract nouns is *glad-ness, complex-ity, efficien-cy, impertinen-ce*. Apparently accidental facts can play a part in the choice of affix: the choice of *-ist* in preference to *-er* with the verb stem *record* for the meaning 'person professionally engaged in *V*ing' seems to be dictated by *recorder* being pre-empted for the meaning 'machine which *V*s'; and the *-al* suffix seems to be preferred (to *-ation* or *-ment*) as a "nomen actionis" in the words *arrival, deprival, survival* because of the phonological accident of their roots ending in /-aɪv/. In a similar way there is no rationale behind the selection of the compound pattern with *-ing* in *playing field* but without it in *playground*.

The meanings of derivational affixes and of compound patterns appear diffuse if we try to generalize about the use of a particular one in all the words it occurs in. At the same time it is also a characteristic of word-formation that the meanings of single lexical items can become quite individualized, or as we described it above, "lexicalized". We have already seen how the derived word *recorder* has become specialized in the meaning of 'machine that records' (as opposed to 'technician who records') and how *darkroom* is specialized to mean 'photographic workroom' rather than, say, 'television room'. But these are just examples of a common characteristic of lexical formations. Consider the items *under-* and *over-* which may both be attached to noun roots designating garments, as in *underclothes, underpants, overshoe, overskirt*, but also to other roots, as in *undergrowth, undercurrent, overlord, overtime*. Both *undercoat* and *overcoat* occur; but whereas the former has been specialized in meaning to 'first or prior coat of paint', the latter has been lexicalized as 'outer coat garment'. (The "partner" of *undercoat* is *top coat*, and the "partner" of *overcoat* is *inner coat* or *jacket*.)

A final aspect of the "particularism" of lexical morphology is the question of PRODUCTIVITY (or is "productiveness" to be preferred?!). Not only are there derivational gaps and anomalies, but derivational affixes – and compound patterns for that matter – vary considerably in the extent to which they are used. Affixes that are available for use in new words are termed "productive". If, for example, not being aware of any abstract noun for 'the state of being pagan', I have a need to use one, I am faced with the possibilities of *paganism, paganity, paganhood, pagancy* and *paganness*. Leaving aside the last item (*-ness* having a rather different status), we might place *-ism* > *-ity* > *-hood* > *-cy* in a descending order of likelihood, i.e. of productivity.

The productivity of an affix is obviously related to the wideness of its present distribution, which, in a sense, is a documentation of past productivity that, other things being equal, is likely to continue. What is more of a puzzle, at least to the diachronic linguist, is how such affixes have become productive, and how previously productive elements have become frozen. Phonological limitations, e.g. the fact that English nominal *-ion* is largely limited to verb stems in *-ate*, e.g. *separate, operate*, clearly restrict the productivity of an item; on the other hand, paradoxically, having a "safe base" (so to speak) ensures that they remain at least moderately productive. Apparently external factors can also influence the actual use of affixes: for instance, the growth of *-isms* and *-ologies* with (higher) education, or the growth or decline in *-ades* (e.g. *limeade, orangeade*) depending on the popularity of coloured fizzy drinks. Compound patterns vary in productivity just as much as derived formations, ranging from the frequency of the *breadcrumb/snowball/fishcake* type to the infrequency of the *bulldog/fountain-pen* type.

Inflectional affixes, as we said earlier, are virtually 100 per cent productive. It is not surprising, therefore, that the most productive derivational affixes of all, like English *-er, -ness*, are partly inflectional in character. This is most clearly seen in their occurrence in transformationally related sentences. If we compare, for instance:

(1) Mozart composed this symphony.
(2) This symphony was composed by Mozart.
(3) Mozart was the composer of this symphony.

we find that the verb *compose* and the noun phrases *Mozart* and *this symphony* may be changed to other values, and sentence 1 will not only transform to a passive sentence 2, but also has a good chance of transforming to a sentence of type 3. (Cf. *Dr Watson was the finder of the vital clue. ?Mary was the see-er of the thief.*) This *-er* is thus highly productive.

However, recalling that derived words are by definition replaceable by simple words (see above, p. 214), we must ask what words could replace *composer* in sentence 3. The answer is that they are almost exclusively derived words in *-er/-or* (e.g. *writer, arranger, editor, backer*), a partial exception being *author (auth-* being a unique morpheme) and a possible full exception being *patron*. It would thus appear that *-er* in such uses is virtually inflectional in character. On the other hand, in a sentence like:

(4) Mozart was a great composer.

where *composer* may be replaced with *figure, man, Austrian*, etc., it is fully derivational. We may also note that the meaning of *composer*, as a derived word, in sentence 4, is limited semantically to the field of music (cf. the similar limitation of *writer* to literature), whereas the *composer* in 1, 2 and 3 could have been of a rhyme, a puzzle, a letter, etc.

The suffix *-ness* in English is perhaps even more productive than *-er*, at least in the transformational uses we have been considering. It may even be used where another suffix is already lexically established: *the longness of the room* is more literally linked to the meaning *long* than is *the length of the room* (the room may be short). We even get spontaneous creations like *the "lived-in-ness" of the room*. Aronoff (1976: 38) would describe such uses of *-ness* as (semantically) "coherent".

Although, then, lexical morphology can be very "particularistic", it is partly grammatical in character. Its grammatical function is, however, more within the word than outside it. Nevertheless the total word always belongs to a grammatical class, and intra-lexeme grammar is largely a matter of describing how the processes of derivation and compounding contribute to the establishment of that class.

Derivational affixes are divided by Robins (1964: 258) into CLASS-MAINTAINING and CLASS-CHANGING types. Whereas both types of affix affect the lexical meaning of the word, class-changing affixes also affect its syntactic value. The English prefix *semi-*, for example, is always class-maintaining whether added to a noun (e.g. *semicircle*) or to an adjective (e.g. *semi-automatic*), whereas the prefix *en-/em-* always converts nouns or adjectives into verbs (e.g. *enslave, embitter*). However, there are affixes which seem to disregard the class-maintaining/class-changing distinction[1] and form words of a particular class, the stem being either of the same class or of a different one: an example is English *de-*, which forms verbs from nouns, e.g. *defrost*, 'remove frost from', or from fellow-verbs, e.g. *decompress*, 'change state in reverse direction from compressing'. Moreover, class-maintaining affixes may signal a change of subclass

---

[1] Presumably, suffixes like *-o(u)r* (as in *horror, terror, splendour*), that form nouns from a bound root, are class-changing, but the root belongs to no syntactic class.

within the class, e.g. German *be-*, 'intransitive > transitive', as in *beantworten, beenden*, or English *-ship* 'animate > abstract (noun)', as in *directorship, authorship*.

Class-maintaining affixes mainly have the function, however, of indicating a particular lexico-semantic characteristic such as female (*-ess*), diminutive (*micro-, let*) collective (*-age*), negative (*un-*), spatio-temporal relations (*pre-, trans-*), etc. They may be compared to modifiers in a subordinative construction. Class-changing affixes, having more abstract meanings, may be seen then as markers of syntactic class within an exocentric construction, and in this sense they perform a function akin to that of markers of subordination like prepositions and conjunctions. It is thus even possible to find a derivational affix like *-ese*, an inflectional affix like *-s* and a preposition like *of* performing somewhat similar functions in *the Japanese coastline, Japan's coastline*, and *the coastline of Japan*.

Patterns of compounding have to be described in somewhat different terms, since the two roots involved each have their own grammatical class. A division of compounds is generally made into: (endocentric) subordinative, where the class of the compound is that of one of its parts; (endocentric) coordinative, where the two constituents are each of the same class as the whole; and exocentric, where the class of the compound differs from that of both of its constituents. The subordinative type is the major one, and the other types may be related to it.

Subordinative compounds may exhibit a whole range of different syntactic-semantic relationships between their parts. In English noun-plus-noun compounds, for instance, where the second noun is invariably the centre (or "head"), the first noun narrows down the meaning of the second by referring to its provenance (*folksong*), its contents (*picture book*), its material (*snowball*), who/what it makes, takes or deals with (*cotton mill, car thief, fire engine*), who/what it is made, caused, driven, etc. by (*steamship, hay fever*), the place or time it operates (*garden party, Christmas tree*), the event that takes place there (*football pitch*) or what it looks like (*bulldog*). In the face of these diverse possibilities, it is obvious that each compound lexeme must be fixed with one particular syntactic-semantic relationship, although, as we saw earlier, this need not be the same for similar-looking items: we then contrasted *airship, steamship* and *cargo ship*, and we might add Jespersen's (1946: 137) examples *goldfish, golddigger, goldmine*. It is also worth remembering that, while ordinary firemen put fires out, a fireman on a (steam) train keeps the fire going.

Coordinative compounds may be either appositive (i.e. the intersection of $N_1$ and $N_2$), e.g. *blue-green, girlfriend*, or copulative (i.e. the union of $N_1$ and $N_2$), e.g. *Schleswig-Holstein, bread-and-butter*. They are relatively uncommon.

Exocentric compounds can mostly be thought of as subordinative compounds that lack an overt centre. For example, the type of compound that Sanskrit grammarians termed *bahu-vrihi* ('much-rice' = 'wealthy man, who has much rice') as exemplified by English *redhead*, 'girl who has a red head (of hair)', can best be accounted for by comparing it with *red-headed girl*, to which it corresponds fairly closely semantically. The compound is thus of a type in which a subordinative pattern obtains, but the centre of the construction has been deleted, or "clipped" (to use Jespersen's term). This not only accounts for a series of similar patterns, as illustrated by *egghead* ('egg-headed person'), *pickpocket* ('person who picks pockets'), but also allows us to explain how *alarm* can acquire the meaning 'alarm clock' and *underground* the meaning 'underground railway'.

Most of the examples of compounding and derivation that we have considered so far have been lexemes with just two constituent morphemes; but any compound or derived word can act as a stem in a further derivation or compounding. It is therefore necessary to understand the constituent structure of these more complicated lexemes. The word *gentlemanly*, for example, obviously relates to *friendly, matronly*, etc. (rather than to *blue-green, \*gentle-brave*) and is therefore *gentle-man* (a compound) + *-ly*. This may have *un*-prefixed to it, and the resultant item may be suffixed with *-ness* (Figure 86). This word could not be construed any other way; an analysis *un-* + *-gentlemanliness*, for instance, would be impossible because *un-* can only be used with nouns to form verbs (e.g. *unseat*).

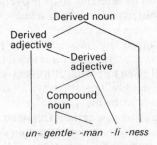

*Figure 86*

The word boundaries of written language are often a poor guide to the analysis of a composite word. *Deputy headmastership*, for instance, is surely to be construed as in Figure 87, rather than as a compound of *deputy* and *headmastership*. Some cases, however, are

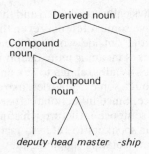

*Figure 87*

less clear. Particularly problematical are words like *hockey player*, which is not simply a particular kind of *player* in the same way that *hockey pitch* is a particular kind of pitch. Rather, we should relate *hockey player* to the construction *play hockey*, as though it were a derived word, based on a phrase. Similarly, words like *red-haired* need to be taken as *red hair* (a phrase) + *-ed*, rather than *red* + *haired*, since there is no word *haired*.

Finally in this chapter we must turn briefly to inflectional morphology. Unlike derivational affixes, inflections are regularly applied to all members of a particular grammatical class or subclass, allowing of course for irregularities in phonological shape, including zero allomorphs. We have already seen how inflectional affixes shape a particular lexeme to play its required part in the sentence, and that inflected forms of the same word, such as *break, breaks, breaking, broke, broken*, may, from the viewpoint of word-formation, be regarded as "allolexes". But, though in one sense the same word, each of the inflected forms of a word represents different grammatico-semantic characteristics (such as number, case, tense) that the word may assume. Thus inflectional affixes may be said to have a dual role: directly expressing these grammatico-semantic categories; and indirectly marking syntactic relations through the patterns of agreement (concord, government) in which these categories participate.

Languages differ greatly in the use they make of inflections, from "isolating" languages like Chinese and Vietnamese that have none to languages like Latin, Sanskrit and Eskimo that have a great many. The most widely used categories are case, gender, number, deixis (including person), voice (including transitivity), tense, aspect, and mood (including modality, mode and positive/negative). These categories may operate exclusively within the noun phrase (e.g. case), exclusively in the verb (e.g. tense, aspect), or in both (e.g. number), although we shall find it necessary to distinguish between the items they are physically attached to and the items they refer to. All the categories have some reference, even though frequently it is an oblique one, to the outside world of meaning (and we shall consider these aspects of meaning more deeply in our next chapter). Gender, for instance, usually relates to sex and animacy, tense to time, and so on, although some categories, like case and mood, have a less direct reference. Since inflectional affixes are, by definition, required parts of a sentence structure, this means that inflecting languages force their speakers to refer to factors such as number and time, which in an isolating language they could avoid.

Inflecting languages seem typically to manifest their categories in a morphophonemically complex way. We saw above how a Greek word like *elelýkete* presents problems of analysis, because the different categories could be interpreted as being manifested in overlapping segments. Matthews (1970: 107–8) takes an Italian example *canterebbero*, 'he would sing', to make the same point: although the whole termination *-rebbero* is uniquely 'conditional', the *-bbero* indicates 'third person' and *-ro* 'plural'. It is normal for an inflectional affix to represent a number of categories in one phonological segment (one morph or one morpheme, according to one's interpretation). Thus Latin *-um* of *bonum* is simultaneously 'masculine', 'accusative' and 'singular'; even English *-s* of *sings* is both 'third person singular' and 'present'. A further typical feature of inflecting languages is morphologically conditioned allomorphy of its affixes. In Latin, for instance, 'genitive plural' can be realized by *-ārum, -ōrum, -um* or *-ium* depending on the declension of the noun. Moreover one phonological sequence, e.g. *-um*, can have quite different values depending on the lexeme it occurs with, 'accusative singular' in *puer-um*, 'boy', but 'genitive plural' in *ped-um*, '(of) feet'. This can give rise to multiple homonymy of inflections, as in Russian where, in typical noun singulars, 'masculine genitive' = 'feminine nominative' (*-(j)a*), 'masculine dative' = 'feminine accusative' (*-(j)u*), etc. The independent signalling value of such inflections is obviously severely limited: the inflections operate within a given class of lexemes.

In agglutinating languages such morphophonemic complexities do not apply. In Turkish, for instance, number and case are separately expressed; we may compare:

| *Latin:* | amīc - īs | 'friend' — 'from plural' |
| *Turkish:* | dost - lar - dan | 'friend' — 'plural' – 'from' |

Moreover virtually all allomorphy of affixes in Turkish is phonologically conditioned. In addition, in languages like Turkish there is relatively little multiple realization of categories like plural, so that a plural marking of the verb is not required when the subject is marked as plural, nor is the plural noun form required after a numeral. It is therefore worth asking whether a suffix like *-lar* in *dostlardan* is really inflectional.

The boundary between inflectional and derivational affixes is in any case not so clear a one as we have perhaps suggested. It will be recalled that the crucial test of a derived word is its ability to be replaced with a simple word wherever it occurs. Consider English manner adverbs in *-ly* such as *quickly, beautifully, carelessly*. Only a tiny minority of such adverbs occur without *-ly*, for example, *well, fast, straight*, so that if these fell into disuse (being replaced by *goodly*, etc.), then the *-ly* would suddenly be inflectional. The comparative *-er* of *quicker, nicer* presents a slightly different problem, in that, while in most contexts it reduces to a simple adjective and is often regarded as a derivational affix, in contexts like *John is quicker than I am* it can only be replaced by an adjective with comparative *-er* or *more*, and must strictly be viewed as inflectional.

The stem to which an inflectional affix is added may be any kind of lexeme from a simple one to the most complex. English plural *-s*, for instance, is added just as easily to *neo-nationalist* as it is to *boy*. Nevertheless inflections retain a close link with the central root in the lexeme, so that the plural of *godchild* is with *-ren* rather than *-s*, and the plural of *brother-in-law* is (at least traditionally) *brothers-in-law*.

Typically, inflectional affixes occupy a position at the extreme end of a lexeme, i.e. initial position for a prefix, final position for a suffix. There are, however, exceptions: Robins (1964: 261) cites Welsh *merch-et-os* 'girl-plural-diminutive = little girls' and *dyn-ion-ach* 'man-plural-diminutive = little men'; we might add the prefix component of German circumfixed *ge—t/ge—en* ('past participle') when it is added to verbs with a "separable" prefix, e.g. *abgereist*, 'travelled away', *ausgegeben*, 'given out'. Whether an inflectional affix is in absolute initial or final position is, however, less crucial than the fact that it forms the outermost layer of morphological structure, a layer that marks relationships between that word and its fellow-words in the sentence.

## Questions for study

1 The definite article is written as a separate word in, for instance, English, French and Welsh, but as part of the noun word in Arabic, Rumanian and Swedish. Is there any way this difference in usage could be justified?

2 Consider the following Aztec data (Zacapoaztla dialect, adapted from Nida, 1949: 11, 156, 169). By comparing minimally different words, make a phonological division of each word into morphemes:

| | | | |
|---|---|---|---|
| nikita | 'I see it' | tikinita | 'you (sing.) see them' |
| kita | 'he sees it' | kinita | 'he sees them' |
| nankitah | 'you (pl.) see it' | kinitah | 'they see them' |
| nikinitak | 'I saw them' | kitak | 'he saw it' |
| kitakeh | 'they saw it' | kinitakeh | 'they saw them' |
| tikitas | 'you (sing.) will see it' | kinitas | 'he will see them' |
| tikitaya | 'you (sing.) were seeing it' | kitaya | 'he was seeing it' |

*N.B.* (i) One morpheme has two allomorphs.
   (ii) It is possible for meanings to be morphologically unmarked (cf. chapter 7) or marked with morphological zero.
   (iii) The precise sequence representing the verb stem 'see' will be unclear from the above. Take it to be *ita*.

3 The Welsh definite article (there is no indefinite article in Welsh) has three different allomorphs, /ə/ *y*, /ər/ *yr* and /r/'*r*, as shown by the examples:

| | | | |
|---|---|---|---|
| dan y siop | 'under the shop' | dan yr ysgol | 'under the school' |
| i'r siop | 'to the shop' | i'r ysgol | 'to the school' |
| o'r siop | 'from the shop' | o'r ysgol | 'from the school' |
| yn y siop | 'in the shop' | yn yr ysgol | 'in the school' |

The prepositions *dan, i, o* and *yn* are pronounced /dan/, /i:/, /o:/, and /ə/ respectively; the nouns *siop* and *ysgol* are pronounced /ʃɔp/ and /'əskɔl/ respectively. What are the conditioning factors for the allomorphs of the article?

4 In a word-and-paradigm approach the singular and plural forms of English nouns might simply be listed as follows:

| SINGULAR | | PLURAL | | | | | |
|---|---|---|---|---|---|---|---|
| /dʌk/ duck | — | /dʌks/ ducks | | /kaʊ/ cow | — | /kaʊz/ cows | |
| /kæt/ cat | — | /kæts/ cats | | /ɒks/ ox | — | /'ɒksən/ oxen | |
| /dɒg/ dog | — | /dɒgz/ dogs | | /gu:s/ goose | — | /gi:s/ geese | |
| /hɔ:s/ horse | — | /'hɔ:sɪz/ horses | | /ʃi:p/ sheep | — | /ʃi:p/ sheep | |
| /maʊs/ mouse | — | /maɪs/ mice | | /fɒks/ fox | — | /'fɒks–ɪz/ foxes | |

234

In an item-and-arrangement account what morphemes might be set up, and what kinds of allomorph and of allomorphic variation would be involved? In an item-and-process account what might the root morphemes be and what process(es) would be involved?

5  Identify the following words as derived or compound. In the case of derived words, what is the class of the derived word, what is the class of the stem, and hence what is the effect of the affix? (For instance, *careless* ADJECTIVE = *care* NOUN + *-less* NOUN>ADJECTIVE.) In the case of compound words, what is the class of the whole word, what are the classes of the constituent stems and what is the relationship between them and the whole? (For instance, *picture rail* NOUN = *picture* NOUN modifying *rail* NOUN.)

   *loathsome, population, smallpox, chainsmoke, seasick, redden.*

6  Can you provide tree diagrams to illustrate the structure of the following words, indicating whether inflection, derivation or compounding is involved at each node on the tree?

   *schoolmasterly, blackboard duster,*
   *United Nations International Children's Emergency Fund*
   (Treat *emergency* as a single morpheme.)

**Further reading**

On words and morphemes: Nida (1949), chapters 2 and 3; Hockett (1958), chapter 19; Robins (1964), chapter 5; Matthews (1974), chapters 1 to 3. On morphology and phonology: Nida (1949), chapters 2 and 3; Gleason (1961), chapters 5 to 7; Matthews (1970); Matthews (1974), chapters 5 to 7. On lexical and inflectional morphology: Matthews (1974), chapters 9 and 10; Allerton (with French) (1975).

*Chapter 11*

# Grammar and meaning

---

## Grammatical classes and meaning

So far we have concerned ourselves mainly with the form of grammatical patterns; but these are not an end in themselves. The point of having different grammatical patterns is to convey different possible meaningful arrangements of words and morphemes. Bloomfield (1935: 166) refers to the meanings of tagmemes, i.e. minimal constructions, as "episememes"; he also (1935: 146) refers to the meanings of their constituent form-classes as "class-meanings". We can thus study either the syntagmatic or the paradigmatic aspect of grammatical meaning. We begin by considering the latter.

In chapter 7 we eschewed the traditional, notional, definition of word-classes in favour of a formal grouping into classes on the basis of common potential for occurrence in key contexts. The words *book, boy, bread*, etc. were all nouns because they all occurred in a common set of contexts like *I noticed the new – yesterday*. But a notional view of the "parts of speech" cannot be totally dismissed. Although there are at first sight many dubious cases such as *arrival, event, blueness, quality*, a substantial majority of English nouns are satisfactorily accommodated under the rubric of 'person, place or thing' or, more generally, 'entity'. And, despite differences in formal definition, the same will hold for a similar category "noun" in most other languages. We may perhaps follow Lyons (1966; 1968: 318) in requiring a formal definition of the class, but allowing a notional determination of the name of the class. Being typically an entity makes the noun a natural choice as theme or subject of a sentence. We typically talk about people, places and things, and this is probably why Jespersen (1924: 96f.) designates the noun as his "primary" category. Difficulties arise, however, when we consider cases where the idea in question can be viewed from different perspectives. The notion of 'thickness', for example, can be thought of as an entity in its own right, when represented by the word *thickness*, but what about the word *thick*? If that, as alleged in the traditional definition of adjective, represents a quality, is it not therefore also an entity? The answer must be that *thick* does not designate an entity IN ITS OWN RIGHT, but a quality that is asserted or presupposed to be attached to some other entity – a person, place or thing. In a similar way, *thicken* also refers to a quality, but this time to one involved in a change of state that is being considered, at least potentially, as taking place. Verbs are traditionally defined as names of actions, processes or states, but this requirement is insufficient without the perspective of the process taking place at some (even if indefinite) time. A significant difference between *arrive* and *arrival* is that only the former is used when an arrival is being asserted as taking place. Adjectives and verbs thus share the characteristic of being asserted or presupposed as part of a predication about a noun-phrase subject or theme, and for this reason many authorities from Plato and Aristotle through Jespersen to generative semanticists like Lakoff and Postal have grouped verbs and adjectives together as a single category. Indeed, in some languages, such as Chinese, it is difficult to make a distinction. Both categories designate what Lyons (1966:233) refers to as "properties", and both may be divided into static (or stative) and dynamic (or non-stative) subtypes, as evidenced by their (non-)occurrence in the progressive aspect in English, cf.:

| | |
|---|---|
| DYNAMIC VERB: | Richard is learning the technique. |
| DYNAMIC ADJECTIVE: | Richard is being dishonest. |
| STATIC VERB: | *Richard is knowing the technique. |
| STATIC ADJECTIVE: | *Richard is being wrong. |

(The verb *to be* that accompanies adjectives in such predicative uses is regarded as an empty surface element.) Conflating the classes of verb and adjective removes the question of why one category, that of adverb, serves to modify both. On the basis of contrasts like *Richard is being an idiot/*Richard is being a genius*, Bach (1968) goes further and adds (predicative) nouns to give a global category CONTENTIVE as the sole lexical word-class. Noun phrases like *the student*, in his scheme, then have a structure analogous to *the one who is a student*. In Jespersen's schema the ranks of modification run from primary to tertiary:

| PRIMARY (I) | SECONDARY (II) | TERTIARY (III) |
|---|---|---|
| noun | verb | adverb |
| | adjective | |

e.g. *The dog barks furiously* (I – II – III), *a furiously barking dog* (III – II – I), *The dog is furiously angry* (I – III – II).

Proponents of dependency grammar, however, follow Tesnière (1959) in regarding the verb rather than the noun as the focal point of the sentence. Tesnière also sees the relationship between word-classes in terms of semantic modification, but for him there is a crucial difference between the predicative and the attributive uses of verbs and adjectives. In its predicative use, the verb is the hub (the "noeud des noeuds") of the sentence, being modified, in different ways, by nouns ("actants") like subject or object and by adverbs ("circonstants"). He would lay out his schema vertically thus:

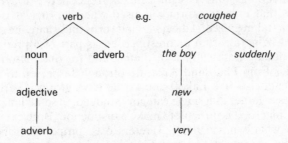

(for the sentence *The very new boy suddenly coughed*). There is something to be said for distinguishing from the outset adverbs that may modify adjectives (such as degree adverbs) from those that may not, but which instead give details of the setting of the verbal action (such as place and time adverbs).

Tesnière's system of word-classes is also interesting in its account of the classes of grammatical word, which he divides into two categories – convertors ("translatifs") and coordinators ("jonctifs"). The latter are simple coordinating conjunctions such as *and*, *or*, which link two equivalent items. Convertors, on the other hand, mark the conversion of one category into another; most prepositions or postpositions, for instance, convert nouns (or noun phrases) into adverbs (or adverbial phrases), e.g. *in* + *the house* → *in the house* = *here*; similarly, *of* converts nouns to adjectives (or better: adnominals), subordinating conjunctions convert sentences (with verbs as their hubs) into nominals, adnominals or adverbials, etc. Determiners, unfortunately, do not seem to find a clear place in Tesnière's system.

To sum up the main points, nouns refer to entities, verbs and adjectives to properties (perhaps subdivided into actions, processes, states, qualities, etc.), adverbials either to degree, frequency or other quantification of verbs and adjectives, or to the setting or venue; and grammatical words simply mark links between the major category words or indicate a (frequently spatio-temporal) relationship along with a change of category.

## Secondary categories and meaning

The major grammatical categories, which we have been discussing so far in this chapter, characterize particular lexemes; the lexeme SING, for instance, is a verb. In most languages, however, there exists a separate set of secondary categories that characterize individual words (or allolexes); the word *sang*, for instance, is past tense, as are also *danced* and *ate*, and yet the three belong to different lexemes. Pastness of tense can, then, characterize any member of the class "verb" in English. These secondary categories are therefore allolexic features or components characterizing a cross-lexeme group of words. In this English example the category (of past tense) is represented by a separate phonological segment, but, as we saw in the last chapter, archetypal inflecting languages often combine different grammatical features in a single affix. Each lexeme, then, already possessing a particular lexical meaning, is further endowed with a set of one or more grammatico-semantic characteristics; in Latin *amīcōs*, 'friend', is endowed with 'plural' and 'accusative'; in Russian писала /pi·sala/, 'write', is endowed with 'past' and 'feminine singular'.

Each secondary category like tense, number, case, gender adds a separate dimension to the array of forms a particular lexeme may take, so that a Latin verb, for example, may have more than a hundred different forms. It will be most useful, however, to survey each dimension individually, assessing its use in different languages. In doing so, we should bear in mind that, although most commonly words are directly endowed with inflectional affixes indicating the subcategory, it frequently happens that a word exhibits its subcategory only in accompanying words that "agree" with it (see chapter 7). We shall find gender a good example of this: for instance, the gender of a French noun like *rat*, 'rat', or *souris*, 'mouse', is only indicated unequivocally by its accompanying articles and adjectives (*le rat blanc*, 'the white rat'; *la souris blanche*, 'the white mouse').

It also happens that a syntactic construction with a grammatical word corresponds to an inflected word: a noun in a particular case, for instance, may correspond to a construction of preposition-plus-noun phrase (cf. German dative *ihm* with *für ihn*, 'for him'). Such uses are usually described as "periphrastic", or "analytic" (as opposed to "synthetic").

Secondary categories characterize nouns, adjectives and verbs,

*Grammar and meaning*

but only rarely adverbs. Since only one category, comparison, is exclusively adjectival, we may say that most categories are associated with nouns or verbs. We shall begin with those most closely associated with nouns.

Although some languages (e.g. Chinese, Ewe, Turkish) lack the feature altogether, the nouns of many languages fall into classes according to the differing inflections they require accompanying words (such as determiners, adjectives and verbs) to have. This subcategory we term GENDER. The gender of a noun must be distinguished from its DECLENSIONAL CLASS. For instance, although Latin first-declension nouns (in *-a*) are predominantly feminine, e.g. *puella*, 'girl', *lupa*, 'she-wolf', *mēnsa*, 'table', a minority are masculine, e.g. *nauta*, 'sailor', *poēta*, 'poet', and therefore require masculine endings in words that agree with them grammatically. A somewhat similar situation arises with Swahili nouns, which fall into six declensional classes, according to their singular and plural prefixes (which include ø):

| | SING. | PLUR. | |
|---|---|---|---|
| 1. | m– | wa– | e.g. geni, 'stranger' |
| 2. | ki– | vi– | e.g. kapu, 'basket' |
| 3. | m– | mi– | e.g. ti, 'tree' |
| 4. | ø– | ø– | e.g. safari, 'journey' |
| 5. | ø– | ma– | e.g. boga, 'pumpkin' |
| 6. | u– | n– | e.g. devu, 'hair'. |

These six classes correlate roughly with six genders, which require similar, though not identical, prefixes in accompanying adjectives, determiners and verbs, so that the sample words given above belong to genders 1, 2, 3, 4, 5 and 6 respectively. However, all animate nouns belong to gender 1, whatever their declensional class, so that we have *kikapu kidogo*, 'basket small', beside *kiboko mdogo*, 'hippopotamus small'.

The number of genders in a language can be as high as in Swahili, or as low as three in German or Russian, or two in French or Dutch. Genders tend to have a rather loose correlation with animacy or sex. In Dutch (or Swedish, etc.) the two genders correlate very roughly with animate (so-called "common" gender) and inanimate ("neuter" gender); but many inanimate nouns are "common", and a few animate ones are "neuter". In languages like French, on the other hand, there is a rough correlation with male v. female (but cf., for instance, *la sentinelle*, 'the sentry'), but inanimates have to be shared between the two genders. Languages with three genders often have a loose classification into male, female and inanimate beings, but most commonly inanimates spill over into the masculine

240

and feminine genders. In Swahili class 1 has the majority of animate nouns, class 2 inanimate objects and class 3 plants.

Gender thus typically correlates loosely with a typology of entities in the real world, but is grammaticalized in that there is a fair degree of arbitrary assignment. This means that, although there are minimal pairs where gender is the crucial difference, the gender difference in these cases does not always correlate simply with sex as in French *un enfant* beside *une enfant*, 'a child', but often with a more complex difference, as in *un voile*, 'a veil', beside *une voile*, 'a (ship's) sail'; and in the vast majority of cases gender is redundant, a given noun having only one possible gender.

Though basically a category inherent to the noun, gender is realized, then, through the noun's "government" (see chapter 7) of other parts of the noun phrase, in particular the determiner and the adjective, and through proform reduction in the pronoun. The gender of the subject (and even object) noun phrase may also be carried over to the verb (as in Russian for the past tense) or to predicative adjectives (in many languages).

NUMBER is also pre-eminently a noun category. In some languages (e.g. Chinese, Malay) number is not grammaticalized at all; in such cases the speaker may speak in a non-committal way of '(one or more) table(s)' but may optionally add 'one', 'two', 'a few', etc. In other languages a subtle categorization is made with dual (e.g. Arabic, Samoan, Czech) and even trial number, although most commonly such refinements are limited to special classes of noun (e.g. parts of the body) or to pronouns. But the vast majority of languages make a distinction between singular ('one entity') and plural ('more than one entity').

The distinction between singular and plural (or between singular, dual and plural) presupposes countability, and in most languages there is a class of nouns that are uncountable or MASS. We saw earlier how English *loaf* and *bread* differ in terms of this feature. Languages differ, however, in the items they assign to these categories: for instance, in German the word *(ein) Möbel*, '(a) piece of furniture', is countable, giving rise to a tendency for the German learner of English to say *\*a furniture*, which is impossible because the English word belongs to the mass (= uncountable) category. Countability places selectional restrictions on the use of determiners, according as they specify counted or massed quantity or either (*a, one, two, several* v. *much* v. *the, my*); and the interaction of the many factors involved causes a number of problematic cases (e.g. *cattle; trousers, scissors, etc.; mess, shambles; politics, phonetics,* etc.).

Number interacts with gender in an interesting way. When a

coordinated noun phrase represents a group of nouns of the same gender, the total noun phrase would obviously be expected to take on the same gender; but when the component nouns are of different genders, a problem arises. It is perhaps for this reason that some languages (e.g. German) neutralize their gender distinction in the plural. Languages retaining a distinction in the plural normally have a system of precedence like French, in which a mixed group is always treated as masculine.

But number is not so directly inherent in the noun as gender. Given that the noun in question is countable, we must look beyond the grammatical character of the noun into the intended meaning to decide on the number of the noun. Number is in fact made most explicit in numerals and other determiners. Unlike gender it is overtly marked on the noun itself in most cases, though not, for instance, in spoken French; and some languages that otherwise mark the noun for plural, leave it in the unmarked, singular, form after numerals, e.g. Welsh *afon*, 'river', *afonydd*, 'rivers', *tri afon*, 'three rivers'. From the noun it is very frequently (more so than gender) transmitted to accompanying determiners and adjectives, and to the verb or predicative adjective; and of course pronouns usually carry the number of the noun (phrase) they replace.

DEIXIS, of which pronominal and verbal PERSON is a special case, is the grammatical category that refers to spatio-temporal proximity relative to the speaker and his speech-act. Every individual speech-act establishes anew the role of speaker, that of addressee (or listener, hearer) and by elimination a third category of non-speaker/non-addressee. This deictic dimension can be seen running across the grammatical classes of determiner, pronoun and adverbial, in that, for example, English *I, my, this, here, now* contrast with *he, his, that, there, then* in terms of (non-)identification with the speaker. The parallel is highlighted in languages like Spanish and Turkish which have a three-way distinction for demonstratives and place adverbs along the lines of older English *this – that – yon, here – there – yonder*. (With the disappearance of *yon* and *yonder*, it became necessary for *that* and *there* to extend their meaning from 'near you' to include 'away from you and me' as well, and *this* and *here* have in consequence encroached somewhat onto previous *that* and *there* territory.) On the other hand, French *ce/cette* represents a neutralization of all three persons, although it can optionally be further specified with *-ci* or *-là* suffixed to the noun, e.g. *ce livre-ci*, 'this book', *ce livre-là*, 'that book'. A comparison of Spanish, English and French (masculine singular) demonstratives could be diagrammed as in Figure 88.

| | 1st person | 2nd person | 3rd person |
|---|---|---|---|
| Spanish | este | ese | aquel |
| English | this | | that |
| French | ce | | |

*Figure 88*

All languages seem to agree, however, in having a three-way distinction in person, at least for singular pronouns. Such pronouns are typically definite, since indefinite pronouns like English *someone* or French *on* may generally be interpreted as including the speaker and the addressee. While the first and second persons are fairly unequivocally defined, the third person can refer to virtually anything else in the universe, and, although use is made of the linguistic and situational context (see chapter 12), any additional identifying clues are invaluable. It is not surprising, therefore, that the third person is more often differentiated than other persons according to whether it is animate or inanimate (*he/she* v. *it*), masculine or feminine (*he* v. *she*), reflexive or non-reflexive (*himself* v. *him*) or in a few languages (e.g. Algonkin languages such as Cree) different from any previously mentioned third person(s) (so-called "obviative") or not.

Like gender, the category of person runs into some difficulty when combining with plural number. Except in the either chaotic or artificial situation of a chorus, there is only one speaker, and so the first person, in the strict sense, is bound to be singular. There may, on the other hand, be a number of addressees (listeners) to give a literal second person plural, just as much as a third person plural. Things become more complex, though, when we consider an admixture of different persons. The following tabulation displays the possibilities of plural persons:

| | | |
|---|---|---|
| 1st+1st | pure (choral) *we* | |
| 1st+2nd[1] | *we*='you and I' | =inclusive *we* |
| 1st+2nd[1]+3rd | *we*='(s)he/they, you and I' | |

[1]  Further distinctions could be made, according whether the second person in these cases is singular or plural.

|       |       |       |
|-------|-------|-------|
| 1st   | + 3rd | *we* = '(s)he/they and I' = exclusive *we* |
| 2nd   | + 2nd | *you*, plural = 'you and you' |
| 2nd[1]| + 3rd | *you*, plural = '(s)he/they and you'. |

It is clear that English, like the majority of languages, classes all groups containing 'I' as *we*, and all those not containing 'I' but containing 'you' as *you*. Some languages, however (e.g. Ojibwa and various other Amerindian languages, Tagalog, Fijian), distinguish *we* that includes 'you' from *we* that excludes 'you'. By means of its dual v. plural distinction, Samoan is also able to keep apart inclusive *we* with and without an additional third person.

With second-person pronouns number appears to be less important, since in some languages, like English, no distinction is made. A different factor, however, may be brought in: second-person pronouns may be subdivided according to the relative familiarity and/or social rank of speaker and addressee. This may be combined with number as in French (*tu*, 'singular familiar', v. *vous*, 'plural or non-familiar') or form a separate dimension as in Spanish (*tú/vosotros*, 'familiar singular/plural'; *Usted/Ustedes*, 'non-familiar singular/plural'). Although this social dimension may be of great complexity, as in Japanese, it rarely complicates grammatical relations like concord, since non-familiar forms invariably take second- or third-person verb forms. Robins (1964: 285), in fact, only accepts person as a grammatical category when it is marked outside the noun phrase, which almost always means in the verb, although Welsh also has personal forms for some prepositions.

The person marked in verb forms is most commonly only the person of the subject of that verb, so that the choice between *was* and *were* in English is determined by the number of the subject noun phrase (except that *you* always counts as plural). Most usually the verb is marked for the person as well as the number of the subject. In some languages, e.g. Basque, Eskimo, Swahili, a "mention" of the object noun phrase is also incorporated into the verb.

Minor nominal categories of inflection include DEFINITENESS, of which differing varieties are to be found in German and in Swedish; in German, for instance, the attributive adjective takes different forms after the definite compared with the indefinite article (surprisingly, possessive determiners like *mein*, 'my', go with the indefinite). Another one is POSSESSION, which is found in Finnish (e.g. *kirjani*, 'my book', *kirjamme*, 'our book', etc. beside *kirja*, 'book'), Turkish, various Amerindian languages, etc.; it might be regarded as a variant of the category of person.

The category of CASE is usually thought of as a category of the noun or noun phrase, but, although it is invariably a nominal inflection, the choice of case is determined outside the noun phrase. There is a less obvious semantic link than with number, gender or person. The case of a noun phrase serves to indicate its syntactic function in the sentence, in particular its connection with a verb or preposition.

The number of cases distinguished in languages can be anything from two (as in Swedish) up to as many as fourteen (as in Finnish) or more. The sentential functions pivoting on the verb include subject, direct and indirect object, and predicative complement; each function has its characteristic semantic value but this is shaped by the character of the particular verb associated with it (– as is also the number of such noun-phrase functions required in a particular sentence. While *sneeze* requires only a subject, *give* requires subject, direct object and indirect object). Thus *defeat* has 'the vanquished' as object, while *lose* has this role as subject. Languages typically have a basic or nominative case, often with zero affix, that occurs in subject position, at least for intransitive verbs, but there may be a separate ergative case, as in Basque or Eskimo, for causative verbs like '(cause to) break'. The direct object may be given the nominative case as in Rumanian or the genitive as in Finnish (but nominative in the plural!), but commonly a separate case form, the accusative, is used. Nevertheless, even where an accusative case does exist, particular verbs may select other cases for their objects such as dative (German), ablative (Latin). Where a dative case exists, it is used for the indirect object. The predicative complement (as in English *(He was) a Frenchman/teacher*.) frequently appears in the nominative, but Russian requires the instrumental for temporary states like that of teacher; Finnish, on the other hand, has two special cases for predicative constructions, the essive for states and the translative for changes of state.

Apart from verb-dependent functions, the other great role of case is to indicate spatio-temporal relations, either independently or in conjunction with prepositions (or postpositions). Some languages have a locative case, either as the sole locational case (as a relic form in Latin) or in contrast with "dynamic", i.e. directional, cases referring to place. The latter situation is exemplified by Turkish, which has locative (*evde*, 'in the house') beside dative (*eve*, 'to the house) and ablative (*evden*, 'from the house'). A further dimension appears in Finnish, which distinguishes interior ('in', 'into', 'out of') and exterior ('on/at', '(on) to', 'away from') local cases, as evidenced by the inflected forms of *laatikko* ('box') – *laatikossa* (inessive), *laatikoon* (illative), *laatikosta* (elative) and *laatikolla* (adessive), *laatikolle* (allative), *laatikolta* (ablative).

Such local cases correspond to constructions with a preposition in most languages, and in case languages the preposition concerned governs a particular case or cases. The cases chosen are usually ones that serve other functions as well (so the (purely) prepositional case of Russian is the exception rather than the rule); and frequently one case is favoured for static (=locative) uses, e.g. Latin ablative, German dative, and another for dynamic uses, especially direction towards, e.g. Latin or German accusative. Temporal uses of the cases, with or without prepositions, most commonly represent figurative extensions of local meanings, as in English *in the evening, around midday* or in the Finnish uses of the elative and the illative for 'from' and 'till' respectively. Other possible adverbial cases include instrumental, as in Russian, and comitative, as in (written) Finnish, referring to 'accompanists' of the subject.

Most case languages have a genitive or possessive case. This stands apart from other cases in typically having an adnominal function: in other words, it marks the embedding of a noun phrase as modifier within a "higher" noun phrase. Thus, it indicates the relationship of a noun phrase not to a verb or a preposition but to another noun phrase, and this relationship is most typically one of possession or belonging, as in *the boy's ball* or *the boy's age*. (The possessive *'s* is probably best regarded as an enclitic particle or postposition now that it is attached to a whole phrase, unlike the Old English genitive case that it derives from.) Case has other nominal functions: a genitive case often has a partitive meaning of 'some but not all of the NP'; Finnish has an independent partitive case; while Turkish, conversely, only puts objects into the accusative when they designate a definite, or complete, amount.

Case, therefore, refers to a variety of relationships that nouns contract to verbs, prepositions or the sentence as a whole. The case may be determined by the character of the verb or preposition or by syntactic function, but it is marked in the noun phrase alone.

Closely allied to case is the verbal category of VOICE. Languages that have voice as a verbal category allow verbs (or at least one class of them) to participate in different sentence patterns according to which of the differently inflected forms of the verb occurs. Typically, in the active voice a verb may structure with two (or more) noun phrases, a subject and one or more objects, while in the passive only one noun phrase is permitted, the one corresponding to the active object but appearing in subject position. Thus, in Latin,

> magister puerum punit.
> 'The master is punishing the boy'.

> puer (ā magistrō) punītur.
> 'The boy is being punished (by the master).'

the verb *punio*, 'I punish', has a distinct passive form (in *-ur*) when the person punished is in subject position (in the nominative case). Ancient Greek has a third "middle" voice with a partly reflexive, partly impersonal, function, though it is not fully differentiated from the passive. Languages that do not allow the reformulation of a sentence through a voice transformation cannot be said to have a category of voice in the full sense. In Hindi, for instance, where the transitive verb has an active-looking construction in the present but a passive-looking one in the past, these must be looked upon as variants. Similarly, ergative languages like Basque and Eskimo, which allow a nominative noun phrase both alone as a "patient" subject and in a transitive sentence as "patient" object, cannot be said to have different voices because the verb form is invariable. But clearly verbal voice and nominal case are closely linked, and both have a sentential role.

The traditional grammatical category of MOOD, which is attached to the verb but seems to make a direct contribution to the character of the whole sentence, appears to have three related strands. The first, which we might term "modality", refers to the attitude the speaker takes towards the reality or truth of what he is asserting. The speaker may, instead of simply asserting what will or did happen, prefer to suggest what could happen or throw doubt on what might (have) happen(ed). Turkish, for instance, has a verbal suffix *-ebil/-abil* for potentiality and a suffix *-(i)miş* (subject to vocal harmony) for dubitative modality, aspects of meaning that might be expressed in English through modal auxiliary verbs like *can, may, must*. Finnish has a special negative conjugation of the verb, whereas most languages simply have an independent particle. A second strand, which we might term "mode", relates to the kind of utterance used by the speaker, whether he is simply asserting (indicative mood), or perhaps asking a question (interrogative mood) or issuing a command (imperative mood) or expressing a wish (optative mood). Many languages have a special verb form for the imperative, and some, like Turkish, have a verbal modification for the interrogative (in Turkish the suffix *-me/ma*). The final strand is what we might term "mood proper" in the sense of verbal categories relating to the grammatical status of the sentence. In this dimension an independent sentence is declarative (indicative), but an embedded subordinate clause may require a different form, perhaps the subjunctive, as in the Romance languages. An embedded sentence may have special non-finite forms such as infinitive, participle or gerund.

The verbal category of TENSE obviously correlates with the time of the verbal action. Some languages, e.g. Malay, lack this category altogether, any reference to time being through an optional adverbial. Languages that do have tense may either, as in Latin, make a three-way division into past ('action entirely in past'), present ('action started in past but continuing into future') and future ('action not yet started); or they may, as in English, simply distinguish between past ('action entirely in past') and present-cum-future ('action partly or wholly in future'). Since the present is a point rather than a period in time (and one that is always relative to the speech-act), there is rarely such a thing as a purely present action.

Further refinement of time reference is generally thought to introduce an additional dimension, which is generally referred to as ASPECT. Aspect involves a number of variables, some of which relate to "timing" (as opposed to the purer notion of "time") and which we may frame in the form of questions:

(1) Is the action known to have taken place at a specific, definite time? ('definite' v. 'indefinite')
(2) Does the action carry on up to a given reference point in time, e.g. the present? Or, if the action is not a durative one, do its effects carry on to the point in time? ('lasting' v. 'non-lasting')
(3) Has the action already started at a given reference point in time, e.g. the present? ('already started' v. 'unstarted')
(4) Is there a completion of a discrete quantum of activity, e.g. reading a complete book? ('complete') Or is there, on the contrary, a clear failure to complete a particular activity? ('incomplete') A neutral unspecified term is possible here.

Aspect (1) would appear to be exemplified by the earlier French difference between past definite (historic) and indefinite (perfect), (2) by the Spanish perfect v. preterite distinction, (3) by the French imperfect v. perfect contrast, and (4) by the Russian perfective and imperfective aspects. The English perfect combines (1) and (2), while the progressive combines (3) and (4). Other more time-independent aspectual contrasts are made in some languages, of which the most important is habitual activity v. non-habitual.

Although it is perhaps partly derivational in character we should mention, finally, an adjectival category that is present in many languages, that of COMPARISON. Every German adjective for which it is semantically plausible may form a comparative form with the meaning 'ADJ. to a higher degree' and a superlative form with the meaning 'ADJ. to the highest degree', e.g. *lang-, länger-, längst-*, 'long, longer, longest'. English has a variant syntactic construction with *more* and *most* for longer words (*more beautiful, most beautiful*), and this is the sole pattern in many languages. A further point of difference is that numerous languages have no distinction between comparative and superlative.

## Grammatical structures and meaning

We turn now from the meanings conveyed by grammatical classes and secondary categories to the meanings of grammatical structures. In chapter 6 we raised the problem of describing the relationship between the constituents in a construction and found that this needed to be done in at least partly semantic terms. (We also noted in chapter 7 that the more delicate our subclassification becomes the closer it correlates with semantic distinctions.) We suggested three possible meanings for the phrase *John's photograph* which depend purely on the relationship between the constituents; but does that really mean that three different syntactic constructions are involved, or merely that three different semantic interpretations are possible? There may be no decisive answer to questions like this, but semantics is bound to play a part in syntactic description (though not necessarily so major a part as generative semanticists have proposed).

An interesting test case for the importance of semantics in describing syntactic structures is the treatment of verbal auxiliary patterns in English. Modal verbs like *will, can*, the progressive *be -ing*, the perfect *have -en/-ed* and present/past tense were traditionally analysed as closely linked to the lexical verb, as their morphology suggests. Thus the discontinuous progressive and perfect forms interweave with each other and with the lexical verb to form structures like Figure 89. The past-tense morpheme (as well as

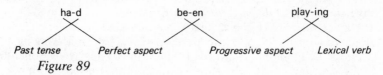

*Figure 89*

the *-en/-ed* morpheme), moreover, combines with the lexical verb in idiosyncratic ways to produce irregular verb forms like *sang, threw, left, went*. It is not therefore too surprising that in Chomsky (1957: 111) we find the rules:

    1. Sentence → NP + VP
    2. VP → Verb + NP
    . . . . . . . . . . . . . .
    8. Verb → Aux + V

249

making the verbal auxiliary elements closer to the lexical verb than its object is. Yet the arguments for this analysis are, as we have seen, morphophonemic, and hence, in the technical sense, "superficial".

It is thus understandable that later Chomsky (1965: 106–7) proposes a rather different analysis making the auxiliary patterns a direct constituent of the Predicate Phrase (a kind of "greater VP"):

(i)  S → NP⁻Predicate Phrase[1]
(ii) Predicate Phrase → Aux⁻VP (Time) (Place)

$$VP \rightarrow \left\{ \begin{array}{l} \text{Copula} \widehat{\ } \text{Predicate} \\ \text{V (NP) (Prep Phrase) (Prep Phrase) (Manner)} \\ \quad \ldots \end{array} \right\}$$

With the exception of the progressive construction, the occurrence of auxiliary elements is not affected by the selection of lexical verb, i.e. any verb may appear in any tense including perfect forms or with any modal. On the other hand, the choice of a verb like *sneeze*, or *give*, in the first case excludes any object, in the second case requires two objects. If, then, the lexical verb is to form its closest bond with its complements (including objects), the auxiliary elements can only form a construction with the VP as a whole, as described in the above rules.

Having allowed the possibility that the auxiliary pattern lies outside the verb phrase, we now consider evidence that it occurs at an even higher level, as an independent sentence constitutent. Elsewhere in Chomsky (1965: 85) we find proposed the rule:

S → NP⁻Aux⁻VP

and we might justify this by pointing to the fact that the first element in the auxiliary pattern, i.e. the tense marker or the modal, is moved away from the verb to initial position in questions (also in negation inversion), e.g. *Did/Can John open the door?*

Rather than make the auxiliary pattern a totally independent sentence constituent, Stockwell *et al.* (1973: 27–8), following up a proposal by Fillmore (1968: 23–4), place the auxiliary component along with the negative particles and certain adverbials within a modality construction, with the rule:

RULE 2: MOD → (NEG) AUX (ADV)

One of the motivations for such a rule is that both *not* and various adverbials of modality like *certainly, surely, possibly* form a close semantic relationship with modal verbs like *must, may, can*; so that,

---

[1]  In this set of rules the symbol ⁻ replaces the more conventional plus sign as the symbol for concatenation.

for instance, *must* occurs commonly with *certainly* but not with *possibly*, while *may* occurs commonly with *possibly* but not with *certainly*. This lexical co-occurrence restriction is indicative of a close semantic bond, but how grammatical a link is it? In terms of class co-occurrence the modal verbs and the modal adverbs are independent of each other; a sentence may have both modal verb and modal adverb, either one alone or neither (tense being the only obligatory auxiliary element). Moreover, while the modal verb is fixed in position, the modal adverb may occur initially, medially or finally, cf.:

> Possibly John may be late.
> John may possibly be late.
> John may be late, possibly.

The grouping of modal adverbs with modal verbs must therefore be on a semantic basis rather than a purely (or surface) syntactic one.

Ross (1969) and Langendoen (1970: 186–9) go even further in declaring the independence of auxiliary verbs: they see them as equivalent to "main verbs", i.e. lexical verbs. In this interpretation auxiliary elements can be viewed as the principal constituents of a verb phrase in a "higher" sentence; so that a sentence like *John may have already arrived* is analysed as in Figure 90, in other words,

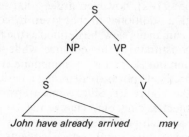

*Figure 90*

making it equivalent to *That John has already arrived may be the case* (= *It may be the case that John has already arrived*). Lakoff (1970a) argues for a similar interpretation of *not* and of adverbials.

Different proposed analyses have thus viewed verbal auxiliaries as a constituent of the verb, of the verb phrase (= predicate phrase), of the sentence, or of a higher sentence. No one of these analyses is correct; no one is incorrect. Each has something to say about their complex grammatical role, which relates partly to "surface" phenomena such as morphology and sequencing and partly to the semantic structure of the sentence. The difficulty of incorporating such diverse characteristics into a single description has caused great perplexity and been responsible for the development of multi-level descriptions.

Nowhere have these problems been more pronounced than in the description of noun-phrase functions like subject and object and their relationship to the lexical verb. Traditional grammar used the functional labels of subject, indirect object and (direct) object to refer to the contributions of such noun phrases as *the doctor, my brother* and *these pills* respectively in a sentence like:

The doctor gave my brother these pills.

These labels have also been constantly emphasized by tagmemicists such as Pike (1958), Longacre (1965), and Cook (1969), who have distinguished functional SLOTS from the classes of elements that act as FILLERS of those slots. Tagmemic grammar stresses that the same class of element, such as noun phrase, may fulfil different functional roles. Their notation for a tagmeme places the slot before the colon and the filler class after, e.g. +S : pn (read 'obligatory subject slot filled by a pronoun'). Halliday also stresses functional roles (1969: 82f.) but derives them from sets of options in a system network: for instance, "the presence of the function 'subject' in the [English] clause realizes the option 'indicative' in the mood system".

Chomsky (1965: 71–2), however, argues that such notions provide no information additional to that given by constituent structure. The subject can, in his view, be defined as the noun phrase that is an immediate constituent of the sentence, while the object can be defined as the noun phrase that is an immediate constituent of the verb phrase (or predicate phrase), assuming a basic sentence structure of a form like Figure 91. Since some transformational rules (passivization, object-raising, etc.) change the identity of the noun phrase occurring in such positions, it is necessary for Chomsky to recognize both deep subjects and surface subjects. For instance, in the sentence

Everyone thought James to be a liberal.

the deep-structure object of *think* would be the non-finite clause *James to be a liberal*. Since, however, there is a passive sentence:

James was thought by everyone to be a liberal.

it is generally assumed that *James* must have been raised (or "promoted") to be the sole object of *think* before passivization takes place, when it becomes the (passive) subject of *think*. An alternative view, not requiring this assumption, is that *James . . . to be a liberal*

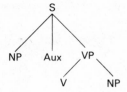

*Figure 91*

becomes the discontinuous subject of *think*, but this interpretation is impossible within a conventional transformational framework.

Fillmore (1968), however, referring to examples like:

John opened/has the box.
John ruined/built the table.

pointed out that no consistent semantic interpretation could be given to the function of "deep subject" any more than to "surface subject", and yet the whole point of deep syntax was to relate a syntactic structure to its semantic interpretation. He argued, therefore (1968: 16–17), that in order to provide for all the syntactic distinctions that are semantically relevant, it was necessary to use labelled functions to represent deep CASES such as agent, experiencer, locative patient, result. This entailed modifying deep structure so as to abolish the verb phrase as a constituent, thereby removing the special status of subject, which becomes nothing more than a verbal complement alongside object, indirect object, etc. The propositional part of the sentence (i.e. the co-constituent of the modality component referred to above) could therefore be viewed as a structure with a verb alongside its required noun and prepositional phrases in the appropriate (deep) "cases". While *John has the box* might be said to have *John* as experiencer or locative, in *John opened the box, John* would be agent. In

The box opened.

on the other hand, *the box* is not an agent, and in fact has a very similar function to the one it has in *John opened the box*: this role is variously described as objective, patient or affected. In ergative languages the two uses of the box would have the same (nominative) case.

Unfortunately, it has not proved possible to give a comprehensive list of roles or "cases", but we may consider the list proposed by Fillmore (1971: 42). The examples below, which are not Fillmore's, have the relevant case manifested by the noun phrase or prepositional phrase *in italics*. The case may be divided into two groups, a central group that are closely tied to the verb, corresponding to Tesnière's "actants":

(1) AGENT: *The student* cleaned the watch.
(2) EXPERIENCER: *The student* lost the watch.
(3) INSTRUMENT: *The solvent* cleaned the watch perfectly.
(4) OBJECT: *The watch* cleaned easily.

and a more peripheral, adverbial, group, corresponding to Tesnière's "circonstants":

(5) SOURCE: The student set out *from the library*.
(6) GOAL: The student set out *for the library*.
(7) LOCATION: The student worked *in the library*.
(8) TIME: The student worked *in the evening*.

Although principally adverbial, some of this second group may occur in subject position, cf.:

LOCATIVE: *The library* contains many books.
TIME: *Last summer* was wet.

but this is relatively rare; and in fact Fillmore makes the claim that there is an order of precedence for taking subject position, the lower numbers having priority over the higher.

This list of cases can be criticized as being incomplete and/or as requiring simplification. Huddleston (1970) argues for a case of FORCE that is an independent instigator of actions as the agent is, but is inanimate like the instrument: it would occur in sentences like

*The sun* dried the watch.

Fillmore himself (1968: 26n., 81f.) mentions BENEFACTIVE (*for the student*) and COMITATIVE (*with the student*). Langendoen (1970: 71f.) divides off RESULT as a subvariety of goal and CAUSE and STIMULUS as subvarieties of source. On the other hand, he apparently merges experiencer and object as PATIENT (1970: 66–71).

The whole area of location is problematical for case grammar. Although the sentence

*The coach* will carry fifty passengers.

has *the coach* as location with no specified orientation, an equivalent prepositional phrase requires a distinction between *in, on, under, behind*, etc. A more serious problem is that, however many distinctions we have, there always seem to be borderline cases (as can be expected in semantics), and there are obvious dangers in resorting to simultaneous or composite occurrence of the categories, as in Langendoen's (1970: 69) interpretation of

John beat *the rug*.

as PATIENT/LOCATION. Similar problems of demarcation confront an attempt like that of Anderson (1971) to see all central cases (and also time) in terms of the "local" ABLATIVE and LOCATIVE. There clearly are semantic links between local and non-local uses of case and prepositions: probably possessive sentences (*Have you got a match* on *you?*) bring this out most clearly, as demonstrated by Lyons (1968: 388–95). But just how far are we entitled to pass over finer semantic details in the cause of achieving a broad generalization? Semantics is by its very nature open-ended and diffuse, and grammatical semantics is in no way an exception.

This problem arises in a special form in the sublexical semantic analysis carried out by generative semanticists. It will be recalled (from chapter 8) that they postulate that all sentences standing in a paraphrase relationship to each other must be accorded the same underlying (semantic) structure. One of the implications of this is that factitive verbs like *kill, clean, open, break*, etc. have to be interpreted as equivalent to 'cause to come to be dead, clean, open, broken etc.'. As a result, superficially simple sentences like *The student cleaned the watch* must be given an analysis like Figure 92.

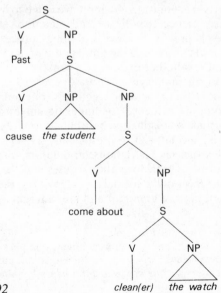

*Figure 92*

There are various arguments for such an analysis: for instance, that it enables us to explain the ambiguity of

The student almost cleaned the watch.

in terms of whether *almost* modifies the "verb" *cause* or the "verb" *clean*; or that it brings out the ambiguity of *clean*, as meaning 'make clean' v. 'make cleaner'. On the other hand, such an analysis loses its validity if we find that the lexical item is not synonymous with the analytic structure, and much evidence has been adduced differentiating *kill* from *cause to die* (cf. Fodor, 1970). But perhaps even more questionable is the basic assumption. Why should semantic equivalence imply syntactic identity? Why should a language not have various syntactic devices and lexical items that in different combinations may produce semantic equivalence? "Surface" functions like subject and object seem to be of inherent value, as witnessed by recent work in "relational grammar" (e.g. Johnson, 1976), which incorporates such functions into a tree-diagram mode of description.

## Grammar, meaning and logic

The more deeply we consider the semantics of grammatical elements, and the more we reject the limitations imposed by the particular words in a language, the more we come to look at the raw data of our experience that lie behind meaning, at Hjelmslev's "purport" (see chapter 2). This world of things, processes, qualities, relations, etc. is of course language-independent, and we are naturally led to wonder whether our deepest semantic structure cannot be common to all languages. Whorf (1956: 233–45) correctly emphasized the differentness of languages, but today we cannot ignore the mounting evidence for linguistic universals. Chomsky (1965: 27–30) makes a distinction between "formal" and "substantive" universals, and later (1968: especially 27–47) proposes abstract principles such as restrictions on deletion transformations, the cyclic ordering of transformational rules and the "A-over-A" principle[1] as instances of the formal type. However, these universals seem to characterize the grammar and grammarian as much as the

---

[1] This principle is intended to explain why it is generally not possible to gain access to a noun phrase within another noun phrase for the purpose of relative-clause formation, *wh*-interrogation, etc., thus excluding sequences like *the boy who John had a book that interested*.

language and we might be excused for taking more interest in the substantive type.

Lyons (1966: 211, 223) suggests that certain categories like sentence, noun and predicator will be needed in all languages. It also seems possible that certain construction types are universal; we might instance modifier-head (= head-modifier), particularly with noun or predicator as head, and relator-axis. Furthermore, some functional categories might also be recognized as universal: Keenan (1976) tries to establish the category "subject" as such.

Such insights lead naturally to the suggestion that a universal grammar be formulated; and, much more controversially, that this then should be viewed as the underlying structure or base for the grammars of particular languages. It is easy enough to agree on the common veins running through languages, but less easy to accept that they must all be seen in the light of a single underlying form, and most difficult of all to settle what form this universal base should take. Nevertheless, having accepted the need for a universal grammatical base, Chomsky finds it natural to explain its universality as a consequence of its being innate, being a part of the human being's inborn *faculté de langage*. Indeed he sees the principal task of linguistic theory as establishing linguistic universals, which may then be taken as corresponding to part of the child's language-acquisition device.

Leaving aside such problems of psycholinguistic theory, we may concentrate on the question of specifying the universal grammatical base, if this should prove feasible. As we saw in chapter 8, generative semanticists have rejected Chomsky's independent deep syntax and advocated a common semantic-syntactic base. This base has turned more and more to logic for a model, and we must consider what fruitful areas of contact exist between logic and grammar.

Logicians, like all philosophers, are concerned with truth, and in particular with the truth (or falsehood) of propositions, i.e. declarative sentences. Propositional calculus is an algebraic system that studies the formation and truth value of complex propositions. Predicate calculus studies the internal structure of simple propositions.

In propositional calculus elementary propositions, usually given as $p$, $q$, etc., may be negated (symbol:~). They may also be combined with other propositions in various relationships, such as conjunction, disjunction and implication. Their relationships are studied by comparing the truth values of the various propositions in a so-called "truth table".

Take the simple sentences:

$p$: The weather is pleasant.

$q$: John is watching the cricket.

Each proposition may be true (T) or false (F). The negation of *p* (or of *q*), i.e. ~*p* (or ~*q*), will clearly have the opposite truth value: when *p* is T, ~*p* will be F; and when *p* is F, ~*p* will be T. Putting this in truth-table form we get:

| *p* | ~*p* |
|-----|------|
| T | F |
| F | T |

This more or less accords with natural language, in so far as the truth of *The weather is pleasant* will entail the falsehood of *The weather is not pleasant*, and vice versa. However, natural language is more complex than logic, in that it allows different kinds of negative, e.g. *The weather is unpleasant*, which are not necessarily equivalent.

The complex proposition $p \wedge q$ (conjunction) is more or less equivalent to linking two propositions with *and* and gives the truth table in (i) below:

| (i) | *p* | *q* | $p \wedge q$ | (ii) | *p* | *q* | $p \vee q$ |
|-----|-----|-----|--------------|------|-----|-----|------------|
| | T | T | T | | T | T | T |
| | T | F | F | | T | F | T |
| | F | T | F | | F | T | T |
| | F | F | F | | F | F | F |

showing that $p \wedge q$ is true only if both *p* and *q* are true. In (ii), on the other hand, we see the values of $p \vee q$ (disjunction), and it is clear that this represents an inclusive *or*, i.e. *or* with the meaning 'and/or', that we find in a sentence like

I hope you have a mackintosh or an umbrella with you.

where it would be quite acceptable to have both. The exclusive *or*, i.e. 'either – or – but not both', that we find in

They all voted Labour or Conservative.

can be represented logically as $(p \vee q) \wedge \sim(p \wedge q)$; but sometimes a special connector ( $\underline{\vee}$ ) is used.

The complex propositions $p \rightarrow q$ (implication, also termed "conditional") and $p \longleftrightarrow q$ (equivalence, also termed "bilateral implication" or "biconditional") are given in truth tables (iii) and (iv) respectively:

| (iii) | *p* | *q* | $p \rightarrow q$ | (iv) | *p* | *q* | $p \longleftrightarrow q$ |
|-------|-----|-----|-------------------|------|-----|-----|---------------------------|
| | T | T | T | | T | T | T |
| | T | F | F | | T | F | F |
| | F | T | T | | F | T | F |
| | F | F | T | | F | F | T |

The value of $p \rightarrow q$ is usually described as the equivalent to *if...*, *then...*, but the last two lines of the truth table belie this. In the case where $p$, i.e. *The weather is pleasant*, is false, can it be said that *If the weather is pleasant, John is watching the cricket* is true? In ordinary life we would say that it is neither true nor false but just not applicable. There is, however, no term of "not applicable" allowed in truth tables, and the "T" in the third and fourth lines of the truth table has to be interpreted as 'not shown to be false'. A more serious objection to equating implication with *if...*, *then...* is that no causal connection is required, so that, in our example, the pleasant weather need not be the cause of John's watching the cricket, but merely a possible concomitant event. Moreover, since to falsify $p \rightarrow q$ we need to show a case of $q$ being F (and $p$ being T), a $q$ proposition that is necessarily true (e.g. *Two plus two equals four*.) is implied by any proposition under the sun. For this reason the logical use of "implication" (the term "material implication" is sometimes preferred) needs to be distinguished from everyday uses of the word.

*The equivalence of* $p \longleftrightarrow q$ is more straightforward: it can be resolved into $(p \rightarrow q) \wedge (q \rightarrow p)$, hence the alternative term "bilateral implication"; it simply means 'if but only if $p$, then $q$'. A further connective that is sometimes introduced is $p \leftarrow q$ (counter-implicative, also termed "replicative"); this is simply the converse of $p \rightarrow q$ (being false only if $q$ is T and $p$ is F) and may be rendered roughly as 'only if $p$, then $q$'.

We can see, then, that logical relations do not always correspond perfectly with the adverbs and conjunctions of natural language. Truth value is at the heart of propositional calculus, and attempts that have been made to define synonymy in terms of truth value (e.g. Lyons, 1968: 450) have to exclude emotive, emphatic and stylistic factors. Thus the three sentences:

Nastase had the match won, but he lost his concentration.

Nastase had the match won, but the idiot lost his concentration.

Nastase had the match won, but the Rumanian lost his concentration.

[where *the idiot/the Rumanian* are unstressed.]

all have the same truth value, but they do not all have precisely the same meaning.

Predicate calculus analyses simple sentences as having a core predicate, which is asserted to pertain to the one or more arguments (most commonly noun phrases) associated with it. Consider, for example, the following sentences, each with a single predicate:

> Smith was a fool.
> Smith was foolish.
> Smith fooled about.
> Smith reported Jones to Robinson.
> It snowed.

In the first three the predicate – a predicated noun phrase (*be a fool*), a predicated adjective (*be foolish*), or an intransitive verb (*fool about*) – is associated with a single noun phrase, its subject *Smith*. We may transcribe the predicate as a function $f$, associated with a variable, the argument $a$, or algebraically $f(a)$. In our fourth example we have the transitive verb *deceive*, which occurs with both subject and object, giving two arguments, formulaically $f(a,b)$ where the ordering of the arguments is distinctive; similarly, *reported* has three arguments and can be rendered as $f(a,b,c)$. A slight difficulty arises with the last example, in that *snow* (also *rain*, etc.) would be a predicate with no lexical argument.

A number of different approaches to the study of verb syntax seem to have been influenced by the predicate-calculus treatment. We have already mentioned Tesnière (1959) and Fillmore (1968), and a number of other theories of dependency or valency grammar (e.g. Hays, 1964; Anderson, 1971; Helbig, 1971; Helbig and Schenkel, 1973) have taken a "verbocentric" view of sentence structure. Amongst generative semanticists, McCawley (1970a) was most prominent in proposing that English (and perhaps every language?) at its deepest level of structure is a VSO language, i.e. a language where the (lexical) verb precedes both subject and object, and thus appears at the head of the sentence.

A further aspect of the logical analysis of propositions concerns the noun phrases that may act as arguments. Considering the sentences:

> Edward VIII (of England) abdicated.
> The last king (of England) but one abdicated.
> A king has abdicated (before now).
> A king may abdicate.

we find considerable variety in the entities occurring in subject position. In the first sentence we have a proper name designating an individual, which forms an argument in its own right, although, of course, the listener must be acquainted with the individual to make sense of the proposition. Alternatively, as in the second sentence, we have a definite description which refers to an individual indirectly, by stating some proposition(s) which can only be true with respect to him (/her/it/them). Thus, in this case, it is presupposed that there are kings of England (as opposed to the situation in France) and that there have been at least two (or, more likely, three, since otherwise we would say *first* rather than *last-but-one*). In the third and fourth sentences we are speaking generically and saying that it is true of at least one king that he may abdicate; or that it is true of any king (or all kings) that he (they) may abdicate.

In dealing with such matters logicians make use of quantifiers. The existential quantifier $\exists$ is used in propositions of the form $\exists x f(x)$ to assert that there is some $x$ (i.e. at least one $x$) such that the proposition with $x$ as an argument of the predicate $f$ is true. For instance, we might assert that there is at least one king such that he has abdicated. The universal quantifier $\forall$ is used in a similar way to assert that the proposition is true of all $x$, e.g. that all kings may abdicate.

Again, generative semanticists (e.g. McCawley, 1970b; Lakoff, 1972) and their associates (e.g. Bach, 1968) have been active in proposing that linguistics should adopt syntactic-semantic descriptions that closely mirror quantifier logic. McCawley, for instance, proposes representing *The man killed the woman* as in Figure 93.

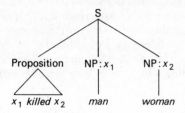

*Figure 93*

Such analyses are attractive when they solve problems that arise with other treatments, and the above analysis is apparently superior when it comes to such problem cases as:

(i)  the ambiguity of sentences like *Nancy wants to marry a Norwegian*, where she may or may not have a particular Norwegian in mind (McCawley, 1968: 175);

(ii)  the so-called Bach-Peters sentences with problems of intersecting cross-reference, e.g. *People who eat vegetables they have grown, generally like them* (Bach 1970);

(iii)  certain difficulties inherent in reflexive constructions, stemming from the need to distinguish, e.g. *The man spoke to himself* from *The man spoke the man*.

(Sentences like this last one occur infrequently, but this one might occur for instance in a desert island situation where a newly shipwrecked couple began talking to a pair of established settlers.) McCawley's analysis is also useful for the kind of quantifier problem that we met in chapter 8, involving the passivization of sentences with *few, many, all*, e.g.:

Many men have kissed few girls.
? → Few girls have been kissed by many men.

A logical viewpoint can thus assist us in unravelling the semantic complexities of noun phrases, definite or indefinite, proper or common, quantified or not.

Logic in general allows us to reformulate the meanings of problematic sentences in an enlightening way. Unfortunately, however, we cannot assume that the clearest, most logically flawless interpretation is the one lying at the heart of most or all languages. Natural languages are, on the contrary, characterized through and through by inconsistencies and illogicalities. There are dangers, therefore, in setting up a logical or quasi-logical system as a universal grammatical base, and of stretching and perhaps distorting languages to fit this system, as traditional grammars once used to with Latin. Logic may well help us understand the semantics of a sentence, but taking it as a model for grammatical patterns is another matter. Even at a semantic level it applies in a straightforward way with only statement utterances, and faces great difficulties with interrogatives, imperatives, exclamations and all expressive uses of language. There are more things in natural language, Horatio. . .

## Questions for study

1 Is a notional definition of the traditional class of ADVERB possible (in English)? If so, what would it be like? If not, why not?

2 Some languages, the so-called isolating languages like Chinese and Vietnamese, lack most or all of the inflectional subcategories discussed in the second section of this chapter. Do you imagine that their speakers simply go without such meanings as number and tense? How can the meanings normally carried by them be conveyed when they are essential?

3 For the purpose of practical language teaching which, if any,

of the different syntactic treatments of verbal auxiliaries
discussed above (pp. 249–51) seems most appropriate:
(a)  for teaching English as a native language?
(b)  for teaching English as a second or foreign language?

4  Distinguish the semantic role of each of the italicized
elements below from the fellow-elements in its set:
(a)  (i)  *The saucepan* cooked beautifully.
      (ii)  *The chef* cooked beautifully.
      (iii)  *The meat* cooked beautifully.

(b)  (i)  John ran *in the stadium.*
      (ii)  John ran *in the house.*
      (iii)  John ran *in the door.*

(c)  (i)  I wrote *the book.*
      (ii)  I read *the book.*
      (iii)  I burnt *the book.*

5  Construct a truth table for the counter-implicative $p \leftarrow q$.
Compare this with the table for $p \rightarrow q$. Construct a further
truth table for the conjunction of the two, i.e. $(p \rightarrow q) \wedge (p \leftarrow q)$, showing this to be equivalent to $p \leftrightarrow q$.

6  How would you explain the following?
(a)  The DIFFERENCE in meaning between:
      (i)  Many people read few books.
      (ii)  Few books are read by many people.

(b)  The EQUIVALENCE of meaning between:
      (i)  Mavis ate few chocolates.
      (ii)  Mavis didn't eat many chocolates.

(c)  The AMBIGUITY of:
      Mavis wouldn't flirt with anyone.

**Further reading**

On grammatical classes and meaning: Jespersen (1924), chapters 4
to 7; Lyons (1966); Tesnière (1959), chapter 32. On secondary
categories and meaning: Hockett (1958), chapter 27; Gleason
(1961), chapter 14; Lyons (1968), chapter 7; Grimes (1975), chapter 5. On grammatical structures and their meaning: Fillmore

(1968); Langendoen (1970), chapters 4 and 6; Stockwell *et al.* (1973), chapters 8 to 12. On grammar, meaning and logic: McCawley (1970a; 1970b); Wall (1972), chapters 2 and 3; Lyons (1977), sections 6.2 and 6.3.

## Chapter 12

# Grammar and discourse

---

## Textual links between sentence-parts

The sentence was traditionally regarded as the upper limit of grammatical analysis. For example, Bloomfield (1935: 170) cites the following short text:

> How are you? It's a fine day. Are you going to play tennis this afternoon?

and declares that "whatever practical connection there may be between these three forms, there is no grammatical arrangement uniting them into one larger form". Bloomfield chose an example which lacks any conjunctions or sentence adverbs such as *so, therefore* or any pronouns that refer back to an earlier sentence such as *he*; but even so the very fact that the three sentences are said in (uninterrupted) sequence by the same speaker means that they form part of a higher unit in the discourse or text in which they occur. The terms DISCOURSE and TEXT are both used for the wider context (e.g. a conversation, a school lesson, a newspaper article, a letter, a novel) in which a sentence occurs. The former term suggests the spoken medium and the latter the written, but we shall NOT use them with this restriction. Sentences are very often meant by the speaker to be interpreted in terms of preceding and/or following sentences: for instance, in Bloomfield's example there is a suggestion that fine weather provides one of the right conditions for playing tennis. But inter-sentential links are not purely semantic: there are also relations of co-occurrence and sequence between sentences, so that, for instance, a question like Bloomfield's last sentence needs to be followed directly by a response (typically *yes* or *no*) by the listener.

An addressee normally expects a speaker's sentences to be semantically linked in some way; and even if there is no apparent connection he will try to find one. As a result, even sentence sequences that might be thought impossible can be provided with a link by the intelligent listener. For instance, the sentence sequence:

> I saw Mary go-go dancing. The General has declared himself president-for-life.

might be thought nonsensical, until it is realized that it is common knowledge amongst Mary's friends that she would only dance again in celebration of some great event.

Semantic links between sentences follow partly from the coherence of the speaker's own thoughts, but he must also ensure that he is carrying the listener with him. In doing this, he depends on the common beliefs and knowledge he shares with the listener, which allow him to leave unsaid certain things that have been said, or at least hinted at, earlier. This shared knowledge is of different kinds:

(a) knowledge of the language, including knowledge of the things, processes, etc. referred to by the words of the language, including not only ordinary words like *man, good, sneeze* but also proper nouns, both unique like *Wolverhampton* and with variable reference like *John*;

(b) knowledge of the world in general, e.g. that houses have windows, that children over a certain age go to school, that (genuine!) sherry comes from Spain, etc.;

(c) knowledge of particular facts, e.g. that Professor X has just got back from Vienna, that my Aunt Grizelda's poodle had toothache on 29th June, etc.

It is, however, difficult to draw a line either between (a) and (b) (that rabbits have long ears?) or between (b) and (c) (that first-class cricket in England is played during the summer months).

Speaker and listener use their common knowledge in conjunction with what Grice (1975: 45) terms the "co-operative principle". By this is meant a tacit understanding of just how much the speaker should actually say, how much leave unsaid, and how meanings are to be "implicated" beyond what is actually said. By this set of conventions what the speaker says should be relevant, sufficient in quantity and adequate in presentation for the purposes of giving the required information, and yet only as detailed as is necessary. For example, if, in answer to the plea

> I'm dying of thirst.

I reply

> There's a packet of tea in the kitchen.

then I might reasonably be taken to be implying that running water is also available along with some means of heating it, that you have my permission to use some of the tea, etc. An essential aspect of these implications is the principle of economy, by which we say what needs to be said in the prevailing circumstances, but no more. This principle does not apply to all uses of language. In some contexts, such as people getting to know each other, speakers mention points they assume to be known by the listener, in order to create a feeling of solidarity between them. In the case of the mass media of communication, only a minimum of shared knowledge can be assumed for all listeners, and sequences like *Captain George Smith, master of the tanker Liquid Assets that went aground near Sandwich on the Kent coast last night, said today that* . . . come to be used.

As a natural result of the coherence of linguistic texts, the same things and events keep on being mentioned, and languages have various devices for signalling identity, similarity or difference of reference compared with some previous item. Such devices provide a way of avoiding duplication and of following the maxim "Be concise"; they are used partly within complex and compound sentences, partly in dependent sentences such as answers to questions, and partly in entirely independent sentences. The devices include the use of a special proform (or "substitute", e.g. *one*) or of a marker of definiteness (e.g. a definite article), and the deleting of a linguistic item that would normally be present ("ellipsis"). Such practices may only be indulged in when it is clear to the listener how he is to reconstruct the missing information. Broadly, he has two sources, TEXTUAL and SITUATIONAL. (Halliday and Hasan (1976) speak of "endophoric" and "exophoric" respectively.) Consider the ways in which the listener ascertains the correct value for *him* in the following cases:[1]

(A.1) [I've arranged for Peter to call in later.]
I thought you might like to have a word with him.
(A.2) I thought you might like to have a word with him.
[– so I've arranged for Peter to call in later.]
(B) [SEES LISTENER HAS NOTICED PETER STANDING IN THE DOORWAY.] I thought you might like to have a word with him.

In the first two cases, the listener refers to the surrounding text to determine the identity of the *he* referred to; in (A.1) he makes an ANAPHORIC (i.e. backwards) reference whereas in (A.2) he makes a CATAPHORIC (i.e. forwards) reference. Cataphoric reference is the exception, and anaphoric the rule, since it is naturally much easier

---

[1] Linguistic contexts are henceforth given in square brackets. SMALL CAPITALS denote "stage directions".

to refer to something already made known to the listener, rather than something he must wait to be introduced to.

In the last case, we have a situational (or exophoric) reference, where the listener is required to look around him and/or think backwards or forwards in time for the most obvious referent. Sometimes it is unclear just how near or far removed the interpretation is from the here-and-now of the current utterance. For instance, the following question:

Well, did you beat him?

might be put to someone dressed for golf or tennis, and reference would most likely be being made to his recently finished sporting encounter; on the other hand, the same question might equally be put to a man in ordinary dress (or even dressed up differently, say as Santa Claus), when he could be forced to rack his brains to think of the occasion being referred to. Even when there has been a linguistic mention to which the speaker refers, this may be only implicit (rather than explicit), as when we might say:

John's house is very cold. The windows all seem to be draughty.

Clearly, the windows referred to are those in John's house, and the listener is expected to use his general knowledge to tell him that all houses, including John's, have windows.

In the examples we have considered so far, it has been the listener's task to identify the particular referent that the speaker has in mind. He (or she) has heard a definite noun phrase, either a pronoun like *him*, or a noun like *student* with a definite determiner like *the, this, my*. In languages that lack a definite article, e.g. Russian, mere occurrence of the noun initially in the sentence, where it is the natural "theme" (see p. 275), is sufficient to identify it as 'given' and therefore in need of identification by the listener. In some cases the identity of the referent is announced as identical with one previously mentioned (*the same*), or as different (*another, the other*, etc.). In any case the listener is required to reconstruct which person, student, etc. the speaker means, using as his basis the linguistic and situational context. Such a phenomenon might be described as "givenness of the referent" realized as DEFINITENESS. (Halliday and Hasan (1976) speaks simply of "reference".)

The kind of givenness we have just described, involving the precise identity of the referent, must be distinguished from givenness of the particular class label (i.e. lexeme) that stands for the referent. Consider these examples:

268

[John's got a red telephone.] We've got a white one.
[When are you going to buy the turkey?] We already have
(done).
[How do you know (that) it's going to rain?] Jack Scott said
so.

In these cases, the words *one, done* and *so* act as substitutes replacing the items *telephone, bought the turkey* and *(that) it's going to rain* respectively, from the immediate context. Each substitute represents a particular class of grammatical element, *one* a noun (but in other cases a noun phrase), *do* (or one of its "allolexes") a verb phrase, and *so* a clause. Bloomfield (1935: 247) used the term "substitute" for such items, but since Harris (1957) the term "proform" has been preferred. We may therefore describe this phenomenon as "givenness of the lexeme(s)" realized by REDUCTION-TO-PROFORM (Halliday and Hasan's term is "substitution"). In addition to proforms, languages have what Halliday and Hasan (1976: 274f.) refer to as "general nouns", e.g. *people, person, man, thing, stuff, matter, question*, which may be used in empty noun phrases in place of pronouns, e.g. *the man*, for *he, the stuff, the thing*, etc. (as appropriate) for *it*.

A lexeme or construction of lexemes that is "given" in this way is most commonly reconstructed anaphorically, as in the examples given above. The missing lexeme(s) can, however, be supplied cataphorically, as in:

If you'd like one, I'll send you a copy of my book.

Occasionally, too, a proform represents something that is evident in the situational context, as when a potential buyer might say:

Have you got any big ones left?

to a market stall-holder who is selling nothing but Christmas trees, for instance.

The interaction of definiteness ("reference") and reduction to proform ("substitution") may be seen clearly in the noun phrase (with or without an adjective), in which the referent and/or the noun lexeme may be "given" or, alternatively, "new", i.e. introduced at this point. This means that, for the English noun phrase *a (blue) book*, we have the possibilities listed below:

|  | LEXEME NEW | LEXEME GIVEN |
|---|---|---|
| REFERENT NEW | a blue book | a blue one |
|  | a book | one |
| REFERENT GIVEN | the blue book | the blue one |
|  | the book | it |

Note that *it* (also *he*, etc.) combines both kinds of givenness. Since noun phrases are often a constituent of an adverbial phrase, givenness can obviously also apply to them (*in the big one*), but in addition adverbs like *there* and *then* seem to involve linguistic or situational reference directly.

As we indicated in chapter 11, definiteness in languages can take different forms, as when in Turkish the accusative case is restricted to objects that are definite: the occurrence of the accusative then requires the listener to identify the given referent. A variant form of definiteness is to be seen in languages like English which have a progressive verb form indicating action still in progress at a particular time, thus forcing the listener to identify the time to which, for instance, *John was mowing the lawn* applies, from either the linguistic or the situational context. Other tense-aspect forms requiring the listener to make a contextual identification of a particular time include past definite in a language like Spanish and pluperfect (past perfect) in a number of languages.

In the case of givenness we have considered so far – definiteness and proform reduction – there has been a linguistic marker of the givenness, a definite article, a proform, etc., that draws the listener's attention to the need to reconstruct something from the context. But in OPTIONAL DELETION (or "ellipsis") the element to be supplied by the listener is totally absent. Commonly (optional) deletion is an alternative to proform reduction, cf.:

[Which kind of soup would you prefer?]
Either (one) would suit me.

(Cf. also the second example on p. 269.) But sometimes deletion occurs when there is no possibility of proform reduction, e.g.:

[John owns seventy ties.]
I only own three (*ones).

(although *ones* would have been required, if the noun phrase had included an adjective, e.g. *three black ones*).

The range of elements that are affected by deletion or reduction-to-proform varies from language to language, but often includes the noun phrase, the head noun in a noun phrase, the verb phrase, the lexical verb, and the whole clause. Generally speaking, proform reduction is more widely available than deletion. The possibilities for deletion, in fact, seem to be fairly language-specific. For example, many languages allow deletion of the head noun in a noun phrase, cf. German *den roten Wagen*, 'the red vehicle' (ACCUSATIVE) – *den roten*, 'the red one' (ACCUSATIVE), but English only allows this in a very limited way; some languages, like Spanish, allow contextual deletion of the subject, leaving a subject-less verb, e.g.:

A. Y María? 'And Maria?'
B. Está mala. '(She) is ill.'
C. Tiene algo grave? 'Has (she) anything serious?'

while English again forbids this. It is a general requirement for the deletion of a noun phrase that the identity of the referent should be recoverable from the context, and thus be definite, e.g.:

Alan pushed hard.
Bill was interested.

where the object will more likely be found in the situation in the first example, but in the text in the second. Cases like *Mary was reading* (beside *Mary was reading something or other*) may be regarded as verbs used intransitively and transitively.

The effect of definiteness, proform reduction and (contextual) deletion is to refer the listener either to the situation or to some other part of the text. In the latter case, it is clear that these manifestations of givenness will have the effect of binding the different parts of the text closer together, or, in Halliday and Hasan's word, achieving COHESION; and they achieve this by using syntactic markers.

In spoken language, intonation may mark a different kind of givenness, not of the individual constituents, but of a combination of them. Consider these three pronunciations of a sentence with a falling intonation nucleus (marked with SMALL CAPITALS) in different places:

[Have you heard the news?]
JOHN'S going out with Mary.
John's going OUT with Mary.
John's going out with MARy.

Most commonly the nucleus or "sentence accent/stress" will be of the LOW FALL type. We disregard the question of minor nuclei on other elements. Each pronunciation of the sentence seems to carry with it different expectations. When *John* takes the nucleus, the suggestion is that there is nothing new about men going out with Mary, but that only now has John done it. If, however, we knew that John had his eye on Mary, and the news is that he is finally going out with her, then *out* will be nuclear. Similarly, Mary will only be nuclear when she is the unpredictable part of the combination. It is thus the item with the greatest NEWS VALUE *vis-à-vis* the others that takes the (major) intonation nucleus. This item is often termed the "focus".

The expectations that influence nucleus placement are at the back of the speaker's mind, but if they have been already expressed in some way, or if some of the items involved have been simply mentioned, then proform reduction or deletion may apply simultaneously, e.g.:

[Is anyone going out with Mary these days?] JOHN is.
[I saw John chatting up Mary.] He's going OUT with her.

Intonation may also play a rather different textual role in its distinction between rising and falling nuclei, a role which links up with definiteness. Comparing the following sentence pronounced with a separate minor intonation group for the final phrase, on the one hand with a low fall, and on the other with a low rise:

I saw MARY | in the BOOKshop.

we find that the rise, but not the fall, implies that the bookshop has been referred to in the last sentence or two.

Returning to the notion of news value of constituents in combination, we have seen that in its negative aspect it amounts to predictability; and it is easy to see that in the extreme case a whole proposition may be taken for granted, amounting to a PRE-SUPPOSITION. In a typical *wh*-question, for instance, the speaker presupposes the truth of a generalized proposition from which one detail is missing and asks the listener to tell him the missing detail. In the question

Who was in Mary's bedroom?

it is presupposed that someone was, while in

How long was John in Mary's bedroom?

it is presupposed that John was. In a simple statement, with no embedding, there is no presupposition but rather an ASSERTION of the proposition, e.g.:

John was in Mary's bedroom last night.

Though it is sometimes argued that there is an "existential presupposition" in respect of all the items assumed as known or given, *John, Mary* and *a bedroom owned by Mary*, in our example. When this has been asserted, it may of course be questioned by the addressee; alternatively, he may accept it, and presuppose it in his next sentence, e.g.:

He was there the night before, too.

Such a sentence, termed a "second instance sentence" by Bolinger

(1952: 35f.), not only has proform reduction and deletion but also presupposes the truth of a closely related sentence.

Presuppositions may also be introduced by particular verbs, adjectives and nouns that take a clause as their complement. In each of the following sentences:

I realize that John was in Mary's bedroom.
I'm glad that John was in Mary's bedroom.
It's a pity that John was in Mary's bedroom.

the speaker presupposes the truth of the *that*-clause, and goes on to describe how it affects someone or something.

Some propositions are neither presupposed nor asserted, but simply presented as a HYPOTHESIS; the obvious example being a typical *yes-no* question like:

Was John in Mary's room last night?

which can also be embedded as in:

I wondered whether (/if) John was in Mary's room last night.

Unfortunately, however, it is virtually impossible to make a clearcut distinction between assertions and hypotheses, as the following series of sentences shows:

John was in Mary's bedroom last night.
Probably John was in Mary's bedroom last night.
Possibly John was in Mary's bedroom last night.
Was John possibly in Mary's bedroom last night?
Was John in Mary's bedroom last night?

At what point along the scale do we change from assertion (or statement) to hypothesis (or question)? Is the traditional question-mark more than just an arbitrary point?

Givenness and presuppositions have been discussed by scholars of the Prague school under the heading of "theme and rheme" and "functional sentence perspective". Items that are given or presupposed form the natural starting point for a sentence, which is sometimes equated with "what the sentence is about", and are termed the THEME, or in the work of American linguists the "topic". But although Mathesius (1939; cf. also Firbas, 1964) wished to link the theme with givenness, Trávníček objected that, while all sentences had a theme, many were made up entirely of new elements. He therefore wished to define the theme purely in psychological terms, as that sentence element which the speaker has in mind as his object of thought and from which his sentence proceeds (1961: 166). This conception is very similar to Halliday's notion of theme, which he describes metaphorically as "the peg on which the sentence is hung" (1970: 161). We may therefore see the theme as the speaker's starting-point in his current sentence, and this may, but need not, take up something already discussed. If we accept theme-rheme as a variable independent of givenness, it is nevertheless easy to see that it is natural for the theme to start from given items and for the sentence-remainder, the rheme (in American work, the "comment"), to present some new information about it, as in:

He'|s run a 3½-minute mile.

(A vertical line is used to separate theme from rheme in this and subsequent examples.) This follows a natural textual progression from the known to the unknown. However, it frequently happens that both theme and rheme are new, as in:

A Kenyan | has run a 3½-minute mile.

A new theme also occurs with a given rheme, giving the reverse of the "natural" pattern, e.g.:

A Kenyan | has done it.

Finally, both theme and rheme may be given, as in:

He|'s done it.

If we take the theme to be the first element in each of the above sentences, it is clear that theme-rheme is a variable that is independent of givenness. But what sort of variable is it? In English the initial element is very often the subject (as in the above examples), but Halliday (1970: 161) also cites cases where another element is the theme, e.g.:

Yesterday | we discussed the financial arrangements.
His spirit | they couldn't kill.

In the first example the adverbial *yesterday* is certainly given prominence by being placed in initial position, but it is perhaps not a starting point for the sentence in the same sense as the subject is; rather it simply places, in advance, a spatio-temporal restriction on the validity of the sentence, providing it, so to speak, with a setting. In the second example, however, the fronted object noun can be seen as a starting point; in fact, it could easily have been the subject of the sentence:

His spirit just couldn't be killed (by them).

Sometimes sentences with fronted objects arise from the fact that the speaker, having announced his theme, is unable to find a suitable verb that takes such a subject with the right meaning. In this interpretation, then, the theme is equated with the planned subject, where the subject is an item that is chosen as sentential starting point and the perspective from which the verbal action is viewed. Thus the difference between the two replies to the following question:

[How did Nastase get on?]
(a) He lost to Borg.
(b) Borg beat him.

would be in the way they present the information, taking the viewpoint of the subject (in (a) he = Nastase; in (b) Borg) and viewing the verbal action with that perspective. In recent years much attention has been given to the problem of the nature of "subjects" and of "theme" or "topic" (cf. Li, 1976), and in Li and Thompson (1976) it is suggested that some languages organize their sentences around subjects and others around topics.

Although the division into theme and rheme is one that is internal to the sentence, it has ramifications in the text at large. Daneš (1974) points out how patterns of theme-rheme within sentence sequences can be organized to give a cohesive text. In one pattern the rheme of one sentence is used as the theme of the next, as in his example (1974: 118):

The first of the antibiotics was discovered by Sir Alexander Fleming in 1928. He was busy at the time . . .

In another pattern the theme is kept constant from sentence to sentence; for instance, the second sentence above could alternatively have began *It was called* . . . In a further sequence pattern different themes in a sentence all stem from a common "hyper-theme", e.g. medical discoveries, cricket.

The same propositional content often needs to be presented with the sentence constituents in different sequences, to suit the purposes of thematic organization of the text. In a language like Russian or Czech, where syntactic distinctions like subject v. object are made morphologically, word order is free to be used for thematic purposes (cf. Dahl, 1975: 351). A language like English, on the other hand, where SUBJECT + LEXICAL VERB + OBJECT is a relatively rigid order, needs to make extensive use of transformations like passivization, object fronting, clefting (cf. chapter 8) to achieve the required thematic order of elements.

275

**Sentence patterning within the text**

We have seen how links may be made between sentences through their sharing common parts: they may share lexical items (shown through proform reduction or deletion); they may share co-reference to the same things (shown through definiteness, etc.); they may be linked by presupposition; or they may be linked through theme-rheme (= topic-comment) structure. But how can sentences as a whole be linked with each other? This may happen in one of two related ways: either they are connected semantically in terms of the propositions they communicate; or they are related textually, in the ways they contribute to the text as a whole.

Sentences that are semantically linked may be involved in a subordinative or in a coordinative relationship. In the subordinative relationship one proposition is seen as a component within another; this is expressed in a number of possible ways:

(i) Embedding the minor sentence either as a subordinate clause or just as a nominalization, and specifying the relationship to the major sentence with a conjunction or a preposition respectively, e.g.: *Although it was raining, we carried on playing; Despite the rain, we carried on playing.*

(ii) Referring to the proposition with a proform and specifying the relationship with a preposition, e.g.: *Despite that, we carried on playing.*

(iii) Simply using a sentence adverbial to mention a relationship to the (contextually recoverable) proposition, e.g.: *Nevertheless, we carried on playing.*

Whereas under (i) the relationship between the propositions has been encompassed within a single sentence, under (ii) and (iii) we have a single sentence that points back to an earlier one. While under (ii) the anaphoric item *that* is used to achieve the link, under (iii) a subcategory of sentence adverbial (we might term it the "contingency" type) is used with a similar effect. The relationship between the sentences (i.e. the "contingency" involved) in the above examples is one of contrast or concession. The other main ones are cause (*for that reason*, etc.) and condition (*in that case, otherwise*, etc.).

When, on the other hand, the propositions are on a par with each other, they may be put into a coordinative relationship. As we saw in chapter 9, two sentences may be coordinated to form a single sentence:

It was raining, but we carried on playing.

but it is also possible to regard them as two separate sentences:

It was raining. But we carried on playing.

The coordinators that link such sentences may express the semantic relationships of addition or grouping together (*and*), choice of alternatives (*or*), contrast (*but, yet*), result or inference (*so*), and reason or cause (*for*, or in spoken English *'cause*).

The other way sentences may be related to each other is in terms of their contribution to the text. Although this is obviously closely related to a sentence's semantic content, it is at least in principle different from it, and may be expressed by one of a whole series of sentence adverbials that have this textual role. In English some of these adverbials mark the way in which the sentence is added together with others to make the same major point, simply reinforcing like *moreover*, or enumerating like *first(ly)*, or summing up like *all in all*; all of these could be said to correspond, in a broad sense, to *and*. A rather different kind of *and* relationship is found with adverbials like *incidentally* and *by the way*, which mark the introduction of a new topic, relatively unconnected with what went before. Corresponding to *or*, we find adverbials that express an appositional relationship between the sentence and its precursor, marking the sentence as a further explanation, like *in other words*, or as an exemplification, like *for instance*. Contrastive or concessive adverbials show that the sentence has to be seen as detracting from what went before and thus either reducing the impact of the previous point or replacing it with a different one: they include *on the contrary, on the other hand, however*. Comparable to *so* is the resultative *therefore*; but to *for* (*'cause*) we find nothing in written English, though spoken English uses *you see, you know*.

Adverbials and conjunctions may thus link sentences which make similar, related, or even different contributions to a text. But precisely what constitutes a similar contribution to a text? It has, for instance, often been pointed out that it is only normal to coordinate sentences of the same type, and so a sentence like:

*? I was surprised to see him, and why did he come?

is ungrammatical. But to fully understand the contribution a sentence makes we must be clear what its function is.

Traditionally a division has been made in utterances between such types as statements (declaratives), questions (interrogatives), commands (imperatives), exclamations; and in more subtle classifications wishes, warnings, requests, etc. and social formulae such as greetings might be added, and questions subdivided into *wh*-questions, *yes-no* questions and alternative (*or*) questions. The basis for such distinctions may be either functional or formal. The

*Grammar and discourse*

functional approach may point to the different purposes the speaker may have in mind (giving information, eliciting information, etc.); or it may draw attention to the characteristic linguistic and situational context of each utterance type: for instance, a *yes-no* question being followed by *yes, no, well*, etc. by the listener, a greeting by a returned (identical or similar) greeting, a command by action (at the appropriate time) or refusal, and so on. Unfortunately neither version of this functional approach, despite its undoubted validity and importance, gives very clear-cut results.

In our search for decisiveness we might then turn to a formal approach to the categorization of sentence types. This would rely on the lexical and grammatical features that mark functional differences. Virtually all languages seem to have the equivalent of *wh*-words; and in many languages *yes-no* questions are marked with a special particle or affix such as Latin *-ne*, Turkish *mi* (with vowel harmony), Japanese *ka*. Many languages have a special verb form for the imperative. The difficulty is, though, that the formal value of a sentence can often be overridden by its accompanying intonation and/or situational context. For instance, in English the textual value of a command like:

Come in.

is matched by the value of the following formally different sentences:

I'd like you to come in.
Would you (like to) come in?

All three sentences are likely to be followed by compliant action along with *Yes, Right*, etc. or refusal along with *No (thanks)*. There are, of course, differences between them, but these are not so great as the formal differences would suggest. We need to explain why such sentences are interpreted in the way they are despite their formal structure. We also need to take account of the fact that a statement pronounced with rising intonation, e.g.:

You're coming?

may be interpreted as a (surprised) question, while some questions, given a falling intonation, e.g.:

Isn't he excited?!

are interpreted as exclamations (the latter might, for instance, be followed by *D'you think so?*).

Such difficulties as these have led linguists to turn to philosophy, and in particular to the work of J. L. Austin and those following him,

278

for a deeper study of the functions of individual sentences. Austin (1962) began from the position that within the traditional class of statements, which have what he calls "constative" value and the potential of being true or false, there lurks a group with a quite different value, which he terms "performative". Performative utterances are characterized as sentences, the uttering of which "is, or is a part of, the doing of an action" rather than "saying something" (1962: 5). Austin's examples of performative utterances included sentences like:

I name this ship the Queen Elizabeth.
[AS UTTERED WHEN SMASHING THE BOTTLE AGAINST THE STERN]
I bet you sixpence it will rain tomorrow.

Such sentences include a first-person singular subject and a present-tense verb denoting some speech-act such as *name, bet, promise, order*; and the sentence does not, as in ordinary descriptive statements, constitute a report on the activity described, but it is itself an instance of the activity described. If I say *I bet* . . . or *I promise* . . . under the appropriate conditions, I have made a bet or a promise respectively. These conditions are said to make the performative happy (= felicitous) or unhappy (= infelicitous). Felicity is said to apply to performatives, while truth and falsehood apply only to constatives. Sometimes the word *hereby* is used to confirm the performative value of the utterance; putting the verb into the past tense, however, immediately changes it back to a constative utterance, i.e. a report.

Even performative utterances are seen by Austin to refer to the world beyond them, however, and he therefore describes them as having both "locutionary force", what they refer to, and "illocutionary force", what kind of speech-act they constitute. (Some sentences also involve "perlocutionary force", the implied effects of the words spoken, on other people for instance, as with a verb like *persuade*, which, though not performative like *advise*, refers to the change of mind the listener will undergo as a result of the speech-act.) It is no big step then for Austin to allow all constative sentences to have implicit illocutionary force so that:

I grow runner beans

can be understood as containing the same illocutionary force as:

I (hereby) state that I grow runner beans.

Thus Austin's initial distinction between constative and performative utterances turns into a distinction between utterances with implicit and explicit illocutionary force.

As we indicated in chapter 11, Ross (1970) goes a step further than Austin by claiming that all declarative sentences, rather than just being implicitly performative, actually have a performative verb in their deep structure. In Ross's view, then, we could partially represent the deep structure of a simple sentence like *It's raining* as in Figure 94. He presents arguments purporting to show that all declarative sentences must contain an *I*, must have a performative verb like *say*, and must contain a *you*. Since much of his data involve uses of pronouns, particularly reflexives, that are difficult for native speakers to agree on, the incorporation of the performative analysis into syntax, albeit a semantically based one, remains controversial. Ross does, however, accept that a pragmatic interpretation of performatives would be equally attractive.

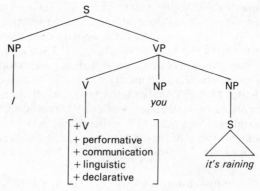

*Figure 94*

A pragmatic view of performative verbs, and of illocutionary force in general, seeks to interpret the value of sentences in their actual situational context. In doing so, the linguist-philosopher must obviously take account of the lexical content and grammatical structure of the sentence but must also see how these carry the propositional content (the locutionary force) and simultaneously its value as a particular kind of speech-act (the illocutionary force). Searle (1969) examines the conditions under which speech-acts such as promises may be said to have been correctly and sincerely uttered: for a promise these would include the propositional requirement that the sentence refer to some future act of the speaker, but also pragmatic requirements, such as that the speaker would not normally be carrying out the act anyway, that the speaker is nevertheless capable of carrying it out, that the listener would wish the act to be carried out, that the speaker intends to actually carry it out (the "sincerity condition"), and that he recognizes he has taken on a responsibility.

Gordon and Lakoff (1971) refer to conditions like these in an attempt to devise "conversational postulates", which will explain how, as we saw above, questions may take on the value of commands or requests, statements may be interpreted as questions, etc. In a sentence like:

Can you hold this vase for me for a moment?

the question may be interpreted as a request because it seeks to establish one of the felicity conditions for a request or command to be operative, i.e. the addressee's capacity for carrying out the activity referred to. Such a question used as a request has been termed a "whimperative". The term "queclaratives" has been devised for questions having something of the force of a statement, e.g. *Do you have to smoke?* (cf. Sadock, 1974).

From examining the contribution of individual sentences within the text at large, we now turn to the text itself and to patterns within it larger than the sentence. Perhaps the crucial question here is one of planning: how big a piece of language can we plan at one time? Without giving this psycholinguistic problem full consideration, we can probably only assert that there is at least a significant difference between the planning of spontaneous spoken texts compared with written. Natural spoken language is used in the cut-and-thrust of conversation or in the impromptu linguistic articulation of a narrative, where planning much beyond the current sentence is a rarely indulged-in luxury. In written language, on the other hand, except for the hastily scribbled note, we have time to plan the whole of what we say, putting it into an appropriate sequence and arranging it into paragraphs and other suitable subunits. This whole area of paragraphs and their structure is one that is in need of further research, as is the problem of their phonological equivalent, "paraphones". Although written language is obviously planned with the reader in mind, his absence from the immediate context makes the written text more like a monologue. In spoken texts, on the other hand, the listener must be taken full account of – indeed, he is likely to butt in with a comment or query at any moment – and this probably means that, even with the best intentions, one speaker's contribution is at most part-planned or short-term planned.

Within sociology ethnomethodologists have made a special study of the contributions of speakers and listeners, in what they term "conversational analysis". Schegloff and Sacks (1973) and others have pointed to various aspects of the structure of conversations, including the rules for initiating them and for closing them. They have demonstrated the existence of so-called "adjacency pairs", which include not only question-and-answer but also greeting-greeting and offer-acceptance/rejection. The significance of these pairs lies partly in the way they determine who holds the conversational "floor" (in the sense of who has the right to speak and remain speaking). Thus a question not only requires the listener to give an answer (thus giving him the "floor") but at the same time places an obligation on him to give another turn to the questioner when the answer is complete. Longer conversations may, of course, cover a whole series of topics, and there has been detailed study of the way topics are chosen, new topics introduced, and so on. What Schegloff and Sacks refer to as "pre-closings", such as *I'd better go*, may be used to invite discussion of any so-far-unmentioned topic. In specialized social situations discourse patterns may develop along slightly different lines. For instance, Sinclair and Coulthard (1975) in their study of teacher-pupil interaction in the classroom describe a common three-part exchange of question (by teacher) + answer (by pupil) + "follow up" (by teacher, e.g. *right!, good!, well done!*).

It is in written language, however, that we would expect to find the highest degree of textual organization. Writers are expected to group their sentences into paragraphs, and normally above this to use higher units such as (possibly) subsections, sections, chapters and even books/volumes. The organizational basis for this potentially complex hierarchy must be semantic. Van Dijk (1972: 140f.) suggests basing textual analysis on the semantic structure of the sentence by reducing each text to a complex sentence, which in turn can be made equivalent to a simple sentence. It is questionable, though, whether such a reduction can do full justice to the nature of a text. A different approach is to seek to analyse the narrative structure of a text into certain basic components, which we might follow Van Dijk (1972: 293) in describing as:

- (i) Orientation (= initial situation of equilibrium),
- (ii) Complication (= rupture of this situation),
- (iii) Evaluation (= arrival/trial of the hero),
- (iv) Resolution (= beneficent action of the hero),
- (v) Coda (= re-establishment of initial situation; hero recompensed).

Such patterning is clearly limited to story-like texts.

Can anything more general be said concerning text structure? To state the obvious: texts have a beginning, a middle and an end. The function of the beginning is perhaps to engage the reader's interest in the topic, problem or situation (e.g. of the hero(ine)). The writer should be aware that the reader has the possibility, at any time, of putting down or even throwing away the text; though it has to be admitted that some texts (e.g. civil service pamphlets) make no attempt to attract the reader's attention, since their writers assume a need or duty on the part of the reader to acquire the information in the text. The reader's attention can be engaged by a prospective introduction, although this can have the effect of (quite helpfully) convincing him that the text is not what he wants. The middle, or body, of the text develops the exposition of the topic, problem or situation – let us say the "plot" – possibly dividing it into a series of "subplots" (including parenthesized "subplots", "subsubplots", etc.). Tension is built up through the non-resolution of the "subplots"; their resolution may be delayed until a final dénouement where all "subplots" are unified in a single "plot" (e.g. in academic texts a series of individual problems is solved with a new macro-theory). Alternatively, an anecdotal structure may be effected through a series of "subplot"-dénouement sequences, as when the macroproblem has been analysed into a series of constituent problems. After the climax has been reached and passed, any following material, such as an epilogue, tends to be anticlimactic. This applies equally, in a non-narrative text, to a résumé or retrospect, which attempts to answer questions like "What was it all for?", "Has the mission been successful?" We shall therefore forgo such a textual element in this particular text.

## Questions for study

1   Consider the italicized proforms in the following sentences. What kind of item does each take as "given"? What kind of givenness, of the referent or of the lexeme, is involved?

>   Here's one of *those* paperweights. John gave *them* to us. He *did it* so ostentatiously as well. I don't know why he has to behave *like that*. Unfortunately I've damaged *mine*.

2   Identify the presuppositions in the following sentences:
    (a)   Why did you choose to take linguistics?
    (b)   Peter was surprised at your success in the exam.
    (c)   How old are your brothers and sisters?
    (d)   Are you still interested in linguistics?

3   Combine each of the following sentence sequences into a single complex sentence, making the first sentence into a subordinate clause:
    (a)   The weather was extremely bad. We therefore ended the meeting early.

(b) They must withdraw their proposal. Otherwise I shall resign.
(c) They protested vigorously. In spite of that I went ahead.
What kind of "contingency" is involved in each case?

4 Study the following text:

I think we shall survive this crisis. Just to name one possibility, we could extend our overdraft. In addition, we could press those owing us money for early payment. Alternatively, we could try to reduce our expenses and our investment. Then we would have less cash to find. On the other hand, we might be overtaken by a general economic collapse, I suppose.

What elements mark textual relations between the sentences? What kind of relationship is involved in each case? Do these relationships impose any structural groupings of sentences within the text that might be presented in the form of a tree diagram?

5 What is the textual value of each of the following sentences? What sort of speech-act does each one function as?
(a) Why don't you ever visit us?
(b) Why don't you visit us next Tuesday?
(c) I'll come on Wednesday, if you like.
(d) I'll come on Wednesday without fail.
(e) Can you come early?
(f) I want you to tell us all about your new book.

**Further reading**

On textual links between sentence parts: Waterhouse (1963); Firbas (1964); Van Dijk (1972), chapter 2; Grice (1975); Halliday and Hasan (1976), chapter 1; Lyons (1977), section 14.3; Allerton (1978b). On sentence patterning within the text: Greenbaum (1969), chapters 1 to 3; Van Dijk (1972), chapter 3; Grimes (1975), chapters 14 to 16; Lyons (1977), chapter 16.

# Bibliography

Allen, W. S. (1956). "Structure and system in Abaza." *Transactions of the Philological Society*. 127–76.

Allerton, D. J. (1969). "The sentence as a linguistic unit." *Lingua* 22. 27–46.

Allerton, D. J. (1970). "Intuitions in grammatical theory." In *Actes du Xième Congrès International des Linguistes*. Bucharest: Éditions de l'Académie de la République Socialiste de Roumanie. 933–9.

Allerton, D. J. (with French, M. A.) (1975). "Morphology: the forms of English." In Bolton (1975), 79–134.

Allerton, D. J. (1978a). "Generating indirect objects in English." *Journal of Linguistics* 14. 21–33.

Allerton, D. J. (1978b). "The notion of 'givenness' and its relation to presupposition and to theme." *Lingua* 44. 133–68.

Allerton, D. J. and Cruttenden, A. (1978). "Syntactic, illocutionary, thematic and attitudinal factors in the intonation of adverbials." *Journal of Pragmatics* 2. 155–88.

Allwood, J., Andersson, L.-G. and Dahl, Ö. (1977). *Logic in Linguistics*. Cambridge: Cambridge University Press.

Anderson, J. M. (1971). *The Grammar of Case*. Cambridge: Cambridge University Press.

Aronoff, M. (1976). *Word Formation in Generative Grammar (Linguistic Inquiry monograph no. 1)*. Cambridge, Mass.: M.I.T. Press.

Austin, J. L. (1962). *How to Do Things with Words*. London: Oxford University Press.

Bach, E. (1968). "Nouns and noun phrases." In Bach and Harms (1968), 91–122.

Bach, E. (1970). "Problominalization." *Linguistic Inquiry* 1. 121–2.

Bach, E. (1974). *Syntactic Theory*. New York: Holt Rinehart.

Bach, E. and Harms, R. T. (eds.) (1968). *Universals in Linguistic Theory*. New York: Holt Rinehart.

Bazell, C. E. (1949a). "On the neutralization of syntactic oppositions." *Travaux du Cercle Linguistique de Copenhague* 5. 77–86. (Reprinted in Hamp *et al.* (1966), 208–15.)

Bazell, C. E. (1949b). "On the problem of the morpheme." *Archivum Linguisticum* 1. 1–15. (Reprinted in Hamp *et al.* (1966), 216–26.)

Bazell, C. E. (1964). "Three misconceptions of grammaticalness." In Stuart, C. I. J. M. (ed.). *Report on the 15th Annual Round Table Meeting on Linguistics and Language Studies (= MSLL 17).* Washington, D.C.: Georgetown University Press. 3–10.

Bazell, C. E., Catford, J. C., Halliday, M. A. K. and Robins, R. H. (eds.) (1966). *In Memory of J. R. Firth*. London: Longman.

Berkeley, G. (1910). *A New Theory of Vision and Other Writings*. (1st edition, 1709.) London: Dent.

Berry, M. (1975). *Introduction to Systemic Linguistics I: Structures and Systems*. London: Batsford.

Berry, M. (1977). *Introduction to Systemic Linguistics II: Levels and Links*. London: Batsford.

Bloch, B. (1946). "Studies in colloquial Japanese II: syntax." *Language* 22. 200–48. (Reprinted in Joos (1957), 154–85.)

Bloch, B. (1947). "English verb inflection." *Language* 23. 399–418. (Reprinted in Joos (1957), 243–54.)

Bloch, B. and Trager, G. L. (1942). *Outline of Linguistic Analysis*. Baltimore: Linguistic Society of America.

Bloomfield, L. (1935). *Language*. London: Allen & Unwin. (American edition, 1933.)

Bolinger, D. L. (1948). "On defining the morpheme." *Word* 4. 18–23.

Bolinger, D. L. (1952). "Linear modification." *Publications of the Modern Language Association of America* 67. 1117–44. (Excerpts reprinted in Householder (1972), 31–50.)

Bolinger, D. L. (1961). *Generality, Gradience and the All-or-none*. The Hague: Mouton.

Bolinger, D. L. (1975). *Aspects of Language*, 2nd edition (1st edition, 1968). New York: Harcourt, Brace, Jovanovitch.

Bolton, W. F. (ed.) (1975). *The English Language. Sphere History of Literature in the English Language, Vol. 10*. London: Sphere Books.

Bresnan, J. (1971). "Sentence stress and syntactic transformations." *Language* 47. 257–81.

Buchler, J. (ed.) (1940). *The Philosophy of Peirce, Selected Writings*. London: Kegan Paul.

Burt, M. K. (1971). *From Deep to Surface Structure*. New York: Harper Row.

Chafe, W. L. (1970). *Meaning and the Structure of Language*. Chicago: University of Chicago Press.

Cherry, C. (1957). *On Human Communication*. New York: Science Editions, Inc.

Chomsky, N. (1957). *Syntactic Structures*. The Hague: Mouton.

Chomsky, N. (1961). "Some methodological remarks on generative grammar." *Word* 17. 219–39.

Chomsky, N. (1964). "Current issues in linguistic theory." In Fodor and Katz (1964), 50–118.

Chomsky, N. (1965). *Aspects of the Theory of Syntax*. Cambridge, *Mass.: M.I.T. Press*.

Chomsky, N. (1968). *Language and Mind*. New York: Harcourt Brace.

Chomsky, N. (1970). "Remarks on nominalization." In Jacobs and Rosenbaum (1970), 184–221.

Chomsky, N. (1971a). "Deep structure, surface structures and semantic interpretation." In Steinberg and Jakobovits (1971), 183–216.

Chomsky, N. (1971b). *Language and Mind*. New York: Harcourt Brace.

Chomsky, N. (1972). "Some empirical issues in the theory of transformational grammar." In Peters (1972b), 63–130.

Chomsky, N. (1976). *Reflections on Language*. London: Temple Smith (in association with Fontana Books).

Chomsky, N. and Halle, M. (1968). *The Sound Pattern of English*. New York: Harper & Row.

Cole, P. and Morgan, J. L. (eds.) (1975). *Syntax and Semantics 3: Speech Acts*. New York: Academic Press.

Comrie, B. (1976). *Aspect: An Introduction to the Study of Verbal Aspect and Related Problems*. Cambridge: Cambridge University Press.

Cook, W. A. (1969). *Introduction to Tagmemic Analysis*. New York: Holt Rinehart.

Dahl, Ö. (1975). Review of Sgall, P., Hajičová, E. and Benešová, E. (1973), *Topic, Focus and Generative Semantics*. *Journal of Linguistics* 11. 347–54.

Daneš, F. (1964). "A three-level approach to syntax." *Travaux Linguistiques de Prague* 1. 225–40.

Daneš, F. (1974). "F.S.P. and the text organization." In Daneš, F. (ed.). *Papers on Functional Sentence Perspective*. Prague: Academia. 106–27.

Dik, S. C. (1968). *Co-ordination: Its Implications for the Theory of General Linguistics*. Amsterdam: North-Holland.

Dineen, F. P. (1967). *An Introduction to General Linguistics*. New York: Holt Rinehart.

Emonds, J. (1972). "A reformulation of certain syntactic transformations." In Peters (1972b), 21–63.

Fillmore, C. J. (1968). "The case for case." In Bach and Harms (1968), 1–88.

Fillmore, C. J. (1971). "Some problems for case grammar." In O'Brien, R. J. (ed.), *Report of the 22nd Annual Round Table Meeting on Linguistics and Language Studies* (= *MSSL 24*). Washington, D.C.: Georgetown University Press. 35–56.

Fillmore, C. J. (1972). "On generativity." In Peters (1972b), 1–20.

Fillmore, C. J. and Langendoen, D. T. (eds.) (1971). *Studies in Linguistic Semantics*. New York: Holt Rinehart.

Firbas, J. (1964). "On defining the theme in Functional Sentence Analysis." *Travaux Linguistiques de Prague* 1. 267–80.

Firth, J. R. (1957). *Papers in Linguistics 1934–51*. London: Oxford University Press.

Fodor, J. A. (1970). "Three reasons for not deriving 'kill' from 'cause to die'." *Linguistic Inquiry* 1. 429–38.

Fodor, J. A. and Katz, J. J. (eds.) (1964). *The Structure of Language, Readings in the Philosophy of Language*. Englewood Cliffs, N.J.: Prentice-Hall.

Fowler, R. (1974). *Understanding Language: An Introduction to Linguistics*. London: Routledge & Kegan Paul.

Fries, C. C. (1952). *The Structure of English: An Introduction to the Construction of English Sentences*. New York: Harcourt Brace.

Frisch, K. von (1950). *Bees, Their Vision, Chemical Sense and Language*. Ithaca: Cornell University Press.

Gaillie, W. B. (1952). *Peirce and Pragmatism*. Harmondsworth: Penguin.

Gimson, A. C. (1962). *An Introduction to the Pronunciation of English*. London: Edward Arnold.

Gleason, H. A., Jr. (1961). *Introduction to Descriptive Linguistics*, 2nd edition (1st edition, 1955). New York: Holt Rinehart.

Glinz, H. (1952). *Die innere Form der Deutschen*. Berne: Francke.

Goethe, J. W. von (1953). *Goethes Werke, in 2 Bänden* (Knaur Klassiker). Munich: Droemersche Verlagsanstalt.

Gordon, D. and Lakoff, G. (1971). "Conversational postulates." In *Papers from the 7th Regional Meeting of the Chicago Linguistic Circle*, 63–84. (Reprinted in Cole and Morgan (1975), 83–106.)

Greenbaum, S. (1969). *Studies in English Adverbial Usage*. London: Longman.

Grice, H. P. (1975). "Logic and conversation." In Cole and Morgan (1975), 41–58.

Grimes, J. E. (1975). *The Thread of Discourse*. The Hague: Mouton.

Haas, W. (1954). "On defining linguistic units." *Transactions of the Philological Society*. 54–84.

Haas, W. (1957). "Zero in linguistic description." In *Studies in Linguistic Analysis* (Special volume of the Philological Society). Oxford: Blackwell.

Haas, W. (1966). "Linguistic relevance." In Bazell *et al.* (1966), 116–47.

Haas, W. (1973a). "Review article on Lyons (1968)." *Journal of Linguistics* 9. 71–113.

Haas, W. (1973b). "Meanings and rules." *Proceedings of the Aristotelian Society* 1972–3. 135–55.

Haas, W. (1976). "Writing: the basic options." In Haas, W. (ed.). *Writing without Letters*. Manchester: Manchester University Press. 131–208.

Halliday, M. A. K. (1961). "Categories of the theory of grammar." *Word* 17. 241–92.

Halliday, M. A. K. (1966a). "Lexis as a linguistic level." In Bazell *et al.* (1966), 148–62.

Halliday, M. A. K. (1966b). "The concept of rank: a reply." *Journal of Linguistics* 2. 110–18.

Halliday, M. A. K. (1967/8). "Notes on transitivity and theme." *Journal of Linguistics* 3. 37–81, 199–24; and 4. 179–216.

Halliday, M. A. K. (1969). "Options and functions in the English clause." *Brno Studies in English*, 8, no. 137. 81–8. (Reprinted in Householder (1972), 248–57.)

Halliday, M. A. K. (1970). "Language structure and language function." In Lyons (1970a), 140–65.

Halliday, M. A. K. and Hasan, R. (1976). *Cohesion in English*. London: Longman.

Hamp, E. P., Householder, F. W. and Austerlitz, R. (1966). *Readings in Linguistics II*. Chicago: University of Chicago Press.

Harris, Z. S. (1946). "From morpheme to utterance." *Language* 22. 161–83. (Reprinted in Joos (1957), 142–53.)

Harris, Z. S. (1951). *Methods in Structural Linguistics*. Chicago: University of Chicago Press. (Reprinted as *Structural Linguistics*, 1961.)

Harris, Z. S. (1952). "Discourse analysis." *Language* 28. 1–30. (Reprinted in Fodor and Katz (1964), 355–83.)

Harris, Z. S. (1957). "Cooccurrence and transformation in linguistic structure." *Language* 33. 283–340. (Reprinted in Fodor and Katz (1964), 155–210; and in Householder (1972), 151–85.)

Haugen, E. (1951). "Directions in modern linguistics." *Language* 27. 211–22. (Reprinted in Joos (1957), 357–63.)

Hays, D. G. (1964). "Dependency theory: a formalism and some observations." *Language* 40. 511–25. (Reprinted in Householder (1972), 223–40.)

Helbig, G. (ed.) (1971). *Beiträge zur Valenztheorie*. The Hague: Mouton.

Helbig, G. and Schenkel, W. (1973). *Wörterbuch zur Valenz und Distribution deutscher Verben*, 2nd edition. Leipzig: V.E.B. Bibliographisches Institut.

Hjelmslev, L. (1961). *Prolegomena to a Theory of Language*. Translated by F. J. Whitfield. (Danish title: *Omkring sprogteoriens grundlæggelse*.) Madison: University of Wisconsin Press.

Hockett, C. F. (1947). "Problems of morphemic analysis." *Language* 23. 321–43. (Reprinted in Joos (1957), 229–42.)

Hockett, C. F. (1954). "Two models of grammatical description." *Word* 10. 210–31. (Reprinted in Joos (1957), 386–99.)

Hockett, C. F. (1955). *A Manual of Phonology* (Memoir 11, Indiana University Publications in Anthropology and Linguistics). Bloomington: Indiana University Press.

Hockett, C. F. (1958). *A Course in Modern Linguistics*. New York: Macmillan.
Hockett, C. F. and Altmann, S. A. (1968). "The design features of language." In Sebeok (1968), 61–72.
Householder, F. W. (1959). "On linguistic primes." *Word* 15. 231–9.
Householder, F. W. (ed.) (1972). *Syntactic Theory I: Structuralist*. Harmondsworth: Penguin.
Huddleston, R. (1970). "Some remarks on case-grammar." *Linguistic Inquiry* 1. 501–11.
Hudson, R. A. (1974). "Systemic generative grammar." *Linguistics* 139. 5–42.

Jackendoff, R. S. (1972). *Semantic Interpretation in Generative Grammar*. Cambridge, Mass.: M.I.T. Press.
Jacobs, R. A. and Rosenbaum, P. S. (1968). *English Transformational Grammar*. Waltham, Mass.: Blaisdell.
Jacobs, R. A. and Rosenbaum, P. S. (eds.) (1970). *Readings in English Transformational Grammar*. Waltham, Mass.: Ginn and Co.
Jakobson, R. (1936). "Beitrag zur allgemeinen Kasuslehre." *Travaux du Cercle Linguistique de Prague* 6. 240–88. (Reprinted in Hamp *et al.* (1966), 51–89.)
Jakobson, R. (1962). *Selected Writings I: Phonological Studies*. The Hague: Mouton.
Jespersen, O. (1924). *The Philosophy of Grammar*. London: Allen & Unwin.
Jespersen, O. (1946). *A Modern English Grammar on Historical Principles*, Vol. 6. London: Allen & Unwin.
Jespersen, O. (1969). *Analytic Syntax*. New York: Holt Rinehart. (First published 1937, London: Allen & Unwin.)
Johnson, D. E. (1976). *Towards a Theory of Relationally-based Grammar*. Bloomington: Indiana University Linguistics Club.
Johnson, W. E. (1964). *Logic, Part I*. New York: Dover Publications. (First published 1921, Cambridge: Cambridge University Press.)
Joos, M. (ed.) (1957). *Readings in Linguistics I*. Chicago: University of Chicago Press.

Katz, J. J. and Postal, P. M. (1964). *An Integrated Theory of Linguistic Descriptions*. Cambridge, Mass.: M.I.T. Press.
Keenan, E. L. (1971). "Two kinds of presupposition." In Fillmore and Langendoen (1971), 45–54.
Keenan, E. L. (1976). "Towards a universal definition of subject." In Li (1976), 247–301.
Koutsoudas, A. C. (1963). "The morpheme reconsidered." *International Journal of American Linguistics* 29. 160–70.
Koutsoudas, A. C. (1966). *Writing Transformational Grammars*. New York: McGraw-Hill.

Lakoff, G. (1968). *Deep and Surface Grammar*. Bloomington: Indiana University Linguistics Club.

Lakoff, G. (1970a). "Pronominalization, negation and the analysis of adverbs." In Jacobs and Rosenbaum (1970), 145–65.

Lakoff, G. (1970b). "Global rules." *Language* 46. 627–39.

Lakoff, G. (1971a). "On generative semantics." In Steinberg and Jakobovits (1971), 232–96.

Lakoff, G. (1971b). *On Syntactic Irregularity*. New York: Holt Rinehart.

Lakoff, G. (1972). "Linguistics and natural logic." In Davidson, D. and Harman, G. (eds.). *Semantics of Natural Languages*. Dordrecht, Holland: Reidel. 545–665.

Lamb, S. M. (1966). *Outline of Stratificational Grammar*. Washington, D.C.: Georgetown University Press.

Langendoen, D. T. (1970). *Essentials of English Grammar*. New York: Holt Rinehart.

Lees, R. B. (1960). *The Grammar of English Nominalizations*. The Hague: Mouton. (Reissued 1963.)

Lévi-Strauss, C. (1945). "L'analyse structurale en linguistique et en anthropologie." *Word* 1. 33–53.

Li, C. N. (ed.) (1976). *Subject and Topic*. New York: Academic Press.

Li, C. N. and Thompson, S. A. (1976). "Subject and topic: a new typology of language." In Li (1976), 457–89.

Lockwood, D. G. (1972). *Introduction to Stratificational Linguistics*. New York: Harcourt Brace.

Longacre, R. E. (1960). "String constituent analysis." *Language* 36. 63–88.

Longacre, R. E. (1964). *Grammar Discovery Procedures*. The Hague: Mouton.

Longacre, R. E. (1965). "Some fundamental insights of tagmemics." *Language* 41. 65–76.

Lyons, J. (1966). "Towards a 'notional' theory of the parts of speech." *Journal of Linguistics* 2. 209–36.

Lyons, J. (1968). *Introduction to Theoretical Linguistics*. Cambridge: Cambridge University Press.

Lyons, J. (ed.) (1970a). *New Horizons in Linguistics*. Harmondsworth: Penguin.

Lyons, J. (1970b). *Chomsky*. London: Fontana/Collins.

Lyons, J. (1977). *Semantics*, volumes 1 and 2. Cambridge: Cambridge University Press.

Malinowski, B. (1949). "The problem of meaning in primitive languages." Supplement I to Ogden and Richards (1949), 296–336.

Martinet, A. (1961). *Éléments de linguistique générale*. Paris: Librairie Armand Colin.

Mathesius, V. (1939). "O tak zvaném aktuálním členění věty." *Slovo a slovesnost* 5. 171–4.

Matthews, P. H. (1966). "The concept of rank in 'Neo-Firthian' grammar." *Journal of Linguistics* 2. 101–10.

Matthews, P. H. (1967). Review of Chomsky (1965). *Journal of Linguistics* 3. 119–52.

Matthews, P. H. (1970). "Recent developments in morphology." In Lyons (1970a), 96–114.

Matthews, P. H. (1974). *Morphology: An Introduction to the Theory of Word Structure*. Cambridge: Cambridge University Press.

McCawley, J. D. (1968). "The role of semantics in a grammar." In Bach and Harms (1968), 125–69.

McCawley, J. D. (1970a). "English as a VSO language." *Language* 46. 286–99.

McCawley, J. D. (1970b). "Where do noun phrases come from?" In Jacobs and Rosenbaum (1970), 166–83.

Mitchell, T. F. (1975). "Syntax (and associated matters)." In Bolton (1975), 135–214.

Morris, C. W. (1946). *Signs, Language and Behavior*. New York: Prentice-Hall.

Nida, E. A. (1949). *Morphology: The Descriptive Analysis of Words*, 2nd edition (1st edition, 1946). Ann Arbor: The University of Michigan Press.

Ogden, C. K. and Richards, I. A. (1949). *The Meaning of Meaning* (1st edition, 1926). London: Routledge & Kegan Paul.

Palmer, F. R. (1971). *Grammar*. Harmondsworth: Penguin.

Palmer, F. R. (1974). *The English Verb*. London: Longman.

Partee-Hall, B. (1971). "On the requirement that transformations preserve meaning." In Fillmore and Langendoen (1971), 1–21.

Pedersen, H. (1959). *The Discovery of Language: Linguistic Science in the Nineteenth Century*, translated by J. W. Spargo. Bloomington: Indiana University Press. (1st edition, 1931.)

Peirce, C. S. (1931–58). *Collected Papers*, edited by C. Harthorne and P. Weiss. Cambridge, Mass.: Harvard University Press.

Perlmutter, D. M. (1970). "Surface structure constraints in syntax." *Linguistic Inquiry* 1. 187–255.

Perlmutter, D. M. (1971). *Deep and Surface Structure Constraints in Syntax*. New York: Holt Rinehart.

Peters, S. (1972a). "The projection problem: how is a grammar to be selected?" In Peters (1972b), 171–88.

Peters, S. (ed.) (1972b). *Goals of Linguistic Theory*. Englewood Cliffs, N.J.: Prentice-Hall.

Piaget, Jean (1968/71). *Le Structuralisme*. Paris: Presses Universitaires de France. (Translated by C. Maschler as *Structuralism*. London: Routledge & Kegan Paul.)

Pike, K. L. (1958). "On tagmemes, née gramemes." *International Journal of American Linguistics* 24. 273–8.

Pike, K. L. (1963). "A syntactic paradigm." *Language* 39. 216–30. (Reprinted in Householder (1972), 195–214.)

Postal, P. M. (1964). "Limitations of Phrase Structure grammars." In Fodor and Katz (1964), 137–51.

Postal, P. M. (1970). "On the surface verb 'remind'." *Linguistic Inquiry* 1. 37–120.

Postal, P. M. (1972). "The best theory." In Peters (1972b), 131–70.

Quirk, R. (1968). *The Use of English.* 2nd edition. With supplements by A. C. Gimson and J. Warburg (1st edition, 1962). London: Longman.

Quirk, R., Greenbaum, S., Leech, G. and Svartvik, J. (1972). *A Grammar of Contemporary English*. London: Longman.

Robins, R. H. (1959). "In defence of WP." *Transactions of the Philological Society*. 116–44.

Robins, R. H. (1964). *General Linguistics: An Introductory Survey*. London: Longman.

Robins, R. H. (1967). *A Short History of Linguistics*. London: Longman.

Ross, J. R. (1967). *Constraints on Variables in Syntax*. Bloomington: Indiana University Linguistics Club.

Ross, J. R. (1969). "Auxiliaries as main verbs." In W. Todd (ed.), *Studies in Philosophical Linguistics* I. Evanston, Ill.: Great Expectations Press.

Ross, J. R. (1970). "On declarative sentences." In Jacobs and Rosenbaum (1970), 222–72.

Russell, B. (1940). *An Enquiry into Meaning and Truth*. London: Allen & Unwin.

Ryle, G. (1949). *The Concept of Mind*. London: Hutchinson.

Ryle, G. (1971). *Collected Papers*, 2 vols. London: Hutchinson.

Sadock, J. (1974) *Towards a Linguistic Theory of Speech Acts*. New York: Academic Press.

Sapir, E. (1921). *Language*. New York: Harcourt Brace.

Saussure, F. de (1962). *Cours de linguistique générale*, 3rd edition (1st edition, 1915). Paris: Payot. (English translation, *Course in General Linguistics*, by W. Baskin. New York: Philosophical Library.)

Schane, S. A. (1968). *French Phonology and Morphology*. Cambridge, Mass.: M.I.T. Press.

Schegloff, E. and Sacks, H. (1973). "Opening up closings." *Semiotica* 8. 289–327. (Reprinted in abridged form in R. Turner (ed.) (1974). *Ethnomethodology*. Harmondsworth: Penguin. 233–64.)

Scott, F. C., Bowley, C. C., Brockett, C. S., Brown, J. G. and Goddard, P. R. (1968). *English Grammar: A Linguistic Study of its Classes and Structures*. London: Heinemann.

Searle, J. R. (1969). *Speech Acts*. Cambridge: Cambridge University Press.

Sebeok, T. A. (ed.) (1968). *Animal Communication, Techniques of*

*Study and Results of Research*. Bloomington: Indiana University Press.

Sebeok, T. A., Hayes, A. S. and Bateson, M. C. (eds.) (1964). *Approaches to Semiotics*. The Hague: Mouton.

Shaumyan, S. K. (1965). *Strukturnaya Lingvistika (Structural Linguistics)*. Moscow: Izdatel'sto 'Nauka'.

Sinclair, J. McH. and Coulthard, R. M. (1975). *Towards an Analysis of Discourse: The English Used by Teachers and Pupils*. London: Oxford University Press.

Steinberg, D. and Jakobovits, L. (1971). *Semantics: An Interdisciplinary Reader in Philosophy, Linguistics and Psychology*. Cambridge: Cambridge University Press.

Stockwell, R. P., Schachter, P. and Hall, B. P. (1973). *The Major Syntactic Structures of English*. New York: Holt Rinehart.

Strang, B. M. H. (1962). *Modern English Structure*. London: Edward Arnold.

Tesnière, L. (1959). *Éléments de syntaxe structurale*. Paris: Klincksieck.

Trávníček, F. (1961). "O takzvaném aktuálním členění větnem." *Slovo a slovesnost* 22. 163–71.

Trubetzkoy, N. S. (1958). *Grundzüge der Phonologie*, 2nd edition (1st edition, 1939). Göttingen: Vandenhoeck & Ruprecht.

Vachek, J. (1964). *A Prague School Reader in Linguistics: Studies in the History and Theory of Linguistics*. Bloomington: Indiana University Press.

Van Dijk, T. A. (1972). *Some Aspects of Text Grammars*. The Hague: Mouton.

Wall, R. (1972). *Introduction to Mathematical Linguistics*. Englewood Cliffs, N.J.: Prentice-Hall.

Waterhouse, V. (1963). "Independent and dependent sentences." *International Journal of American Linguistics* 29. 45–54. (Reprinted in Householder (1972), 65–81.)

Wells, R. S. (1947). "Immediate constituents." *Language* 23. 81–117. (Reprinted in Joos (1957), 186–207.)

Wenner, A. M. (1968). "Honey bees." Chapter 11 of Sebeok (1968), 217–43.

Whorf, B. L. (1956). *Language, Thought and Reality*. (*Selected writings of Benjamin Lee Whorf*, ed. John B. Carroll.) Cambridge, Mass.: M.I.T. Press, and New York: Wiley.

Wittgenstein, L. (1953). *Philosophical Investigations*. Oxford: Blackwell.

# Index

ablative (case), 245, 246, 255
accentual pattern, 106, 116, 148,
    203, 208, 221
accusative (case), 144–5, 151,
    232, 245, 270
"actant", 238, 254
active and passive, 85, 90, 156–7
additive coordination, 127–9
addressee, 13–15, 24, 266–75,
    278–82
adessive (case), 245
adjacency of morphemes, 124–5
adjacency pairs, 282
adjective, 10, 46–7, 117, 119–20,
    129, 146–7, 148, 156, 184,
    198, 228, 235, 237–8, 240–1,
    242
adjective phrase, 70, 185, 198
adjunct, 136
adjunction transformation, 176,
    177–8
adverb (= Advb), 46–7, 101, 125,
    129, 146, 148, 184, 237–8, 262
adverbial (= Adv), 83–4, 114,
    115, 136–7, 149, 161, 167–8,
    185, 190–1, 198, 203, 238,
    248, 250, 251, 254, 276, 277
affix, 48, 148, 213–15, 219–23,
    224, 225–9, 231–3, 234
agent (role), 130, 253–4
agent-deletion transformation,
    170–1
agglutinating language, 232
agreement (grammatical), 43,
    149–52, 154, 239

Alexandrians, 2
Algonkin languages, 243
allative (case), 245
Allen, W. S., 11
Allerton, D. J., 57, 92, 209, 235,
    284
allolex, 215, 231, 239
allomorph, 36, 37, 216–19, 224,
    234
allomorphy, 36, 37
allophone, 35–6, 37
alternative coordination, 127–9
ambiguity, syntactic, 12, 85, 95,
    116–18, 145, 198–200, 201,
    261, 263
Amerindian languages, 212, 243,
    244
anaphora/-ic, 125, 267, 276
Anderson, J., 255, 260
animacy, 43–4, 240–1
animal language, 30
anti-mentalism, 94
applicational grammar, 5
appositive coordination, 127–9
Arabic, 124, 150, 220, 233, 241
arbitrariness, 19, 23, 27–8, 29
argument, 259–60
Aristotle, 2, 237
Aronoff, M., 224, 228
article, 10, 216–17, 233, 234,
    239, 244; see also determiner
aspect, verbal, 105, 248, 249, 270
assertion, 272–3
attributive adjective, 147, 237–8
Austin, J. L., 2, 14, 278–9, 280

# Index

subject, grammatical, 125,
138–40, 236, 238, 245, 252–3,
256–7, 274–5
subject-predicate construction,
150
subordinating conjunction, 129,
193, 196, 238, 276–7
subordinative compound (word),
229, 230
subordinative construction, 127–9,
131, 229; links between
sentences, 276
"substance", *see* "form" v.
"substance"
substitute, *see* proform
substitution (test), 46–7, 98–9,
214; transformation, 175
subtractive morph, 222–3
suffix, 220, 223, 233
superfix, 221
superlative, 36, 148
suppletion, 219n
surface restraint, 179
surface structure, 3, 86, 87, 124,
150, 158–60, 163–73, 188
Swahili, 150, 151, 240, 241, 244
Swedish, 233, 240, 244, 245
symbol, 18–20, 24–5; logical,
mathematical and musical, 24–5
synchronic (v. diachronic), 5, 11
syncretism, 143
synonymous sentences, 95
syntactic feature, 61, 84, 138–42,
149, 154, 157, 219
syntactic independence, 211–12
syntagmatic relations, 34, 35, 40,
109f; rule, 83–4
syntax, 25, 29–30, 36, 37, 38, 39,
42–8, 60–209, 236–84 (*see also*
morphology and syntax); deep,
*see* deep structure
system network, 140–2, 252
systemic grammar, 6, 7, 138, 140–2,
183, 185–6, 193, 205, 252

systematicness, 9, 26

"tactics", 5
Tagalog, 220, 244
tag-formation transformation, 181
tagmeme, 4, 37, 236
tagmemics, 4, 7, 138, 183, 185,
186–7, 193, 205, 252
talking (and walking), 1–2
telegrams, 21
tendency (v. rule), 37–9, 41, 46,
56
tense, 105, 140, 145, 153, 232,
247–8, 249, 270
terminal symbol, 71–2, 84
terminology, 9
Tesnière, L., 6, 7, 129, 238, 254,
260, 263
text, 202–3, 265–84
text structure, 282–3
textual links between sentences,
275–84; links between sentence
parts, 265–75, 283, 284;
progression, 274, 275, 282–3;
reconstruction, 267–8
thematic organization of text, 275
theme, 268, 273–5
*there*-insertion transformation,
170, 181
thinking, 13
time adverbial, 136–7; (role), 254
"togetherness", 109, 116, 125;
*see also* coherence
token, *see* type and token
topic, *see* theme
traditional grammar, 1, 2, 9, 10,
53–4, 60, 93, 133
transform, 157
transformations, 3, 4, 84–7, 97,
103–4, 154–82, 227, 252, 275;
conditions on, 161, 179; format
of rules, 160–3; functions of,
159, 163–9; in generative
grammar, 84–5, 159–73, 182;